Clifton Park - Halfmoon Public Library
475 Moe Road
Clifton Park, New York 12065

W9-ATG-774

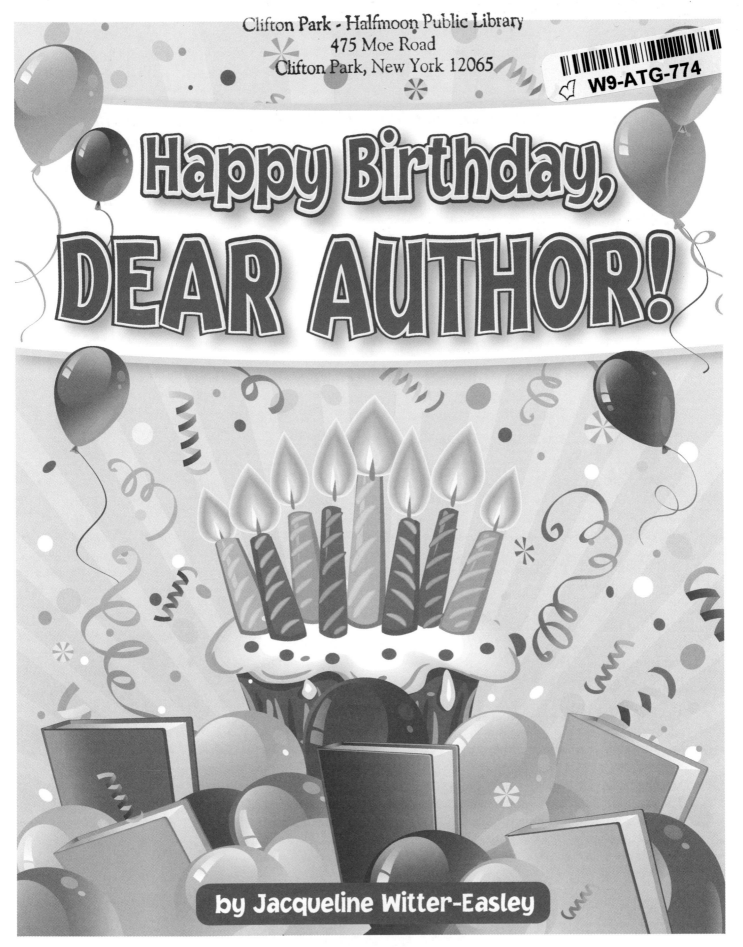

Happy Birthday, DEAR AUTHOR!

by Jacqueline Witter-Easley

UpstartBooks

Madison, Wisconsin

To my wonderful husband, Chuck. Thank you for all of your loving support and encouragement throughout the writing of this book. And to my children, Sabrina and Liam. You are, and always will be, my constant joy and inspiration. I thank God every day for you.

—J. W.

Published by UpstartBooks
4810 Forest Run Road
Madison, WI 53704

1-800-448-4887

2746

© 2012 Highsmith, LLC
By Jacqueline Witter-Easley

The paper used in this publication meets the minimum requirements of American National Standard for Information Science — Permanence of Paper for Printed Library Material. ANSI/NISO Z39.48-1992.

All rights reserved. Printed in the United States of America.
The purchase of this book entitles the individual librarian or teacher to reproduce copies for use in the library or classroom. The reproduction of any part for an entire school system or for commercial use is strictly prohibited. No form of this work may be reproduced or transmitted or recorded without written permission from the publisher.

Table of Contents

Happy Birthday, Dear Authors Born in March!

Happy Birthday, Dear Authors Born in April!

Happy Birthday, Dear Authors Born in May!

Resources

Introduction

It was an autumn Sunday afternoon at my local public library, where I worked as an assistant children's librarian. I stood nervously in the center of our program room, which I'd just finished decorating with streamers, balloons, and a colorful poster that proclaimed, "Happy Birthday, Paul Goble!" I looked around the room, surveying the prepared activities, trays of refreshments, and author's book display. I was ready. I walked over to the door where sixteen first, second, and third graders waited expectantly. I opened the door and collected their invitations to our birthday party honoring Paul Goble and his inspiring picture books about Native American cultures.

Once the children filed in, they stood awkwardly near the tables and chairs, not sure what to do. They did not know each other because they attended different schools in the area. Finally, Rachel, a second grader, looked at the other boys and girls and confidently asked, "So, which was your favorite Paul Goble book?" The party had begun!

As a former classroom teacher, I witnessed the powerful connection that beginning readers made to children's literature every day because I integrated author studies throughout the year. My first grade students acquired the necessary decoding and comprehension skills to function as members of society's literacy club (Smith, 1988) by reading and responding to picture books. More importantly, they also developed and nurtured their desire to read because they were immersed in positive, authentic reading and writing experiences through our author studies. They debated the qualities of their favorite authors, recommended new titles, and participated meaningfully in thoughtful discussions. This balanced approach fostered a positive attitude toward literacy, and many of my beginning readers saw themselves as competent readers.

Once I began working part time in the children's department of my local public library, I wanted to bring those same positive experiences to our young patrons. Many parents and children enter the children's department and become overwhelmed with the vast collection of picture books. This collection is shelved alphabetically by the authors' last names. Unless the parents and children are familiar with award-winning children's authors, they will not feel confident in selecting books that pertain to their interests, have been written in an engaging style, reinforce specific topical insights, or promote creativity. I decided to adapt my successful author program from its classroom format to make it conducive to beginning readers in a library setting. Our "Happy Birthday, Dear Author!" Reading Club for grades 1–3 was born—and now, with this book, the ideas that have made it a success in my library are in your hands.

In this book, you will find detailed programming ideas for author birthday parties that are geared toward beginning readers. The activities are appropriate in both a classroom and school library setting during the school year, from September to May. If your goal is to promote literacy skills via a balanced approach for your students, the activities in this book will be ideal. If your goal is to increase recreational reading among your primary-level patrons, you will find open-ended, fun activities to create a monthly reading club for your library community.

Grab your books and let the celebrations begin!

—Jacqueline Witter-Easley

Smith, F. (1988). *Joining the Literacy Club: Further Essays into Education.* Portsmouth, NH: Heinemann Library.

Chapter One

Components for a Successful Author Celebration Program

To ensure a successful author birthday celebration, certain program components should be considered and adapted for your classroom or library setting. As you read through the following hints, note that some suggestions are for classroom teachers, and others for school librarians. The main difference these educators will experience when implementing author celebration programs lies in student participation. For teachers, it is likely easier to require student participation, as the students are a "captive audience." Librarians may need to promote the program and entice students to sign up for this extracurricular activity.

1. **Select living authors.**
   Teachers and Librarians: This program is most effective if you select authors who are still living. Obtain author addresses (most publishers will forward mail; otherwise, some authors share their residence or office address) so that the children will be able to send birthday greetings to authors as part of the festivities. There are many ways to correspond with an author—the possibilities are limited only by your own creativity! Each author's style or story topics will provide a framework from which to devise your birthday greeting's format. Some authors are even available via Skype™! Imagine the excitement of providing a video conversation with a famous author to your students! When writing to an author, the best assurance for a response is to put all the children's greetings into one large 10" x 13" envelope and include a cover letter explaining your program. Include a self-addressed stamped envelope. One year, I also included an 8-inch fabric square for the author/illustrator to decorate and return to us. By the end of the year, we had a beautiful author quilt to display in our classroom and in my public library's children's services department!

Hearing back from an author can be one of the most motivating components of the program for children. When an author makes contact with them, they experience a true reading and writing connection, and they realize the author/illustrator is a real person! When you receive your reply, be sure to share it with the children at the next author birthday celebration. You'll soon hear them asking about whether the author wrote back the moment they enter the party room.

Librarians: Since your author birthday celebrations will most likely include children in grades 1–3, you will need to select authors on a three-year cycle to avoid repetition. Therefore, this book contains celebration ideas for at least three different authors' birthdays during each month of the school year.

2. **Provide ample amounts of the author's/ illustrator's books for circulation.**

   Librarians: Consider temporarily adjusting the loan period to one week so the books can be circulated in a timely fashion and the children will not become frustrated trying to obtain books in order to participate in the program. Additionally, it's best to have multiple copies of each author's more popular works available for participants. You should also inform the primary-level teachers about your program and give them a list of the authors your club will celebrate throughout the school year. Encourage the teachers to stock their classroom libraries with several copies of the authors' books. This will alleviate the burden of circulating enough copies of the authors' books and help the students to successfully read their books for participation in your program.

   Teachers: Meet with your school librarians early in the year and request that they order a sufficient number of books by the authors you plan to study. Be sure to stock your own classroom library, too!

3. **Create a book list and reading log.**

   NOTE: Sample reproducible book lists and reading logs for the authors featured in this book can be found at the end of their respective author sections. Use these, or feel free to create your own!

   Librarians: Provide each program registrant with a book list and reading log for that month's featured author. This will create a framework from which children can select books to read by that author. Format this handout by listing the books by that author that are available in your library's collection on one side (be sure to include the call number next to each book).

   Photocopy the reading log on the reverse side of the book list. Be sure to include a space for parent/guardian signatures on the reading log. When parents/guardians sign after their child has read each book, students are participating in a system of accountability, while also promoting parent involvement in your program. Make the handout appealing to first, second, and third graders, so use colorful graphics and inviting fonts that relate to the author's works. Since you will not see your students every day, you will need to have the book list and reading log for the following month's author ready to hand out at the end of each author party.

   Teachers: Provide students with a book list and reading log for that month's featured author. This will provide guidance for their self-selected reading options. Format this handout by listing the author's books and indicate those books that are held in your classroom library and school library. Photocopy the reading log on the reverse side. Be sure to include a space for either your signature, or a parent/guardian signature. If your students read the books during silent reading time, you will sign their reading log for each book. If they read the books at home, their parents or guardians can sign the log. Make the handout appealing to first, second, and third graders by using colorful graphics and inviting fonts that relate to the author's works.

4. **Keep the featured author's books in a central location.**

   Librarians: While the book list will provide children with call numbers for each of the author's books in the library's collection, children will experience more success if the books by the current month's featured author are placed together in an appealing display. Consider choosing an area of high traffic so the program becomes visible to many children. Include a colorful, visually stimulating poster with all the pertinent information in a clear, concise, easy-to-read format. Provide informative and attractive flyers for students and parents to take with them for extra publicity. As the featured author's books circulate, be sure to replenish the display with returned books as soon as possible to avoid difficulties in obtaining the books in a timely fashion.

   Teachers: Pull all of the featured author's books from your classroom library and arrange them in an attractive display. If you have shelf space near a bulletin board, you can use the bulletin board as a permanent display area for each month's featured author. By creating a special display, you will promote more fluid usage of the books, as students will select books for silent reading, etc. This will also encourage impromptu student discussions as they gather informally around the display to select their books. Furthermore, you will be able to pull the author's books quickly to integrate them into your curriculum.

5. **Basic Requirements for All Participants**
Librarians: Since the children will have one month to read the author's works, and the majority of the authors suggested in this book write picture books, a realistic requirement is for children to read five books. Divide the reading log into five lines or sections. In each section, the child will write the title of the book he/she finished reading, and the parent will sign it for validation. Since some members of this program are beginning readers, be sure to emphasize that children can meet the requirements by listening to an adult read the books aloud.
Teachers: You will most likely involve the students in an author's books by reading several aloud throughout the month. You may also integrate the author's books into your curriculum, and use them in literature circles. However, in an effort to promote lifelong reading habits, you might consider requiring your students to read two to three additional books on their own. They should keep track of all books read in class activities and independently on their reading logs. Encourage your students to check out books from either the school or public library and have their parents sign their logs to verify at-home reading, too.

6. **Plan to celebrate the author as close to the author's real birthdate as possible, and reward the children with a birthday party invitation.**
Librarians: As children turn in their completed reading logs, give them a fun invitation to attend the birthday celebration. Create invitations that relate to the author's themes or topics. Now that the children are experts on the author's works, they will "get" the invitation's connection to the books right away! Be sure the invitation accurately conveys the key information: date, time, place of celebration, and library information (address, phone number, website). The children must bring their invitation with them on the day of the party to use as a "ticket" for admission to the event. Use a spreadsheet program to keep track of the students enrolled in the club, and check off those who have earned a party invitation. This quick organizational tool will prove indispensible for gauging enrollment in the overall program, celebration attendance, etc.
Teachers: A few days before the author birthday party, distribute colorful invitations to your students. If you use a classroom mailbox, place the invitations inside to create a fun surprise! Be sure to create invitations that connect to the author's themes, characters, or topics. Now that the children are experts on the author's works, they will "get" the invitation's connection to the books right away! Indicate the date and class period or time when the party will take place. Keep track of your students' independent reading so that they will complete their requirements in time for the party.

Chapter Two

General Celebration Ideas

Every author or illustrator has his own style, genre, and topics of interest. All these can lend themselves to unique thematic author parties. Of course, once you start planning your celebrations and develop your program throughout the school year, you will most likely create a wide variety of games, activities, snacks, and decorations to suit your own style, too! However, if you find that the parties have begun to exhaust your creativity every month, consider incorporating the general ideas provided in this chapter into your celebrations. The format, time frame, and setting will all vary depending on the location of your party, so remember to make adjustments accordingly. Additionally, be sure to consult the resources section on page 189 for more ideas to augment your celebrations.

1. **"Happy Birthday, Dear Author!" Birthday Cards**
   A key component of every celebration should involve children making a special birthday greeting to mail to the featured author. Children could make their own birthday cards and sign their first names; they could collaborate to make a birthday banner or mural; they could dictate a birthday poem or jingle that emulates an author's writing style, etc. The birthday greeting format should reflect the author's writing style, genre, or specific topics. For example, an author who writes animal stories might enjoy a mural of a zoo, with each child pasting on an animal that he or she has drawn and labeled with a special message.

2. **Create a Festive Environment**
   Whether you are a classroom teacher or a librarian, you need to transform your daily environment into a party room to create a celebratory atmosphere for your students/book club members. Arrive at school early in the morning and hang up streamers, balloons, posters of the author, book jackets, etc. Place the author's books along ledges in the room (window sills, white or chalkboard ledges, etc.). If you are a classroom teacher, you will likely integrate the author's books into the entire school day, so you should have the room decorated before the students arrive. Keep the celebration day special. By attending to such details as festive decorations, you are conveying to your students and book club members that this celebration is truly a special event.

3. **About the Author**
   Be sure to reserve time during the birthday celebration to tell the students the story of the author's life. This should be an interactive storytelling event. Be creative! Develop a draw-and-tell story and use a few key props to help tell the story; or make a mural, adding pieces to the design as you relay various events about the author to your students. Specific ideas and techniques will be described for each featured author in this book. Many authors have websites with autobiographical information that you can use to assist you in gathering your data. Another key resource is the vast collection titled *Something About the Author* (SATA) from Gale Group Publishers. This 200+ volume set is found in many public and university libraries, and can also be accessed online at www.gale.com with a subscription. Each author in the collection is indexed and easy to find.

   Additionally, many public libraries contain author biographies, cataloged in the 921 section alphabetically by the subject's last name. (If you are a teacher, check your school or local library for these resources.) Once you've gathered enough information, plan out how you will orally tell the author's life story to your students during the party.

4. **Go on a Treasure Hunt!**
A treasure hunt is a fun, noncompetitive party game. Divide the students into groups of four and have each group follow their own set of clues that lead to a special treasure. Create clues related to the author's books and have the students use the clues to find a hidden treasure. For example, after reading Eric Carle's books, the children might scour the classroom or library for small creatures (spiders, ladybugs, caterpillars, etc.) with clues attached. After finding each creature, the students must read the clue and determine the location of the next creature. This is especially effective in the library, where students could learn about the Dewey Decimal system if the librarian hides the items in different sections of the library. Each clue would lead the children to another section of the collection. The final item found is the treasure: a decorated box filled with materials for making a craft, activity sheets rolled into scrolls and tied with ribbon, or whatever you feel is appropriate for your students.

5. **Play Traditional Party Games with a Twist**
Once you start thinking about transforming traditional party games, the possibilities are endless! Here are a few ideas to get you started:
   - "Pin the Tail on the Donkey" could be transformed into almost any theme, such as: "Pin the Glasses on Arthur" (for Marc Brown's books), "Pin the Crown on Lily" (for Kevin Henkes' books), etc.
   - Another favorite party game, the beanbag toss, could be adapted to any author's or illustrator's books. For example, the children could 'feed' Tacky (for Helen Lester's books) by throwing beanbags at a poster-sized drawing of this lovable penguin with his beak opened wide!
   - Charades are always fun to play! Write the names of characters from the featured author's books on small slips of paper. Students draw a slip of paper,

pantomime that character's action in the books, and try to stump their classmates! This also works for Pictionary™ games.
   - Bingo can be adapted for specific characters and/or author's book titles. For an extra challenge, give the game a critical thinking twist by reading a clue aloud, and having students scan their Bingo cards for an appropriate corresponding answer. (For instance, the clue might be, "This main character in Helen Lester's books has a name that also means, "Showy, flashy, or tasteless." Students whose Bingo cards have a square with "Tacky" in them would cover that square with a playing piece.) Whoever has marked five squares, four corners, or some other predetermined goal on her Bingo card wins the game!
   - Hot Potato is fun when it features the antagonist from an author's series of books, such as passing around a stuffed black spider for Anansi (from Eric Kimmel's retellings), or the mischievous duck (from Doreen Cronin's books). Nobody wants to be stuck with Anansi—keep that potato going!

6. **Mathematics + Books = Critical Thinkers**
Make a natural link to mathematics by incorporating the following activities into your author party:
   - **Graphs:** Create picture graphs onto which the children affix a shape or picture for their choice of: favorite book, favorite author/illustrator featured so far, favorite character, etc. Older students can create bar graphs and arrange the findings into histograms. Leave the graphs up in the classroom or library for children to refer to throughout the school year or semester. Talk about the graphs. ("Why do you like _____ best?" ; "Which book do more children prefer?" ; "How many more children like this character better than that character?" ; "What percentage of students read this book?", etc.)

- **Venn Diagrams:** Students can collect information about the author's books and sort the ideas into categories, such as funniest, saddest, and most informative books. Create Venn Diagrams to reveal their findings. Do any books belong in more than one category? What other categories can they create for this particular author's works?

- **Story Cards:** Younger children will enjoy using story cards based on the featured author's books to act out word problems. For example, draw a penguin wearing a Hawaiian shirt to represent Tacky the Penguin (Lester, 1992). Distribute a snack bag of Goldfish™ crackers and pose various problems to the students, such as: "Five fish were swimming in the water. One jumped up and Tacky ate it. How many are left?" Older students can group the items into sets to review multiplication facts. Many small objects, such as shaped crackers, jelly beans, chocolate-coated candies, miniature pumpkins, etc., will lend themselves to this activity. Simply create a story card with a picture and setting related to the featured author's books and use a corresponding object as the manipulative.

7. **Include Birthday Presents**
Obtain the latest book by the featured author and wrap it in colorful paper. Dramatically open it and read it to the children. Other gift ideas include: puppets of book characters (a hedgehog for Jan Brett's books, for example), small stuffed characters, materials to use for a craft, a DVD of one of the author's books, or a CD of music related to an author's themes. After sharing this present with the students, prominently display it for children to play with or use on their own.

8. **Scrapbooks of Memories**
At the end of each session, have the students draw a picture of a character from one of the author's books. They will label their paper with the author's name and write a brief journal entry about their favorite books, characters, or activities. Have the students assemble these pages into a binder, along with their completed reading logs. By the end of the school year, each student will have a scrapbook of memories related to the author program. This gift will increase the likelihood that the children will continue to explore more books by these authors, even after the school year ends—and that they'll want to participate in author birthday parties when the school year begins again.

9. **Refreshments**
Provide a simple refreshment to add to the festive atmosphere. This could range from cupcakes to single-serve ice cream cups, to fruit and popcorn or brownies (be aware of any student allergies). If possible, provide round sugar cookies that the children can decorate to resemble a character from the author's books. Another possibility might be to provide a lollipop taped to a paper cut into a shape that reinforces a theme of the author's books. For instance, if your featured author is Lois Ehlert, tape a flower shape to the lollipop as a token of the author's garden-oriented books. Be sure that you have extra supervision on hand and that snacks are appropriate for the age of your students. No matter the treat, remember that you must always lead the class in singing a rousing rendition of "Happy Birthday, Dear Author" before enjoying the food!

10. **Technology**
Given the amazing technological advances this generation of children has experienced in their lifetimes, vast opportunities exist for using technology during your birthday celebration. Here are some ideas:

- **Interactive White Boards:** What a fun way to draw-and-tell a story about the author: on a computer board! Another great use of this technology would be a game show venue. Create a true/false quiz about the author that is filled with silly facts, and the students can answer using the hand-held devices that accompany these boards.

- **Websites:** Before the celebration, use a search engine to find various appropriate websites pertaining to your featured author. If your school or library has an overhead projector for your laptop, you can project the website on a screen for all to see. This would also lend itself well to participating in a webquest activity.
- **MP3 Players:** Download a series of songs that relate to the themes/topics of your author's books. Play portions of the songs to the students and have them "Name That Tune" and explain why it was selected for this particular author's books.
- **Digital Photo Treasure Hunt:** Take photos of artifacts that relate to the author's books and insert them into a PowerPoint™ slide show. As each image is projected, students must try to write the corresponding book title.

Happy Birthday, Dear Authors Born in September!

September 1	Jim Arnosky		September 13	Else Holmelund Minarik
September 2	Bernard Most		September 14	Diane Goode
	Ellen Stoll Walsh		September 15	Tomie de Paola
September 3	Aliki		September 20	Arthur Geisert
September 4	Syd Hoff		September 21	Taro Yashima
	Kate Waters		September 25	Jim Murphy
September 5	Paul Fleischman			Andrea Davis Pinkney
	Gloria Jean Pinkney		September 27	**Paul Goble***
September 7	Alexandra Day			G. Brian Karas
September 8	Byron Barton			Bernard Waber
	Michael Hague		September 29	Stan Berenstain
	Kevin O'Malley			Marissa Moss
	Jack Prelutsky*		September 30	Alvin Tresselt
	Jon Scieszka*			Janet S. Wong
September 10	Babette Cole			
September 11	Anthony Browne			

*Author featured in this chapter

Happy Birthday, Dear Jack Prelutsky!

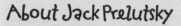

About Jack Prelutsky

- Birthday: September 8, 1940
- Hobbies and Talents: Singing, playing guitar, photography, carpentry, collage art
- Family: Wife, Carolynn
- Residence: Seattle, Washington
- First Children's Poet Laureate in 2006
- If he could have one wish it would be to sing the national anthem for the opening game of the World Series at Safeco Field!

Celebration Activities

Author's Story

Tell about Jack Prelutsky through a limerick. Leave the rhyming lines blank. Place the words in a word bank for students to select and fill in as the poem is read aloud. For beginning readers (first graders), focus on rhyming patterns. For more advanced readers (second and third graders), include in the word bank words that don't belong in the poem and focus on context clues as well as word patterns.

Limerick

There once was a boy from New York
Whose behavior made teachers blow their
_____ (corks).
He was wiggly and spry,
He had ideas to _____ (try).
This boy from Brooklyn, New York.

This young man from New York loved to sing.
He would put a tune to most _____ (anything).
He sang out quite loud
To appreciative _____ (crowds),
This young man who just loved to sing.

After pottery, cab driving, and carpentry,
This man tried drawing and _____ (poetry).
"You make magic with words," an editor said.
"Your poems are some of the best that I've _____ (read)."
She told this great poet, Jack Prelutsky!

Birthday Greetings

Have the students create colorful birthday cards and encourage them to write a poem as their greeting. Younger students can write couplets; older students can write their own limericks. Mail these to the author in a large manila envelope with a cover letter explaining your program. Remember to include a self-addressed stamped envelope!

Ride a Purple Pelican Treasure Hunt

Overview

Students will follow the clues from state to state, based on poems from Prelutsky's book, *Ride a Purple Pelican* (1986). As each state is found, students will color it on a blank United States map. After locating their set of states (4–5 total), they will bring their completed maps to the group and use them to play USA Bingo, or simply show them to you and collect a small prize (stickers, pencil, bookmark, etc.). Make sure you have enough prizes for everyone!

Preparations

1. Before the celebration, plan how you will divide the students into small groups of 3–4 students.
2. Read through the book and select five poems that mention the name of a state, or, for a challenge, add poems that name cities in certain states.

3. Reproduce and cut out the pelican template from page 18 (one for each *group),* and the blank U.S. map from page 17 (one for each *student).*

4. On the back of each pelican, write the name of a state that the students must "ride" to, such as: "Ride to Delaware." (The states you use will depend on which ones you choose from those mentioned in the poems from the book.)

5. Using an online image search or your own artistic skills, create a large outline of the five states that students will be visiting. On the back of each state, write the poem from the book that names *another* state (or hints at another state with a city name) that the students will "ride" to. (So, for instance, if you were to use Oklahoma, Wyoming, Delaware, Arkansas, and California, you would write a poem from *another* state on the back of each outline.)

6. Hang the outline of each state around the perimeter of the room, or along the bookshelves.

7. Reproduce and enlarge the map of the United States of America on page 19 for yourself.

Game Time

Give each student a crayon and a blank map. Put the students in their groups, and give each group a pelican with the name of the first state they must ride to written on the back. At your signal, each group will set out to find their first state outline, based on the pelican's directions. When they find their state outline, they will turn it over to find the poem from Prelutsky's book written on the back. They will read the poem together, and when they read the state named in the poem, they will search the classroom or library for the outline of the next state. When they find it, they will color the state in on their personal maps, and read the new poem. As play continues, groups of students will travel around the room to the different state stations, often where their peers have just left. When they get to the last state, the poem on the back will name the state that they started with (such as Dela-

ware, for the group whose pelican told them to "Ride to Delaware"). This will be their last poem. The first group to return to you with their completed map is the winner. Be sure all groups "win" a prize, as described above.

Extension Ideas

- **USA Bingo:** The students could use their completed maps to play a few rounds of USA Bingo. Tell students to color in five additional states on their maps. Read a poem from Prelutsky's book. If a student colored in the state named in the poem, she can place a marker on it. The first student to reach five states can yell, "Bingo!"

- **Creative Writing:** Read aloud a poem from the book and discuss with the students how Prelutsky often focuses on a food or animal found in that particular state. Brainstorm a list of foods, animals, landmarks, and other key features of your home state and have the students write a poem about it. Tell the students to focus on one particular feature for their poems. Post a large outline of your state on a classroom bulletin board and scatter the students' poems around it for an attractive display.

Poetry Coffee House

You and the students will read aloud your favorite poems from Prelutsky's many poetry books. Give students a few minutes to practice reading their favorite poems. Encourage them to work with a partner and "perform" their poem, using movement, choral reading, and/or props. This simple activity promotes a love of poetry, critical thinking in determining one's favorite poem, practice in oral reading fluency, and development in public speaking skills.

For Laughing Out Loud . . . Or Not!

Instruct students to sit in a circle. Begin play by having one student read aloud one of Prelutsky's poems from his book, *For Laughing Out Loud* (1991). At the end of the poem, the reader yells, "Ha!" to the player on his right. That player then yells, "Ha, ha!" to the next player to the right, and so on around the circle. Any player who laughs or makes a mistake must go into the middle of the circle. The players in the middle may try to make other players laugh by repeating lines from Prelutsky's poem and making funny faces. The player who lasts the longest without laughing, wins!

Sing-along Fun

Many of Jack Prelutsky's poems are actually songs. He has created a CD of many of his holiday poetry collections (see book list). Play this CD as background music during the celebration time, or teach a few of the songs to the students.

Who Is Who in this Haiku?

Share the haiku poems by Jack Prelutsky from his book, *If Not For the Cat* (2004). First, read the haiku aloud without showing the illustrations. Field guesses as to what animal the haiku is about, then reveal the art. Prelutsky included an answer key on the final page, titled "Who is Who." This might serve as inspiration for the children to create their own haiku poems about a favorite animal. They could then create a class book with an answer key at the back, too!

jackprelutsky.com

Jack Prelutsky's website is a colorful, audiovisual experience for children and teachers. It is conducive to projecting onto a screen and sharing it with the whole class. Jack Prelutsky juggles icons that serve as links to such topics as frequently asked questions, songs (starring Prelutsky, himself), photos, biography, fan letters, book lists, and sports cards. This is a fun way to pass the time while the students are eating the snack or birthday treat.

Craft Project: Collage Art

One of Jack Prelutsky's favorite artistic endeavors is creating collages. This visual art form is a natural way to connect art to poetry. Provide several Jack Prelutsky books for students to browse, and have each child select a favorite poem. Once they have selected a poem, provide them with a wide variety of materials, such as magazines, patterned papers, newspapers, wallpaper samples, clip art images, ribbons, construction paper, felt, buttons, sea shells, and any other small objects that may inspire creativity. Tell the students to read their poems several times and list the images their poems convey. Have them use the collage materials to express the images and feelings they get from the poem by arranging the materials on a 9" x 12" piece of card stock. Discuss the concepts of balance and composition, as well as the use of color and shape to convey feelings. Students should copy the poem in their best writing (or type them up for keyboarding practice) and assemble the poem and collage on a 12" x 18" sheet of construction paper for a beautiful classroom display.

Party Favors

Magnetic Poetry: Type up 100 or more random words, using a size 16- or 18-point font and allowing three spaces between each word. Run the words through a laminator that takes magnetic laminate rolls. Make one set for each student. Cut apart each word and place the set into a small cellophane bag (approximately 3" x 5", available at most craft stores). Cut card stock into 3" x 2" rectangles, and write: "Magnetic Poetry in Honor of Jack Prelutsky's Birthday Celebration!" On the reverse side, you can place a birthday sticker, or type up this poem:

> I'm so happy on this day,
> I could jump and shout, "Hooray!"
> I could march and sing and play,
> But for now, I will simply say,
> "Today is Jack Prelutsky's birthday!"

Party Food

Since Jack Prelutsky loves baseball, and most foods that start with /ch/ (see his website for his answer to the question, "What is your favorite food, writer, and sport?"), serve old-fashioned ballpark food: hot dogs and chips! If this is not possible in your library or classroom, serve ball park snacks: peanuts, popcorn, or cotton candy (be aware of allergies). Serve the snacks in snack bags and call out, "Get your peanuts, popcorn, or cotton candy here!" Once everyone has a snack, sing "Happy Birthday" to Jack Prelutsky and yell, "Play ball!" at the end!

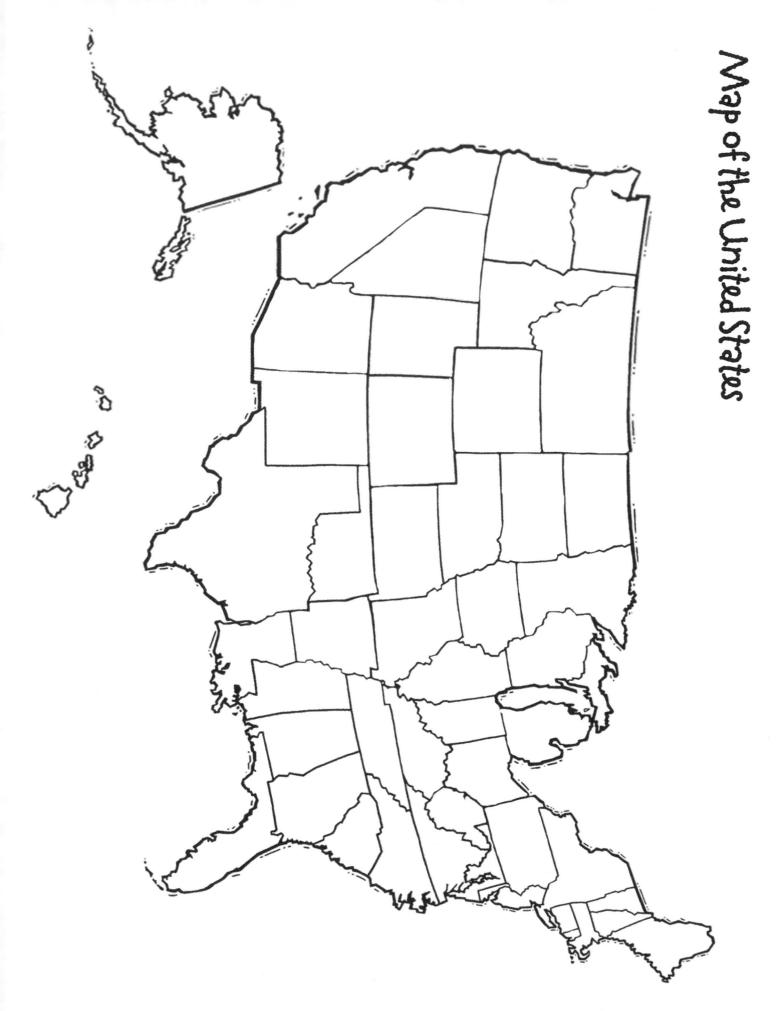

Pelican

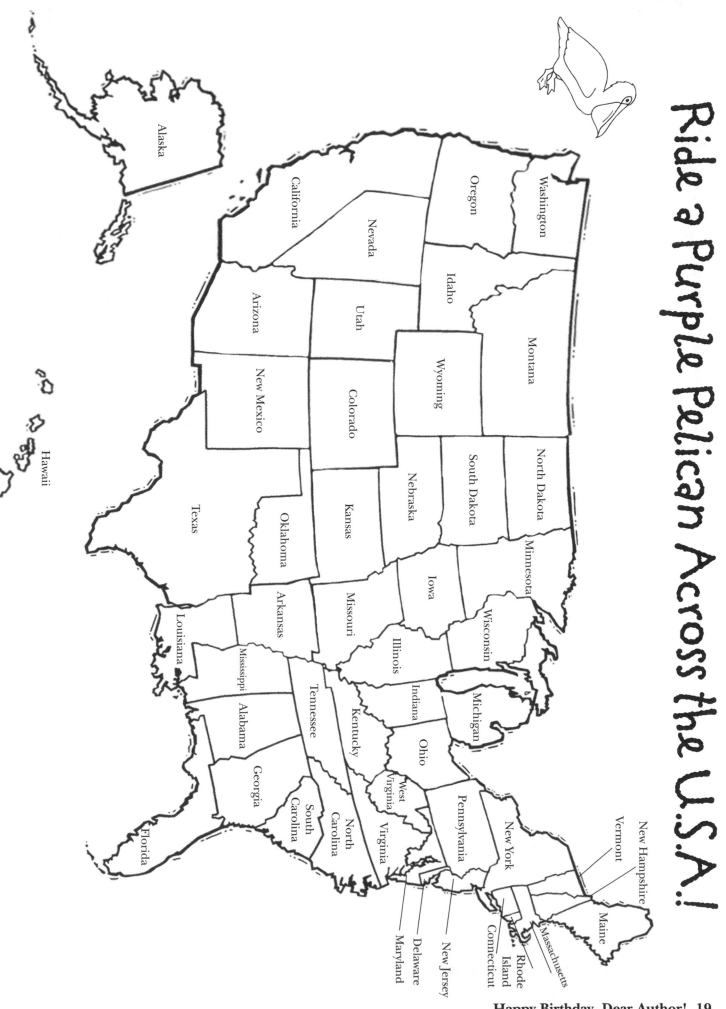

Ride a Purple Pelican Across the U.S.A.!

Happy Birthday, Jack Prelutsky!

Born September 8, 1940

Picture Books

- *Beneath a Blue Umbrella*
- *Dog Days: Rhymes Around the Year*
- *Read Aloud Rhymes For The Very Young*
- *Rolling Harvey Down The Hill*
- *Wild Witches' Ball*
- *The Wizard*

Easy Readers

- *It's Christmas!*
- *It's Halloween!*
- *It's Thanksgiving!*
- *It's Valentine's Day!*
- *Rainy, Rainy Saturday*

Nonfiction—Poetry

- *A. Nonny Mouse Writes Again*
- *Awful Ogre's Awful Day*
- *Awful Ogre Running Wild*
- *The Baby Uggs Are Hatching*
- *The Beauty of the Beast: Poems from the Animal Kingdom*
- *Behold the Bold Umbrellaphant*
- *The Dragons Are Singing Tonight*
- *For Laughing Out Loud*
- *The Frogs Wore Red Suspenders*
- *The Gargoyle On The Roof*
- *Good Sports*
- *The Headless Horseman Rides Tonight*
- *If Not For the Cat*
- *Imagine That! Poems of Never Was*
- *In Aunt Giraffe's Green Garden*

- *It's Raining Pigs & Noodles*
- *It's Snowing! It's Snowing!*
- *Monday's Troll*
- *My Dog May Be a Genius*
- *My Parents Think I'm Sleeping*
- *The New Kid On The Block*
- *Nightmares: Poems to Trouble Your Sleep*
- *A Pizza The Size of the Sun*
- *Pizza, Pigs, and Poetry: How to Write a Poem*
- *Poems of A. Nonny Mouse*
- *Read a Rhyme, Write a Rhyme*
- *Ride A Purple Pelican*
- *Scranimals*
- *Something BIG Has Been Here*
- *The Way of Living Things*
- *What a Day It Was At School*

Compact Disc

- Jack Prelutsky Holiday CD

Jack Prelutsky Reading Log

Read 5 books by **September** _____.

On each line, write the title you've read and have your parent/guardian sign that you read it.

Bring this completed reading log to me by **September** _____ and receive your invitation to attend our birthday celebration on

_____.

Date/Time

_____

Title   Parent/Guardian Signature

_____

Title   Parent/Guardian Signature

_____

Title   Parent/Guardian Signature

_____

Title   Parent/Guardian Signature

_____

Title   Parent/Guardian Signature

Happy Birthday, Dear Jon Scieszka!

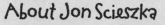

About Jon Scieszka

- Birthday: September 8, 1954
- His last name rhymes with "Fresca"!
- He is the second oldest of six boys, with no sisters.
- He earned a Master of Fine Arts in Writing at Columbia University.
- He has taught elementary school, mostly grades 1–4. The years he spent in the classroom taught him that children learn through playing and humor.
- He has created a non-profit organization called *Guys Read*, and he has a website dedicated to motivating boys to read at www.guysread.com.
- In 2008, Jon Scieszka was appointed by the Library of Congress to be the first National Ambassador for Young People's Literature.

Celebration Ideas

Author's Story: The True Story of Jon Scieszka!

Imitate the cover of *The True Story of the 3 Little Pigs* (1989) by covering the front page of a newspaper with headings created on a word processor that relate to significant events in Jon Scieszka's life. An excellent source for creative headings and biographical information is his autobiography, *Knucklehead: Tall Tales & Mostly True Stories About Growing Up Scieszka* (Scieszka, 2008). His website is also a good source: www. jsworldwide.com.

Before the party, cut out a 5" x 5" square from a sheet of newspaper and tape it over a similar layout on an inside page of the newspaper you will use to tell Scieszka's story. By placing the square of newspaper over a similar layout, the square will blend in and remain unnoticed by the students when you page through the paper. Tape the square on three sides, leaving the top open to create a pocket. Place bookmarks or stickers in the pocket before the students arrive.

Once the party begins, share biographical information about Jon Scieszka with students by paging through the newspaper you have created. When you have finished reading the headlines, close the paper and say, "That's the story of how Jon Scieszka brought new magic into the world of storytelling." As you say this, fold the paper in half and turn it upside down, allowing the bookmarks/stickers to magically fall out of the paper!

Oink, Oink . . . Guess Who!

This circle game is based on *The True Story of the 3 Little Pigs: By A. Wolf*. To play, have all the children sit in a circle. Select one child to stand in the middle and be Alexander T. Wolf ("Al"). Blindfold the wolf and turn her around three times. The wolf will point to anyone in the circle, who then states, "Oink, oink!" The wolf must guess who the voice belongs to by saying, "May I borrow a cup of sugar, (name)?" If the wolf names the correct person, the players trade places. If the wolf cannot guess three players' names correctly, have the wolf trade places with another player anyway, to keep the game moving.

Happily Ever After?

This improvisation activity is based on *The Frog Prince, Continued*. Before the party, write the names of famous couples from fairy tales on slips of paper, such as Cinderella and Prince

Charming; Snow White and the Prince; Sleeping Beauty and the Prince; Beauty and the Beast; Rapunzel and the Prince; etc. Place the slips of paper in a box that you've wrapped like a birthday present.

- During the party, discuss this book's purpose: to explore how a well-known fairy tale might end if the story continued on after the marriage ceremony. Pair up the children and have one member of each pair pick a slip of paper from the decorated box. Instruct the partners to talk about what might happen between these couples after the wedding. Have them brainstorm some ideas that are specific to the characters, such as Cinderella being a compulsive cleaner, Snow White constantly singing to the birds, etc. Then have each pair act out a scene for the class. Give out silly award ribbons, such as Most Creative Ending or Silliest Story.

Hot on the Trail of the Stinky Cheese Man

Divide the students into groups of three or four and have each group use clues that you provide to figure out where the Stinky Cheese Man is hiding. Place a picture of the Stinky Cheese Man in the final location, along with a small prize for each group member. Sample clues might be

- Run, run as fast as you can . . . you can't catch me, I'm the Stinky Cheese Man!
- I ran past the shelves with board books of all sorts, and now I'm cruising on past the videos really fast!
- I passed the videos for all you kid-eos and now I'm bouncing like a ball to the Author Wall!
- I ran past the videos for all you kid-eos, I bounced like a ball past the Author Wall, and soon I'll play by the Autumn display!
- I ran past the board books with all sorts of looks, I bounced like a ball past the Author Wall, I was able to play by the Autumn display, and now I'll go by the sitting scarecrow!
- Run, run as fast as you can! You caught me, the Stinky Cheese Man!

Howdy, Pardner!

Cowboy & Octopus is comprised of several brief, comedic episodes in which a cowboy and an octopus develop a new friendship. Have students partner up and share a unique story about themselves, such as the silliest Halloween costume they've ever worn (based on an episode in the book), or their favorite food, etc. Once they've established the beginnings of a friendship, give each partner set a booklet of fun partner games, such as a page of tic-tac-toe grids or dots for the Dot Game (in which players take turns connecting dots in order to make boxes; see www.su perkids.com/aweb/tools/logic/dots for sample game, which can be played on a simple piece of graph paper). Games make a great activity to start off the party because you can form partners as children enter the party area. It gives them something fun to do while you set up other activities, or distribute the party treats—and it can be a great ice breaker.

Time Warp Activities

Scieszka's popular Time Warp Trio series serves as the inspiration for the following activities. Before you dive in, consider asking one or more of these questions to get students thinking:

- What year would you like to travel to? Why?
- Why do you think the author wrote these books?
- Would your mom let you use the "Book" to travel through time?
- Who are you most like: Joe, Sam, or Fred?

Parachute Game

Have all the students stand around a parachute and hold onto it. Choose one child at a time to go under it and crawl through the "time warp" (the parachute) while the rest of the children shake the parachute. As the chosen child crawls under the parachute, show the students a famous year in history that they would all have knowledge about, such as 1776 (signing of the Declaration of Independence), 1969 (first moon landing), 1849 (gold is discovered in California), etc. Once the child emerges from the parachute, the students can raise their hands to give the time-traveling student clues about what year they've traveled to. Choose years from the book series, too, to give students more ideas to draw from.

Craft: Time Capsule Book

In honor of Scieszka's Time Warp Trio series, make time capsules! Before the celebration, cut poster board into 5 ½" x 8 ½" sheets (enough for two for each student). These sheets will serve as book covers. Cut plain paper into the same dimensions, enough for five pages for each student. Staple the covers and five pages together to make a book for each student. Take a Polaroid or digital photo of each child, have them fill out a questionnaire about themselves, and then place the books in a box that all the students can decorate.

During the party, talk about the idea of time travel and preserving personal histories for future generations. Distribute the blank books and have the students make a cover for them. On the pages, have students write responses to the following prompts: Name, age, favorite color, favorite food, hobbies, favorite school subjects, best friends' names, favorite books, goals for future career(s), important current events for future generations to know, etc. Collect the books in the time capsule. At the end of the school year, open the capsule and return the books to their owners. Ask students how things have changed, even over the course of a year. What is the same? What is different? Allow time for sharing.

Fibonacci Nature Hunt

In *Math Curse,* the teacher's name is Mrs. Fibonacci, the same name as the man who discovered the golden ratio in nature and developed the Fibonacci pattern. The golden ratio is based on the progression of natural objects as they grow from 1 to 2, to 3, to 5, to 8, etc., in size dimensions, in reproduction, and in appendages (flower petals, plant leaves, etc.). Hide the following items or images around the room:

pine cone, pineapple, seashell, rose, sunflower, photo of a human hand, and other Fibonacci-related images.

Collect other images of Fibonacci in nature and show the patterns to students. Then show them the pattern: 1, 1, 2, 3, 5, 8, and ask them to look carefully at the pattern and try to determine what numbers come next.

Divide the students into groups and have them find the hidden items. To make it more challenging, give them clues or riddles to solve that will lead them to the object, such as, "You can hear the ocean within my curved walls, and I am the home to small creatures." Once they guess that the object is a seashell, they can look for it and place it in a paper bag. The first group to collect all of their artifacts wins. Prizes could be pencils with colorful eraser tops, or other items to use in math class.

Rhyme Time!

In *Science Verse,* Jon Scieszka presents scientific concepts through poems written in the style of other famous poets. Give each small group the tune to a familiar song (either a different tune for each group, or the same for all). Sample tunes might include "Three Blind Mice," "She'll Be Comin' Round the Mountain," or "Twinkle, Twinkle, Little Star." Have the students make a list of key ideas about a current science unit. Each group must use their list to create lyrics that match up to their assigned tune. They will write a song about the science unit and sing it to the class.

Seen Art?

This creative book about seeing art throughout the Museum of Modern Art (MoMA) can be easily integrated into a celebration and/or art class. Here are a few ideas:

- Choose any artist and conduct a lesson about his/her work by simply showing the artwork from Internet searches. Display it on the overhead projector in chronological order to show the progression of the artist's works, styles, and inspirations. Select a specific style for the students to learn about and imitate in their own art projects.

- Visit the website of your own local art museum and enjoy a virtual tour of the artwork housed in that location. Are there some local artists featured in the museum? If so, focus on their artwork and the local inspirations behind the work. For example, perhaps they painted or photographed a local street, store, or monument. Have the students create artwork of the same point of interest using a variety of media.
- Create a webquest for the Museum of Modern Art's website and have the students follow the clues to find works of art by featured artists.
- What is art? Have the students decorate paper towel tubes and use them as "Artiscopes." Allow them to slowly walk around the classroom, library, playground, etc., using the artiscope to focus on, and locate, details that they may not otherwise notice in these familiar environments. Have them choose one particular detail that pleases them and draw it using oil pastels, charcoal, or any other uncommon media. Talk about the fact that art is everywhere if one pays attention to his/her environment and captures it in a unique way. Revisit Scieszka's book and focus on the subjects that the artists used to create their own masterpieces.

Celebration Food
- Stinky Cheeseman cheese and cracker tray (based on *The Stinky Cheeseman and Other Fairly Stupid Tales*)
- Alexander T. Wolf's Granny's birthday cake
- "Artistic Cookies" (based on *Seen Art?*): provide round sugar cookies with frosting and sprinkles for students to decorate and create their own creations before eating them
- "Cupcake Conundrums" (based on *Math Curse*): display a tray of cupcakes and ask various math problems, such as "What fraction of the cupcakes has green frosting?" Partners can work together to solve the problems and the first pair to raise their hands and provide the correct answer can each get a cupcake. Tailor this activity to match the math skills of your students.

Party Favors

Markers designed for blowing air into them to spatter their colors on paper (create small labels a la "Alexander T. Wolf's Huff-&-Puff Pens"), small brain teasers (in honor of *Math Curse),* small sand timers (Time Warp Trio series), etc.

Birthday Greetings

One way to contact Jon Scieszka is via email. Go to his website (jsworldwide.com) and link to his email. Have the students each dictate a sentence to include in a class birthday card and email it to him. If you have an interactive white board, the students could each draw a picture and sign it; this could then be attached to the email for a more personalized greeting. Digital photos of the class's birthday celebration would also be a nice way to enhance an email note.

Happy Birthday, Jon Scieszka!

Born September 8, 1954

Picture Books

- *Baloney, Henry P.*
- *The Book That Jack Wrote*
- *Cowboy & Octopus*
- *The Frog Prince, Continued*
- *Math Curse*
- *Robot Zot!*
- *Seen Art?*
- *The True Story of the 3 Little Pigs*

Time Warp Trio Series

- *Knights of the Kitchen Table* (#1)
- *The Not-So-Jolly Roger* (#2)
- *The Good, The Bad & the Goofy* (#3)
- *Your Mother was a Neanderthal* (#4)
- *2095* (#5)
- *Tut, Tut* (#6)
- *Summer Reading is Killing Me* (#7)
- *It's All Greek To Me* (#8)
- *See You Later, Gladiator* (#9)
- *Sam Samurai* (#10)
- *Hey Kid, Want to Buy a Bridge?* (#11)
- *Viking It and Liking It* (#12)
- *Me Oh Maya* (#13)
- *Da Wild, Da Crazy da Vinci* (#14)
- *Oh Say, I Can't See* (#15)
- *Marco? Polo!* (#16)

Other Titles

- *Guys Write for Guys Read* (ed. by Jon Scieszka)
- *Knucklehead: Tall Tales & Mostly True Stories About Growing Up Scieszka*
- *Science Verse*
- *Spaceheads: SPHDZ Book 1*
- *Squids Will Be Squids*
- *The Stinky Cheese Man and Other Fairly Stupid Tales*

Jon Scieszka Reading Log

Read 5 books by **September** ____.

On each line, write the title you've read and have your parent/guardian sign that you read it.

Bring this completed reading log to me by **September** ____ and receive your invitation to attend our birthday celebration on

_____.

Date/Time

_____
Title   Parent/Guardian Signature

_____
Title   Parent/Guardian Signature

_____
Title   Parent/Guardian Signature

_____
Title   Parent/Guardian Signature

_____
Title   Parent/Guardian Signature

Happy Birthday, Dear Paul Goble!

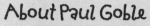

About Paul Goble

- Birthday: September 27, 1933
- Birth place: Haslemere, England
- Paul Goble became a permanent U.S. resident in 1977 and won the Caldecott Award for *The Girl Who Loved Wild Horses* soon after.
- He has been formally adopted by the Lakota and the Yakima peoples.
- He donated many of his original paintings to the South Dakota Art Museum. You can explore them at www.southdakotaartmuseum.com/explore_paul.htm.
- He has been fascinated by Native Americans since he was a young boy when his mother would read books about Native Americans to him.

Celebration Ideas

Paul Goble's Story

Provide crayons and torn pieces of brown butcher paper to students and tell them about key events in Paul Goble's life (see sample script at right). Before you begin, explain that many Native American tribes lived in tipis, including the Lakota tribe. Tipi walls were often made of buffalo hides and painted with symbols that depicted the tribe's history. Pass around copies of *Tipi: Home of the Nomadic Buffalo Hunters* and tell students to imagine that their torn pieces of paper are buffalo hides, and that their crayons are paints. Explain to students that as you relate this story, they are to create symbols on the torn paper that they feel represent key events in the story. For younger students, use prompts to help inspire them, if necessary.

As you tell the story, pause for a little while after each part to give students a chance to draw. When the story is finished, give each child another piece of butcher paper. Let the children decorate it with symbols that tell about their own histories. Use Paul Goble's autobiographical work, *Hau Kola: Hello Friend*, as a source for story information.

Sample Story Script: Hau Kola! (Hello, Friend!)

On September 27, 1933, in England, Paul Goble was born.

[Students might draw a symbol for baby]

He lived in a small home with a beautiful garden and a pond. This was his favorite spot to sit and think. "The place helped me grow in my mind," he said.

[Students might draw a symbol for knowledge]

He would often search for wild flowers or sketch small birds. But one of his favorite pastimes was to go into the newly plowed fields and search for stone-age tools and arrowheads.

[Students might draw a symbol for arrows]

The arrowheads made him wonder about the people who lived long ago. He became fascinated by the history of native peoples, and he read many books about them. His mom even made a tipi for him!

[Students might draw a tipi]

Now he lives in America, where he still loves to learn about native peoples. He and his wife, Janet, and their son, Robert, live in South Dakota. Here, Paul Goble can visit Native American tribes and learn about their folklore.

[Students might draw a symbol for friendship and/or community]

Once Paul Goble has a new story to tell, he works at home to turn that story into a new picture book. He works many hours each day to get the words and pictures just the way he wants them.

[Students might draw a symbol for books]

He reads many books and visits Native American museums to make sure his details are correct.

[Students might draw a symbol for wisdom]

Paul Goble asks, "Do you like to write or paint? Do you sometimes feel disappointed with the results of your hard work? I also feel like that, and yet, if we are patient, the spirits do come. Do not be discouraged. Try again. May the wanagi help you."

[Students might draw a symbol for encouragement]

Iktomi Treasure Hunt

Iktomi is a character in several books by Paul Goble. Iktomi is a trickster, but he often falls victim to his own tricks! Tell the students that Iktomi has lost his horse, and they must follow the clues to find the missing horse.

Preparations

Create 4 sets of 5 clues, 1 set of 5 clues for 4 teams of students. The clues should lead the students to various landmarks around the classroom, or to various sections of the library. For instance,

a. Help Iktomi find his horse! He was seen wandering over by the DVDs.
b. You just missed him! Did you see him gallop away? He headed over to the biography section.
c. The horse liked these books, but then he got hungry! He is grazing by the fairy tale display.
d. Oh, that horse is as tricky as Iktomi! He finished grazing over here, and now he is resting by the fish tank. Tiptoe over to the tank quietly . . . maybe you can sneak up on him before he gallops away!

e. You found the horse! Trot over to (your desk or a general gathering place) to get your reward!

Print out the horses reproducible on page 32. Print out five copies of each horse, cut them out, and glue or tape your clues onto the back of each horse. Follow your clues and hide the horses in their appropriate spots. You will give each team the first horse/clue to get them started on their hunt.

Game Time

Set the scene by reviewing a few of Goble's Iktomi tales. Tell the students that Iktomi has lost his horse, so they need to follow the clues to find it. Then divide the group into four teams. Give each team its first horse clue and review the directions. The first group to find Iktomi's horse wins the game (of course, you'll have enough small prizes for everyone once all the groups have found their horses). Prizes might be bookmarks made with Lakota symbols, stickers, small bag of candy, pencils, etc.

Create a Museum Display

Read *Storm Maker's Tipi* and discuss the illustrations of the Native American camp. On the last page of the book, Goble has provided a template of a tipi for readers to photocopy. Provide photocopies of this tipi on cards tock and have the students use symbols to decorate the tipi. Then follow the directions for cutting and assembly. Provide a table top that you have covered with green butcher paper, and have the students arrange their tipis on the table top for a museum display of how the Napi people set up their camp. Include information about cottonwood trees, since their leaves inspired the Napi's construction of the tipi. Have students research these people, and include interesting notes and captions for the display.

Become a Wild Horse

This is a game that focuses on Goble's popular award-winning book, *The Girl Who Loved Wild Horses*. It is noncompetitive, so the fun is in the game and not in getting a prize!

Directions

Read through the directions below and explain the game to students before playing.

1. Blindfold all the players, and stand in the middle of the room.
2. Tell the players to start bumping into each other asking "Wild Horse?"
3. If the other player answers back, "Wild Horse?" then that player is not the Wild Horse.
4. After about 30 seconds, you will tap someone on the shoulder and whisper, "You are the Wild Horse."
5. The Wild Horse may open his eyes, but he is not allowed to talk.
6. Once someone bumps into the Wild Horse and asks "Wild Horse?", the Wild Horse still must not answer. This will signal to the first player that she has found the Wild Horse. She may then open her eyes and hold the Wild Horse's hand, thereby becoming the Wild Horse, too.
7. Play continues, and the Wild Horse grows as a chain of students develops.
8. Eventually, all the students will form one continuous chain, holding hands and becoming the Wild Horse!

Craft: Make a Love Flute

In Goble's book, *Love Flute,* a shy Native American woos a young woman by playing beautiful music on a flute given to him by the birds. Have the children make their own flutes. You will need 12-inch cardboard tubes (preferably from wrapping paper), colored plastic tape, and markers.

Directions

a. Before the party, cut a ¾" x ¼" rectangle approximately 2 inches from one end of the tube. This will be the mouthpiece.
b. Next, use a sharpened pencil to puncture six holes along the length of the tube, each approximately 1 inch apart. These will be the holes that the students will cover with their fingers to change the tone and pitch of the notes.
c. The students can use four pieces of plastic tape to cover the end of the tube that is closest to the mouthpiece. This will direct the air to flow out of the other end.
d. The students can use markers to decorate their flutes.
e. The students can experiment with playing their flutes. Teach them how to play the flute softly as they blow air over the mouthpiece. Model reverence for this genre of music.

Symbolgram Identities

As a class, make a list of positive characteristics that they would like to cultivate in their own personalities (i.e., trustworthiness, honor, respect, love, happiness, kindness, love of nature, etc.). Next, have the students brainstorm symbols that they feel would represent each characteristic. For example, perhaps a shield would symbolize honor, or a heart could symbolize love. They could even discuss specific colors and what moods and ideals each one conveys (i.e., blue might make them think of calm, serenity, coolness, sorrow, etc.). Have the students list some characteristics that reflect their own identities and create a symbolgram of themselves by arranging the symbols for each characteristic into a pleasing shape or composition, and using colors that convey the ideals of each characteristic. Students could cut out the symbol shapes from colored construction paper and arrange them on a larger sheet of butcher paper. Hang them up in the room, on the backs of their chairs, or on a bulletin board. Be sure to create a symbolgram for yourself!

Birthday Greetings

Have students select a shape, such as a tipi, horse, or buffalo. Each student can color their shape and write a brief birthday greeting on it, then glue it onto a large paper. Fill in the landscape around the shapes with trees, Native Americans, etc. Mail this class-made mural to Paul Goble, expressing your gratitude to him for his wonderful books that have enlightened so many of us on the cultures of various Native American tribes.

Party Favors

Provide students with dreamcatchers (available from party catalogs), small plastic horses, and a smooth pebble with a word on it to inspire students, such as "love," "faith," "truth," or "honor." Put these items into a small bag and create a label that reads, "Happy Birthday, Paul Goble!" to adhere to each bag.

Party Food

Serve sugar cookies cut into horse shapes. Frost and decorate them before the party. Sing "Happy Birthday" to Paul Goble and enjoy!

Climb the Mountain!

Play this game in honor of the hills, bluffs, and mountains of the western states, where many of Goble's books take place. To play the game, draw a large outline of a mountain on the board. Next, draw three horizontal lines, each one a third of the way up the height of the mountain:

Before the Celebration

Prepare a set of questions about Goble's books and his life story.

During the Celebration

Give each child an index card on which they must write their names. Tell them to hold onto their cards. Read aloud one of your questions and call on the first student to raise her hand. If her answer is correct, he/she may tape the index card on the base of the mountain. If she is incorrect, call on another student until the correct answer is given. Once students are on the mountain base, they can move their index card into the next zone for each subsequent correct answer. The first to climb the mountain and reach its peak (in Zone 3) is the winner!

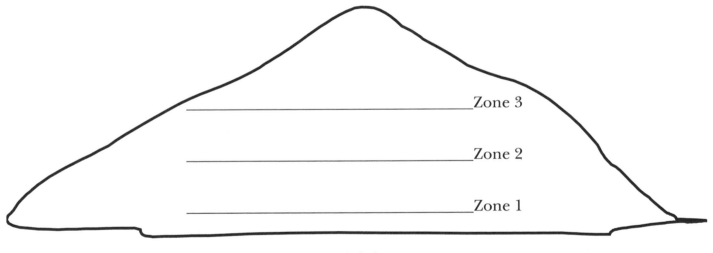

mountain's base

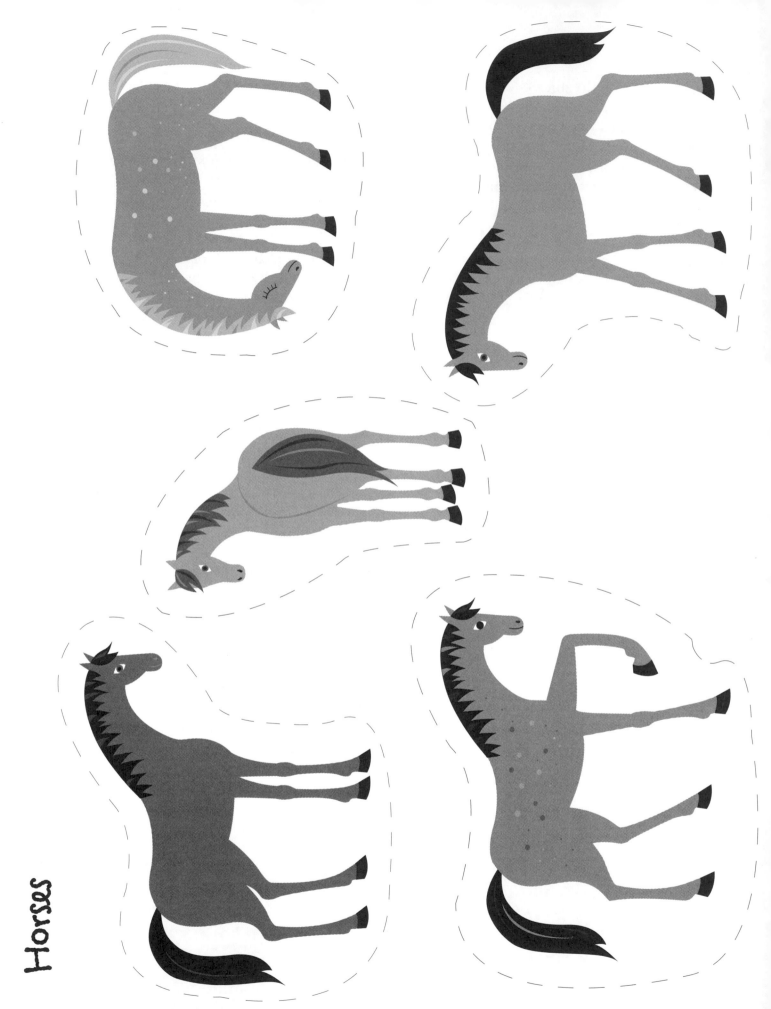

Horses

Happy Birthday, Paul Goble!

Born September 27, 1933

Picture Books

- *Adopted by the Eagles*
- *Beyond the Ridge*
- *Buffalo Woman*
- *Death of the Iron Horse*
- *The Gift of the Sacred Dog*
- *The Girl Who Loved Wild Horses*
- *The Great Race of the Birds and Animals*
- *Her Seven Brothers*
- *Iktomi and the Berries*
- *Iktomi and the Boulder*
- *Iktomi and the Buffalo Skull*
- *Iktomi and the Buzzards*
- *Iktomi and the Ducks*
- *Iktomi Loses His Eyes*
- *The Earth Made Me New: Plains Indians' Stories of Creation*
- *The Legend of the White Buffalo Woman*
- *Love Flute*
- *Mystic Horse*
- *Remaking the Earth*
- *The Return of the Buffalo*
- *Star Boy*
- *Storm Maker's Tipi*
- *The Woman Who Lived With Wolves and Other Stories from the Tipi*

Folktales

- *All Our Relatives: Traditional Native American Thoughts About Nature*
- *The Boy and His Mud Horses and Other Stories from the Tipi*
- *Crow Chief*

Informational Picture Books

- *Tipi: Home of the Nomadic Buffalo Hunters* (with Rodney Frey)

Autobiographical

- *Hau Kola: Hello Friend* (Meet the Author, with Gerry Perrin)

Paul Goble Reading Log

Read 5 books by **September** ____.

On each line, write the title you've read and have your parent/guardian sign that you read it.

Bring this completed reading log to me by **September** ____ and receive your invitation to attend our birthday celebration on

_____.

Date/Time

_____

Title   Parent/Guardian Signature

_____

Title   Parent/Guardian Signature

_____

Title   Parent/Guardian Signature

_____

Title   Parent/Guardian Signature

_____

Title   Parent/Guardian Signature

Happy Birthday, Dear Authors Born in October!

October 1	Ann Morris	October 15	Katheirne Ayres
October 2	David Diaz		Barry Moser
October 3	James Herriot	October 16	**Joseph Bruchac***
	Marilyn Singer	October 18	Nancy Winslow Parker
October 5	David Shannon		Ntozake Shange
	Gene Zion	October 19	Ed Emberley
October 7	Susan Jeffers		Dan Gutman
October 8	Faith Ringgold	October 20	Nikki Grimes
	Mike Thaler		Crockett Johnson
October 9	Johanna Hurwitz	October 21	Ann Cameron
October 10	Nancy L. Carson	October 25	Carolyn Bailey
	Daniel San Souci	October 26	**Steven Kellogg***
	Robert D. San Souci*		Eric Rohmann
October 11	Russell Freedman	October 29	Valerie Worth
October 14	Miriam Cohen	October 30	Eric Kimmel
	Elisa Kevlin		

*Author featured in this chapter

Happy Birthday, Dear Robert D. San Souci!

About Robert D. San Souci

- Robert D. San Souci was born October 10, 1946.
- His last name is pronounced "San Soo-see."
- He has lived in San Francisco all his life.
- When he was a boy, he mowed neighbors' lawns for 25¢ an hour and used that money to buy used books!
- He wrote the script for Disney's™ movie, *Mulan*.
- His brother, Daniel San Souci, is an award-winning picture book illustrator. The two brothers have worked together on nine books!

Celebration Activities

Tell Robert San Souci's Story

In honor of San Souci's volumes of scary stories, such as *Short and Shivery: Thirty Chilling Tales*, *More Short and Shivery: Thirty Terrifying Tales*, and *A Terrifying Taste of Short and Shivery*, tell San Souci's biography like you would a scary story: turn out the lights, draw sketches of key events with glow-in-the-dark chalk, use a sinister voice . . . have fun with it! Here is a sample story that you can tell near a chalk or smart board:

Many years ago, on a shivery October day in 1946, a young boy was born. *(Draw a leafless tree and a baby.)*

This boy grew up with a brother named Daniel. He told Daniel a story that he had heard, and Daniel was mesmerized! Daniel laughed, and he gasped at the scary parts; he was a captive audience!

Soon this young boy knew in his heart that he wanted to be a storyteller. *(Draw a heart.)*

(With large eyes and scary voice) This boy entered high school and crept down the dark corridor of the hallway after school (walk in place on tiptoe, as if creeping along). He walked up to a darkened room, where he heard other voices talking about new events at the school. He opened the door and realized (with voice's pitch increasing for dramatic effect) this was the school newspaper club! *(Draw a newspaper.)*

He wrote his stories for the school newspaper and the yearbook throughout his high school years. He knew that these clubs would help him to become a writer and storyteller. *(Draw a pen.)*

Once in college, he majored in creative writing and world literature. He spent many dark nights combing through the folktales of many cultures. *(Draw a moon.)*

After college, he continued to study folklore. He traveled around the world through his extensive reading of books about many cultures. *(Draw the earth.)*

Finally, after working for a bookstore and telling creepy stories to his friends and customers, this man published his first children's book! *(Draw a book.)*

Who is this man who can send shivers up our spines with one of his scary stories, yet also make us learn more about different cultures? Why, it's Robert D. San Souci! *BOO!* And guess who illustrated his first book? His brother, Daniel San Souci!

(Turn on the lights and review the key events of his life by talking about the drawings with the class.)

Craft: Make Glow-in-the-dark Chalk

Use the recipe from *The Ultimate Book of Kid Concoctions* (Thomas & Pagel, 1988).

Ingredients:

- 1/3 cup quick-setting Plaster of Paris
- 1 Tbsp. glow-in-the-dark paint, such as Glo Away by Plaid®
- 3 Tbsp. water
- Plastic cookie cutter, candy mold, or toilet paper tube

Instructions:

1. Mix plaster, paint, and water together in a small bowl.
2. Spoon the mixture into the mold.
3. Let the chalk dry for 30–45 minutes.
4. Carefully pop the chalk out of the mold.
5. Provide instructions for home use: Draw design on paper or sidewalk, and shine a flashlight directly on it to energize the glowing capacity.

Write to the Author

Create a Halloween Mural. Provide students with templates of bats, stars, knotty trees, owls, etc. Students trace the shape's outline onto light colored paper and write a brief birthday message on it. Cut it out and glue it onto dark blue butcher paper to create a group mural, and mail it to Robert San Souci. His contact information is available on his website (www.rsansouci.com).

Treasure Hunt

Find the five dogs to save the girl from the Hobyahs! This treasure hunt is based on *The Hobyahs*.

Before the Celebration

Create a sequence of five clues, one for each dog. For example, Clue #1 would say, "We [the dogs] are hiding in the Nonfiction Forest! You will find Dog #1 (Turpie) hanging out by the folktales. Go to the aisle with call # 398.2." Hide the next clue, which has a copy of Turpie on one side and Clue #2 on the reverse side, so that it is partially visible once the students enter the correct aisle. Clue #2 will then lead them to the next dog, Topie, and Clue #3. Once the students find the fifth dog, have them report to you to receive a small prize.

Ultimately, you will have 4–5 small groups playing, so you will need to create 4–5 sets of clues.

During the Celebration

Divide the students into 4–5 small groups and give each group its first clue. Then, send them on the treasure hunt! This is a great way for students to review the Dewey Decimal system and get to know their school library!

Foolish Fisherman Games

In honor of San Souci's Cajun version of *Six Foolish Fishermen*, have the students participate in a variety of silly/foolish games.

- Banana Pass: Line up the students into teams of six (for the six fishermen). Give the first student in each team's line a banana. The student places the banana between his knees and must pass it to the knees of the next student in line. The first team to get the banana passed to the last player in line, wins!

- Dizzy Lizzy: This game must be played on a grassy play area. Give each team of six players one baseball or wiffle ball bat. The players will take turns putting their foreheads to the bat's handle, with the bat standing on end. They must keep their forehead on the bat while running around it 2–3 times. Then, they will let the bat fall to the ground and run to a finish line. Most runners will have difficulty running in a straight line!

- Silly Olympics: Use straws for a "javelin throw," use paper balls for the "shot put," and use paper plates for the "discus throw."

A Weave of Words

Teach students a simple weaving project, such as paper placemats. Have the students weave 1-inch strips of construction paper into a 9" x 12" paper. They could use Halloween colors and set out their placemats for the class Halloween party. Older students could learn to weave a small pouch, using yarn and a cardboard frame. An excellent resource for this project is *You Can Weave! Projects for Young Weavers* (Monaghan & Joyner, 2000). The step-by-step directions presented in this book are geared toward children, ages seven and up. You can also consult a website such as www.wikihow.com/Make-Placemats-by-Weaving-Paper-Strips.

Magic Show

Several of San Souci's folktales involve magical transformations, especially *The Hired Hand: An African-American*, *The Silver Charm: A Folktale from Japan*, and *The White Cat: An Old French Fairy*. Allow time for students to volunteer their participation in a magic show. Bring in several children's books that demonstrate a variety of tricks. Have students sign up for the show and have them share their skills during the celebration. Here are a few tricks that the teacher can perform during the party, too:

- Party Potion: Before the celebration, empty the contents of a fruit drink mix into a clear plastic pitcher. Fill a second pitcher with cold water. Tell the students that you will transform this pitcher of water into fruit punch and pour the water into the prepared clear pitcher. As the water interacts with the powdered mix, it will change into the color of the drink mix!

- Crayon Resist Story: Before the celebration, use a thick white crayon to write out a story or a birthday message on white construction paper. Hang this up on the front chalkboard and tell the students, "Robert San Souci is a master of folktales; he magically turns blank paper into stories of adventure and fantasy. In honor of his wonderful talent, I will transform this blank paper into a story with the stroke of a paintbrush!" Dip a thick brush into purple or blue watercolor (use a deep hue so the white crayon words will appear with ease). Slowly paint over each word, encouraging the students to read the story or message aloud as each word is revealed.

- Guess My Favorite Book: Place a decorative party bag on a table and hold a pad of paper in your hands. Tell the students to think about which San Souci book was their favorite, and ask students to raise their hands to volunteer their answers. Call on a student, and write down the title that is volunteered by that student. Then fold the paper, and put it into the party bag. Continue to write this same title on new paper, no matter what title the subsequent students tell you. By the end of this activity, the party bag should be filled with folded pieces of paper that all contain the same title on them. Shake the bag dramatically, and hand it to one student. Have the student close her eyes, reach into the bag, and draw a folded piece of paper. Have her read the title and not tell anyone else the name of the title. Tell the class that you will guess which title is on the paper. Ham it up, saying, "Okay, it's becoming clearer . . . I see the word, 'folktale' in the title . . .", etc. Guess the title and have the student reveal that you were correct! This and other good ideas can be found in *Leading Kids to Books Through Magic* by Caroline Feller Bauer (1993).

Sukey's Treasure: Based on *Sukey and the Mermaid*

In this activity, students will try to solve riddles in order to win chocolate gold coins, which can easily be purchased online.

Before the Celebration

Type up a variety of riddles. These could be based on current science or social studies topics, or mathematical riddles. Place 3–5 riddles in a party bag (written on individual strips of paper and folded in half).

During the Celebration

Divide the students into teams of 4–5 and give each team one bag of riddles. Have one student on the first team draw a paper from the bag and read the riddle aloud. Teams should then put their heads together to solve the riddle. The first team to raise their hands and tell the correct answer wins a gold coin. Continue until all of the riddles have been solved. The team with most gold coins wins the game; however, be sure to provide at least one gold coin to all of the other students, too.

Cinderella Silliness

San Souci has retold a variety of Cinderella variants, including: *Sootface: An Ojibwa Cinderella Story, Cendrillon: A Caribbean Cinderella, Little Gold Star: A Spanish-American Cinderella*, and *The Talking Eggs*. Here are several activities related to elements of Cinderella tales.

- Older primary students could fill in a graph in which they record the basic elements found in San Souci's Cinderella variants, including Cinderella character; stepmother; siblings; magic source; goal; rags-to-riches event; token (i.e., glass slipper). They could also find variants by other folklorists to add to their chart and create their own Cinderella story set in modern times (using the chart headings to scaffold them in the construction of their stories).
- Race: Help Cinderella get ready for the special event (dance, ball, etc.). Divide students into two teams, and have each team stand behind the finish line. Give each leader one suitcase with a variety of fancy clothes packed inside. Upon command, each team member must run with the suitcase to a finish line, open the case and put on the garments, then run back to the start line, remove the garments, and hand the suitcase to the next player. Play continues until one team finishes first.
- What Would Cinderella Do? All Cinderella characters share common characteristics that show their integrity. Brainstorm a list of such characteristics with the students.

Before the Celebration

Type several scenarios in which a person is faced with a difficult dilemma. Place these scenarios in a party bag.

During the Celebration

Divide students into small groups. Have a representative of each group pick a slip of paper from the bag and bring it to the group. Instruct the groups to discuss what Cinderella would do in that situation, and tell them to draw a picture of their scenario. Provide time for each group to share their scenario with the class. Encourage them to use the brainstormed list of words to help them.

Party Favors

Gold coins (chocolate or plastic), for *Sukey and the Mermaid*; plastic eggs filled with small candies, for *The Talking Eggs*; a small bead kit for making their own silver charms, for *The Silver Charm: A Folktale From Japan*; or a small notebook and pencil to encourage students to write down their own retellings of folktales.

Happy Birthday, Robert San Souci!

Born October 10, 1946

Folktales

- *Brave Margaret*
- *Cendrillon: A Caribbean Cinderella*
- *Cinderella Skeleton*
- *Cut From the Same Cloth: American Women of Myth, Legend, and Tall Tale*
- *The Enchanted Tapestry: A Chinese Folktale*
- *Even More Short and Shivery: Thirty Spine-Tingling Stories*
- *Fa Mulan: The Story of a Woman Warrior*
- *The Faithful Friend*
- *Feathertop: Based on the Tale by Nathaniel Hawthorne*
- *The Firebird*
- *The Hired Hand*
- *The Hobyahs*
- *Larger Than Life: The Adventures of American Legendary Heroes*
- *The Legend of Scarface*
- *The Legend of Sleepy Hollow*
- *Little Gold Star: A Spanish-American Cinderella*
- *More Short and Shivery: Thirty Terrifying Tales*
- *Nicholas Pipe*
- *Pedro and the Monkey*
- *The Samarai's Daughter: A Japanese Legend*
- *The Secret of the Stones*
- *Short and Shivery: Thirty Chilling Tales*
- *The Silver Charm: A Folktale from Japan*
- *Six Foolish Fishermen*
- *Sootface: An Ojibwa Cinderella Story*
- *Sukey and the Mermaid*
- *The Talking Eggs: A Folktale from the American South*
- *Tarzan*
- *A Terrifying Taste of Short and Shivery*
- *The Twins and the Bird of Darkness*
- *Two Bear Cubs*
- *A Weave of Words: An Armenian Tale*
- *The White Cat: An Old French Fairy Tale*
- *Young Arthur*
- *Young Guinevere*
- *Young Lancelot*
- *Young Merlin*

Biography

- *Kate Shelley: Bound For Legend*

Picture Book

- *The Christmas Ark*

Robert San Souci Reading Log

Read 5 books by **October** _____.

On each line, write the title you've read and have your parent/guardian sign that you read it.

Bring this completed reading log to me by **October** _____ and receive your invitation to attend our birthday celebration on

_____.

Date/Time

_____
Title   Parent/Guardian Signature

_____
Title   Parent/Guardian Signature

_____
Title   Parent/Guardian Signature

_____
Title   Parent/Guardian Signature

_____
Title   Parent/Guardian Signature

Happy Birthday, Dear Joseph Bruchac!

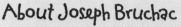

About Joseph Bruchac

- Joseph Bruchac was born on October 16, 1942 in Saratoga Springs, New York.
- His last name is pronounced "Brew-shack".
- He was raised by his Abenaki grandparents.
- His grandfather passed along a knowledge of nature by taking Joseph for many walks in the woods behind their home.
- Joseph wanted to become a naturalist when he grew up.
- He married his college sweetheart, Carol.
- He has two grown sons: James and Jake.

Celebration Ideas

Joseph Bruchac: Dreamweaver and Native American Storyteller

Relate a story about Joseph Bruchac using a dreamcatcher as the vehicle for telling the story.

<u>Before the Celebration</u>

Cut yarn into 20-foot lengths, one per student. On one end of each length of yarn, attach a small word card. Each card's word will relate to a significant part of Joseph Bruchac's life. Arrange the yarn lengths on the floor, loosely forming the shape of a dreamcatcher (see _www. dream-catchers.org_ for images and instructions for making a dreamcatcher). The following words could be used for the cards:

1. **October 16**—The date of Joseph Bruchac's birth.
2. **Maternal Grandparents**—These are the people who raised Joseph. They owned a store in the Adirondack Mountains called Bowman's Store. Here, Joseph sat behind the wood-burning stove and listened to the people gathered in the store, telling their stories.
3. **Abenaki**—Joseph's maternal grandparents were Native Americans from the Abenaki tribe. Joseph's father was from a country in Central Europe called Czechoslovakia, which is now two countries: the Czech Republic and Slovakia.
4. **Shame**—His maternal grandparents never spoke of their Native American heritage because, back then, it was shameful to admit to being Native American. His grandfather, Grandpa Jesse, was very dark skinned and would tell people that he was French because he was ashamed.
5. **Library**—Growing up, Joseph loved to read, so his Grandpa Jesse often took him to the library. Grandpa Jesse dropped out of school in fourth grade because he was tired of enduring the harassment and prejudice of his classmates. He was not a good reader, and, therefore, he was very proud of Joseph's excellent reading ability. Joseph has said that he had two favorite places to be when he was a child, and the library was #1!
6. **Nature**—Joseph also loved nature. His second favorite place to be was in the woods, behind his childhood home. His grandfather often took him into the woods and taught him how to follow animal tracks, identify plants, and how to be very observant. These wonderful experiences inspired Joseph's desire to be a naturalist.
7. **Poetry**—Joseph began writing poetry in second grade and continued all through high school. It wasn't until he took a creative writing class at Cornell, however, that he began to see himself as a writer. He switched his major to English.

8. **James & Jesse**—Carol and Joseph are the proud parents of two sons, James and Jesse. James is a teacher of Native outdoor awareness and Jesse is a storyteller of Abenaki heritage tales.

9. **Culture**—Joseph Bruchac has dedicated his life to preserving Native American culture. He works diligently to change the view his grandparents had of their heritage by sharing his stories with all of us.

10. **Spirituality**—Joseph says that an important theme in his books is spirituality; we need to work at developing our inner strengths of character, respect, and connection to the earth, rather than only focusing on material objects, like getting toys and gadgets.

11. **Circle**—Just like the dreamcatcher started as a circle, we must remember that life is a circle, always connected to each other. Joseph Bruchac knows this; his autobiography is titled *Seeing the Circle**.

    *If you have it handy, read page 19 from his autobiography aloud. It talks about the significance of the circle.

During the Celebration

Have the children stand around the perimeter of the dreamcatcher, each one next to one end of a length of yarn. Tell the students that dreamcatchers are significant to various tribes of Native Americans.

"Legend has it that when a dreamcatcher is placed near a person's bedside, all of the good dreams will filter through it, while all of the bad dreams will be caught in the threads of the dreamcatcher. Joseph Bruchac leads a life dedicated to catching good dreams and thoughts about Native American people and writing them down for all of us to read about. Each one of you is standing in front of a piece of the dreamcatcher. When I call your name, gently pull on your yarn length until the word card at the end of it comes into your hand. Read your word card aloud, and I will tell you what that word means to the life of Joseph Bruchac."

Birthday Greetings: Circle Cards

Give each child two paper circles. Each circle should be divided into four equal sections. Instruct the students to cut out one section from one of the circles; this will become a window. Next, Have the students write a happy birthday message to Joseph Bruchac on the circle that has had one section cut out. Set that circle aside. On the second circle, have the students think about four things they love about Joseph Bruchac's books and draw/write about each book in one of the sections. Finally, lay the first circle (with the window) on top of the second circle. Distribute a brass brad to each student, have them puncture the center of the circles with the brad, and fold over the brad's ends to connect the circles together. They have just completed circle cards, emulating the circle of life that Bruchac conveys through his many books! Be sure the students have signed their cards!

*Joseph Bruchac's address is available at his website: www.josephbruchac.com.

Party Food

- Strawberries, strawberry shortcakes (based on *The First Strawberries: A Cherokee Story*).
- Journey Cakes: These were flat types of cornbread that traveling Northeastern Native Americans took along on journeys.

  Recipe: 1 cup corn meal

  1 tsp. salt

  1 ½ tsp. sugar

  2 Tbsp. butter

  1 cup boiling water

  1 egg

  1. Add water to dry ingredients and mix.
  2. Add egg and beat together.
  3. Make into small cakes and bake at 400°F for 20 minutes. You may want to add whipped cream and strawberries for sweeter flavor!

Turn this into an activity by having the students work in small groups, following the recipe on individual recipe cards. As the journey cakes cook, tell one of Bruchac's stories from one of his anthologies, such as *Native American Animal Stories* or *Native Plant Stories*.

Trail Marker Hunt

Divide the students into groups of three or four, and assign a color to each group. Each group must follow a "trail," which is indicated on colored paper (a different color for each group) using trail markers similar to those used by Native Americans. The trail markers will lead to a prize, such as bookmarks with candy bags.

<u>Before the Celebration</u>

Consult a camping or outdoor skills book for trail marker symbols. One particularly good resource is Jessica Loy's (2003) *Follow the Trail: A Young Person's Guide to the Great Outdoors*. This book contains basic symbols that are easy to draw (such as a large rock with a small rock perched on the right side of it, meaning "turn right"). Use colored paper, approximately five sheets per group, and make one symbol on each paper. Use a different color of paper for each group. Then place each colored set around the room, providing a trail for the students to follow, and place a set of small prizes at the end of each trail. Finally, make a trail marker key for each student to use while navigating his/her way along the color trail.

Indoor Race Games

Joseph Bruchac co-authored two picture books with his son, James, that focus on animal races: *Turtle's Race with Beaver*, and *Raccoon's Last Race*. After talking about these two Native American folktales with the students, tell them that they will participate in a race, too. Try out one or two of the following:

- Turtle and Beaver: Choose one student to be the turtle, and another to be the beaver. The rest of the students form a circle around the turtle and join hands. Beaver stays outside of the circle while the turtle starts running inside the circle. Players

holding hands begin to lift and lower their joined hands, allowing the turtle to dart outside of the circle, where the beaver can try to tag the turtle. The beaver cannot run inside the circle, so the turtle must use strategy to choose the right moments to enter and exit the circle. Players will lift their hands to help the turtle escape into the circle if the beaver gets too close. Once the beaver tags the turtle, choose a new beaver and turtle.

- Cross the River I: You will need four carpet squares, or other such shapes, for this race. Divide the group into two teams, and give each team two carpet squares. Have the teams line up behind a start line (the river bank) and point to the finish line (the opposite side of the river). Tell the students that they each have two stepping stones (carpet squares) and they have to use them to cross the river. Each person goes, one at a time, and then slides the carpet squares back to the next teammate, waiting in line at the riverbank. The first team to get everyone across the river wins the race. If anyone steps off of one of the stones, that player has fallen into the water and must go back and start again.

- Cross the River II: In this version of the game, you will need two jump ropes. Stretch out the jump ropes so that they are parallel to each other, about one foot apart. Tell the students that each rope represents the riverbank, and they need to jump over the river. Line them up behind one of the ropes and have them each take a turn jumping over the river. After everyone has had a turn, move the ropes a little further apart and have the students jump again. Continue to lengthen the distance between the jump ropes until one child remains who has successfully jumped across the river.

- Animal Races: Choose an animal from one of Bruchac's books, such as a raccoon, beaver, or turtle. Have the students line up on one end of the room, playground, or gymnasium. At your signal, have the students move like that animal from one side of the play area to the other. Whoever reaches the other side first, wins!

Why Stories

Joseph and James Bruchac also co-authored *How Chipmunk Got His Stripes*. This is a *pourquoi* (French, meaning *why*) tale, because it answers the question, "Why do chipmunks have stripes?" Brainstorm a list of forest animals and their unique characteristics, such as:

- Skunks—black with one white stripe
- Owls—heads turn all around their necks
- Snakes—forked tongues

Children can choose one animal and make a paper bag sculpture of that animal. Use the bottom of the bag as the foundation, and attach arms and legs to hang freely from the sides and bottom of the bag. Make the animal's head, and attach that at the top, by the bag's opening. Fill the bag with crumpled tissue paper or newspaper, and staple it closed. Give the students a sheet of paper, cut to fit the back of the paper bag. The students can write a brief story about how their animal got its unique characteristic, and tape the story to the backs of the animal sculpture. Line them up on a classroom or library shelf for a display titled A Zoo Full of Pourquoi Tales!

Wishes Can Come True

In Bruchac's *Gluskabe and the Four Wishes*, four Abenaki men ask Gluskabe to grant a wish. Gluskabe gives each man a pouch and tells him that his wish is granted, but he must wait to open the pouch until he is home. The first three men cannot wait, and each receives his wish in a way that leads to his demise. The fourth man listened to Gluskabe and was granted his wish: to be a good hunter and provide food for his family.

Discuss the themes of this legend with the students: We must truly listen to one another, and we must seek self-improvement that will benefit others. Challenge each student to think about and list several wishes that involve self-improvement (to be a better friend, to try to do well in school; etc.). Hand out small party bags, each filled with the following: a pencil, a small notebook (miniature notebooks are available in sets of four for $1.00 at most dollar stores), a small seashell, a packet of seeds, a small super ball, and other small, inexpensive objects that would inspire students to think creatively. As you hand out the "pouches," tell them not to look inside until they have all returned to their seats—just like Gluskabe told the Abenaki men to wait until they were home. Once they have looked in their bags, have them take out the items and use the pencil and notebook to jot down their wish, and to write out how each object can represent a way to make their wish happen. For example, the pencil and paper will provide them with the tools to stop and write about their ideas, to think through a problem, to observe the world around them; the shell will remind them to listen and hear the ocean, just like they need to pause and listen to their friends, family, and teachers; the seeds will remind them to be patient and nurturing, allowing their ideas to grow; the super ball will remind them to be flexible, go with the flow, or to be enthusiastic about other people's ideas, etc. You may need to get them going by thinking aloud about one or two objects first, then allow time for them to consider their objects independently, or with a partner. Ask them what other objects they would include in the bag. Tell them to decorate the bag and then put it in a special place in their bedrooms to remind them to make their wish come true each morning before they start the day.

Moon Poems

Use *Thirteen Moons on Turtle's Back: A Native American Year of Moons* as inspiration for creating poems about the night sky. As a whole class, dictate a list of descriptive words about the moon. You may need to read a few poems from this book to help the students think about unique words, other than round, bright, etc. Give each student a large white circle cut from construction paper. Tell them to use the words to make a poem about the moon. For younger children, their poem could be a word list; older students could create acrostic poems, cinquains, haiku, or narrative poems. Once they have finished writing their poems on scratch paper, have them write them on the moon-shaped construction paper.

Star Shapes

In *The Earth Under Sky Bear's Feet: Native American Poems of the Land,* Joseph Bruchac reminds his readers, ". . . there can be as much to see in the living night as in the more familiar light of day." Ask them if they have ever seen the Big Dipper in the night sky. Tell them that many Native Americans consider this constellation to be part of a larger set of stars that outline a bear shape. Show the illustration in the back of this book to help the students see the bear shape. Talk about other shapes that they might see when they take the time to really look at the night sky. Distribute sheets of black construction paper and white paint. Tell them to use scratch paper first to sketch out an outline of an animal and then to show points where they would put the stars. Once they have created a picture that is pleasing to them, have them use the white paint to make stars on their black paper that outline the animal shape they've chosen. Sit in a circle and have each child hold up his constellation picture, challenging the other students to guess what animal they see. When there are no additional guesses, the student can reveal the name of the animal that he created in the constellation.

Party Favors

Small dreamcatcher key chains (available at party supply catalog companies), peppermint patties for Bruchac's commit-MINT to preserving his Native American heritage through his books, or small animal-shaped erasers to represent the many animal stories he has retold.

Curriculum Connections

For creative ideas on how to link Bruchac's books to science, social studies, art, and reading/language arts, consult the following resources:

- *Keepers of the Animals: Native American Stories and Wildlife Activities for Children* by Michael J. Caduto and Joseph Bruchac. Fulcrum Publishing, 1991.
- *Keepers of the Earth: Native American Stories and Environmental Activities for Children* by Michael J. Caduto and Joseph Bruchac. Fulcrum Publishing, 1988.

Happy Birthday, Joseph Bruchac!

Born October 16, 1942

Picture Books

- *The First Strawberries: A Cherokee Story*
- *The Great Ball Game: A Muskogee Story*
- *How Chipmunk Got His Stripes*
- *Raccoon's Last Race*
- *Turtle's Race With Beaver*

Nonfiction

- *Between Earth and Sky: Legends of Native America*
- *The Boy Who Lived With The Bears and Other Iroquois Stories*
- *The Earth Under Sky Bear's Feet: Native American Poems of the Land*
- *Gluskabe and the Four Wishes*
- *Many Nations: An Alphabet of Native Americans*
- *Native American Animal Stories*

Poetry

- *A Circle of Thanks: Thanksgiving*
- *Pushing Up The Sky and Other Native American Plays For Children*
- *Thirteen Moons on Turtle's Back: A Native American Year of Moons*

Biography

- *A Boy Called Slow: Sitting Bull*
- *Crazy Horse's Vision*
- *Seeing The Circle: Autobiography of Joseph Bruchac*
- *Squanto's Journey*

Easy Readers

- *The Trail of Tears*

Juvenile Fiction

- *Eagle Song*

Anthologies

- *Native American Animal Stories*
- *Native Plant Stories*

Joseph Bruchac Reading Log

Read 5 books by **October** _____.

On each line, write the title you've read and have your parent/guardian sign that you read it.

Bring this completed reading log to me by **October** _____ and receive your invitation to attend our birthday celebration on _____.

Date/Time

_____

Title   Parent/Guardian Signature

_____

Title   Parent/Guardian Signature

_____

Title   Parent/Guardian Signature

_____

Title   Parent/Guardian Signature

_____

Title   Parent/Guardian Signature

Happy Birthday, Dear Steven Kellogg!

About Steven Kellogg

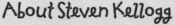

- Steven Kellogg was born on October 26, 1941.
- Steven Kellogg has been writing and illustrating children's books for over 25 years, and he has published more than 90 books!
- He has loved to draw animal pictures since he was a child.
- He always knew he would make a living as an artist.
- Pinkerton is Steven's real pet Great Dane!

Celebration Ideas

Draw-n-Tell Story about Steven Kellogg

Tell the story of this talented author/illustrator by incorporating biographical information into a line drawing of a dog that will resemble Pinkerton! Before you begin, here is a hint for drawing the outline of Pinkerton's face: Trace an image of Pinkerton from one of the book covers, using very faint pencil marks. During the story, use a thick black marker to draw over the pencil marks as you create the outline of Pinkerton.

Sample Story

a. Steven Kellogg was a happy, energetic boy who loved to draw!
(Draw a triangle for the dog's nose.)

b. He had two younger sisters: Patty *(draw a circle and color it in for one eye)* and Martha *(draw a circle and color it in for the second eye).*

c. He loved to sit in front of them and tell them stories.
(Draw a mouth with a slurpy tongue coming out of it.)
He and his sisters called these "telling stories on paper" because he drew pictures to enhance his stories.

d. After he drew a picture, he passed it to Martha.
(Draw a curving line from the tongue/chin area, up around the right eye.)

e. She looked at it *(draw an oblong oval to make an ear)* . . .

f. . . . and passed it on to her sister, Patty *(draw a curved line from the ear along the top of the dog's head).*

g. Patty looked at it *(draw the second ear)…*

h. . . . and passed it back to her brother, Steven *(draw a curving line to form the left side of the face, connecting it to the tongue).*

This is how Steven Kellogg started his career as an author and illustrator! When he grew up, he went to college at the Rhode Island School of Design; married his wife, Helen; and moved into a beautiful farmhouse in Connecticut, where he adopted a Great Dane and named him Pinkerton. The rest is history!

Party Food

Try one of the following recipes:

Pinkerton's Puppy Chow Snack Mix

Ingredients:
- ½ cup peanut butter
- ¼ cup butter
- 1 cup chocolate chips
- ½ tsp. vanilla
- 9 cups Crispix™ cereal
- 1 ½ cups powdered sugar

Instructions:
1. Combine peanut butter, butter, and chocolate chips in a microwaveable bowl and microwave for one minute.
2. Blend ingredients together, adding vanilla.
3. Place the Crispix™ cereal in a large bowl, and pour the peanut butter mixture over the cereal, mixing and coating all of the cereal.
4. Sprinkle powdered sugar evenly over cereal.

Johnny Appleseed's Favorite Caramel Apples

Ingredients (for every four students):
- 1 – 14 oz. package caramels
- 2 Tbsp. water
- 4 large apples and 4 wooden sticks
- 2 cups chopped pecans
- 1 cup semisweet chocolate chips
- 1 tsp. shortening
- 1 cup toffee bits

Instructions:
1. In a microwaveable bowl, combine caramels and water, microwaving for 1 minute.
2. Stir and microwave 30–45 seconds more, until caramels have melted.
3. Insert wooden sticks into apples and dip into caramel mixture. Coat with pecans; set on waxed paper to cool.
4. Melt chocolate chips and shortening in the microwave. Drizzle chocolate over caramel apples and sprinkle with toffee bits.
5. Allow time to cool before eating!

Dog-gone Good Birthday Cake

Make a sheet cake of any flavor and cut it to resemble a dog bone. Frost and decorate, complete with candles to blow out after the children sing "Happy Birthday" to Steven Kellogg.

Pinkerton Party Ideas

- **Paw Print Graphs:** Print and cut out several copies of the paw print on page 52, enough for each student to have one. Post a question on a bulletin board, such as, "What is your favorite Pinkerton Book?" or "If you were Pinkerton, what would your favorite activity be?" Across the bottom of the board, list three or four options for answers to each question. Then, have students answer the question by placing their paw print in a column above their response. The tallest column will indicate the majority preference!

- **Find Pinkerton's Dog Bones:** Before the celebration, fill a cardboard tube for each student with small candies, bookmark, eraser, stickers, etc., and wrap in white butcher paper, tying both ends securely with a white curling ribbon. These will be Pinkerton's dog bones. On each bone, print the answer to a question, such as "cats"—which will answer the question, "What animal do dogs like to chase?" Create a question (typed on a strip of paper) and an answer (written on a bone) for each student. Ask questions related to various content areas you have been learning about in class. Hide the bones around the room and place the question strips into a doggy dish.

During the celebration, tell the students, "Pinkerton has hidden many bones around the room. You each need to find one bone, using the clue written on the strip of paper that you will pick from his doggy dish. Look for the bone that has your question's answer written on it. If you find a bone that does not have your answer on it, quietly replace it so that it can be found by the right person!" Once everyone has found their correct "bone," allow them to open them.

- Play "Steven Kellogg Says": Tell the students to pretend that they are Steven Kellogg's dog, Pinkerton, and he is trying to train them to behave. Have one student volunteer to be Steven Kellogg and stand in the front of the room. She will say, "Pinkerton, sit still!" The students must all sit still. If the leader does not preface the command with "Pinkerton," the students should not obey—just like the traditional game of "Simon Says." Distribute blue ribbons to all students for their excellent behavior!

Tall Tale Fun

Steven Kellogg has retold and illustrated several tall tales. Here are some fun ways to extend the students' enjoyment of these stories.

- **Take the Tall Tale Challenge!** Do you have what it takes to be a Tall Tale Hero? Try these challenging tasks:
  - Pecos Bill's Snake Jump: Use a long jump rope and ask a student to hold one end while the teacher holds the other end. Lay the rope flat on the ground and shake it side-to-side. Students line up to jump over the "snake." Continue to increase the level of difficulty, eventually raising the rope and creating transverse waves.
  - Mike Fink's Strong Brain-Strong Arms Challenge: Before the celebration, inflate two black balloons, and tape one on each end of a wrapping paper tube. Students line up and take turns answer-

ing a question; if they are correct, they can lift the "barbell." Start with easy questions and progress to more difficult questions to see whose brain is as strong as her arms!
  - Paul Bunyan's Expert Tree Identifier: Partner up students, giving each pair one bandanna, and lead them outside for this activity. This activity is best suited for a playground with trees nearby. One partner will use the bandanna to cover his eyes. The other partner will lead her blindfolded friend to a tree. The blindfolded friend must hug the tree, feel its texture, and use his senses to get to know the tree. Then the leader will lead the partner back to the group, remove the blindfold, and challenge him to find the tree! Reverse roles and continue the game.
  - Johnny Appleseed's Balancing Act: Line students up on one side of the room, and give each student an apple to balance on her head. See who can reach the other side of the room with the apple still on his head!

Much Bigger Than Martin Scavenger Hunt

Before the celebration, create a scavenger hunt list of items for students to measure. Challenge them to find items that meet specific criteria, such as "Find three things in this room that are less than 6 inches long," or list specific items to measure and have them record the measurement (such as, "How many inches long is your science book?"). Students could work in small groups, or individually depending on your time and the students' ability levels. Award the students with new rulers, or a packet of Fruit by the Foot™!

Mystery Mayhem

In honor of Kellogg's picture book mysteries, *The Mystery of the Missing Red Mitten, The Mystery of the Stolen Blue Paint,* and *The Mystery of the Flying Orange Pumpkin,* play a game of "Mystery Squares." Draw a 3 x 3 grid on the chalkboard. Inside each grid, write a number or word related to Kellogg's biography and/or picture books.

Before the celebration, create clues for each number or word, and select one number or word to be the "Mystery Number/Word." The students answer the clues in order to eliminate the numbers/words until one final word or number remains. For example, if one of the numbers is 70, the clue could be: "It is NOT the number for how old Steven Kellogg was in 2011" (if the year is 2012, since he was born in 1941). Students raise their hand and say the answer: 70. Draw an "X" over this number and continue on to the next clue. Combine math and reading skills with your clues, such as: "It is NOT a word that is the opposite of Tall Tale HERO" (Answer: Villain).

Halloween Fun

- Have the students design a Halloween costume for Pinkerton and display them on a bulletin board.
- Write the names of characters from Kellogg's books and place them into a plastic pumpkin. Students pick a name and act it out, charades style, for their classmates to guess the character's name!
- In honor of Kellogg's *The Island of the Skog* and *The Mysterious Tadpole,* have students create their own mystery monsters on 12" x 18" sheets of construction paper. They could make up a name and a story about it, too!

Birthday Greetings

Since Kellogg creates stories about animals based on real pets of his own, such as Pinkerton, Secondhand Rose (*A Rose for Pinkerton*), and Goldensilverwind (*Best Friends*), have students draw a picture of themselves with their own pets, or a pet they wish they owned. Each student could draw this on the front of a card and write a personalized greeting and note about the pet inside the card. Go to Kellogg's website at <u>www.stevenkellogg.com</u> for his contact information.

Party Favors

- Small stuffed dogs with dog collars tied around their necks, saying "I had a dog-gone good time at Steven Kellogg's Birthday Party!"
- A handout that lists and describes several fun partner games that students could play with a friend, in homage to *Best Friends* and *Won't Somebody Play With Me?*
- Small packet of crayons, in honor of Kellogg because he's known as "The Boy Born with a Crayon in His Hand!"

Paw Print

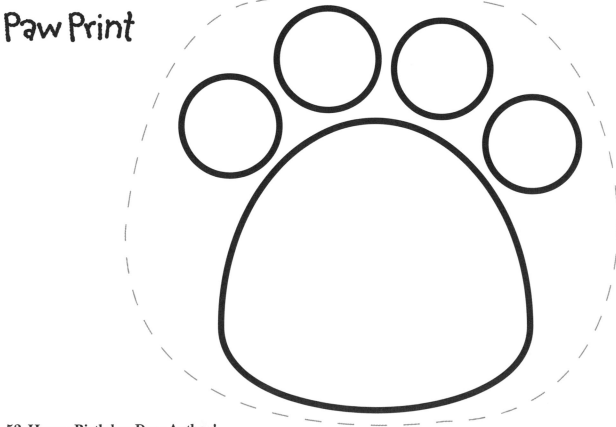

Happy Birthday, Steven Kellogg!

Born October 26, 1941

Book List

- *A-Hunting We Will Go!*
- *Best Friends*
- *Can I Keep Him?*
- *Chicken Little*
- *The Christmas Witch*
- *Give the Dog a Bone*
- *The Island of the Skog*
- *Jack and the Beanstalk*
- *Johnny Appleseed*
- *Mike Fink: A Tall Tale*
- *The Missing Mitten Mystery*
- *Much Bigger Than Martin*
- *The Mysterious Tadpole*
- *The Mystery of the Flying Orange Pumpkin*
- *The Mystery of the Stolen Blue Paint*
- *Paul Bunyan: A Tall Tale*
- *Pecos Bill: A Tall Tale*
- *Pinkerton, Behave!*
- *A Penguin Pup for Pinkerton*
- *The Pied Piper's Magic*
- *Prehistoric Pinkerton*
- *A Rose for Pinkerton*
- *Ralph's Secret Weapon*
- *Sally Ann Thunder Ann Whirlwind Crockett*
- *Tallyho, Pinkerton!*
- *There Was an Old Woman*
- *The Three Little Pigs*
- *The Three Sillies*
- *The Wicked Kings of Bloon*
- *Won't Somebody Play With Me?*
- *Yankee Doodle*

. . . and many other titles written by various authors and illustrated by Steven Kellogg!

Steven Kellogg Reading Log

Read 5 books by **October** ____.

On each line, write the title you've read and have your parent/guardian sign that you read it.

Bring this completed reading log to me by **October** ____ and receive your invitation to attend our birthday celebration on

_____.

Date/Time

_____

Title   Parent/Guardian Signature

_____

Title   Parent/Guardian Signature

_____

Title   Parent/Guardian Signature

_____

Title   Parent/Guardian Signature

_____

Title   Parent/Guardian Signature

Happy Birthday, Dear Authors Born in November!

November 1	Hilary Knight	November 16	Jean Fritz
	Nicholasa Mohr	November 18	Nancy Van Laan
November 2	Jeannie Baker	November 21	Leo Politi
	Natalie Kinsey-Warnock	November 22	Jamie Lee Curtis
November 3	Janell Cannon	November 23	Marc Simont
November 5	Raymond Bial	November 24	Gloria Houston
			Frances Hodson Burnett
November 7	Sneed B. Collard, III	November 25	Marc Brown
			Charles Schulz
November 8	Marianna Mayer		Crescent Dragonwagon
November 9	**Lois Ehlert***	November 27	Kevin Henkes
November 11	Peg Kehret	November 28	Tomi Ungerer
November 12	Marjorie Weinman		**Ed Young***
November 13	Jez Alborough	November 29	David M. Schwartz
14 Nancy Tafuri, Astrid Lindgren,			*Madeline L'Engle* *Louisa May Alcott*
November 15	Maira Kalman *& Wm. Steig*	November 30	Margot Zemach
			Mark Twain
	Daniel Pinkwater*		*Jonathan Swift*

*Author featured in this chapter

Happy Birthday, Dear Daniel Pinkwater!

About Daniel Pinkwater

- Daniel Pinkwater was born on November 15, 1941, in Memphis, Tennessee.
- He grew up in Chicago, Illinois, and played out the adventures from favorite books with his neighborhood friends.
- He lives with his wife, Jill Schutz Pinkwater, in New York.
- His wife has illustrated several of his books.
- He has written over 70 books for children.
- He has illustrated over half of his books.
- He has been a commentator on NPR's *All Things Considered* radio show since 1987.
- Dan Pinkwater studied sculpture and writing at Bard College.

Celebration Ideas

Big, Colorful Splot Hats

Give each child a white baseball cap (available through craft catalogs) and have them talk to a partner about their favorite colors and symbols that would show people what is unique about them. Once their ideas are flowing, have them use colorful fabric paints to paint their colors and symbols onto their hats. Have them proudly wear their hats to showcase their individuality. Fabric markers work well to add words or phrases. (Based on *The Big Orange Splot*.)

Hunt Activity: Werewolf Club Members Unite!

Tell the students that aliens have rewritten the answers to questions about Daniel Pinkwater. Give each student a secret coded question to solve. Once each child has successfully solved the answer, she must hunt for a party bag that is labeled with the corresponding answer. This activity is based on Pinkwater's Werewolf Club series of books.

Before the Celebration

Reproduce and cut apart the following questions, and give each child one strip to solve. Answers are, respectively: Ice cream; 1941; G/E/A/N/R/O = Orange; Polar bear; Hoboken

Questions

- This must be a favorite food of Daniel Pinkwater's because it plays a role in several of his books. Circle every third letter to spell out this secret word.

  L X I T E C Q A E
  K W C T Y R Z P E U I A P V M

- When was Daniel Pinkwater born? Subtract three from each number to find the year of his birth:
  4 12 7 4 = ___ ___ ___ ___

- What is Mr. Plumbean's favorite color? Write the first letter of each picture and then unscramble the letters to find the answer!

  ___ ___ ___ ___ ___ ___

- Circle every second letter to answer this question: What type of bear is Larry?

  G P E O G L A A Y R
  P B I E V A S R

- In what city does Pinkwater's Chicken Emergency take place? Find the letter that matches each numeral and write the answer.

A = 13	B = 12	C = 11	D = 10
E = 9	F = 8	G = 7	H = 6
I = 5	J = 4	K = 3	L = 2
M = 1	N = 14	O = 15	P = 16
Q = 17	R = 18	S = 19	T = 20
U = 21	V = 22	W = 23	X = 24
Y = 25	Z = 26		

6   15   12   15   3   9   14

__ __ __ __ __ __ __

More Question Ideas

If the riddles are too easy or too difficult for your students, here are other question and answer ideas that you can use to build your own riddles and codes:

- What is the author's middle name?

- What is the name of the club of kids who work together to solve mysteries?

- Mr. Plumbean's house is the opposite of this mystery word:

- Solve the clues to reveal the word for Mr. Pinkwater's occupation.

- How old is Daniel Pinkwater?

- What type of stories does Mr. Pinkwater write?

- Where can you find lots of great books?

- Jill Pinkwater, Daniel's wife, has contributed to his books by being the _____.

- Irving and Muktuk are known as the _____.

Create at least one question per child in attendance. Answers are, respectively: Manus; Werewolf Club; Answer for mystery word is *plain*, opposite = fancy; Author; Subtract 1941 from current year; Silly stories, picture books, etc.; The library; Illustrator; Two Bad Bears

Author's Story

Use the answers from the hunt activity above as key touchpoints for telling this story about Daniel Pinkwater. As the story unfolds, have the students with the appropriate answer step forward and hold up their answer card at that time.

Mr. Pinkwater was born in _____ (1941) in Memphis, TN. He is ____ (current age) years old. When he was 28, he married Jill Schutz. Now, her name is Jill Pinkwater and she often draws the pictures for Daniel's books. This makes her the _____ (illustrator) of his books.

His first book was *Bear's Picture*. He used his middle name when he wrote this book. His middle name is _____ (Manus). He illustrated this book himself because he is also an artist. In 2008, this book was re-illustrated by D. B. Johnson.

Now, Daniel Pinkwater has written over 75 books for children! One of his most famous books is *The Big Orange Splot*. Mr. Pinkwater loves colors, especially _____ (orange)! He created many _____ (fancy) houses in this book. He also wrote about a chicken emergency in a town called _____ (Hoboken). Mr. Pinkwater loves to make up _____ (silly) stories and many of them are about _____ (polar bears) and loving food like _____ (ice cream), and just being yourself! Irving and Muktuk are two characters who learn to behave after acting like _____ (Two Bad Bears) in their books. If you want to read about a bunch of kids who turn into werewolves at night and solve mysteries, then his recent series called _____ (The Werewolf Club) is for you!

Daniel Manus Pinkwater is a very talented children's book _____ (author) and you can find many of his books at your _____ (library)! If you want to listen to Mr. Pinkwater, turn on your radio and tune into your National Public Radio station to hear him talk on the show called "All Things Considered."

The Yo-Yo Man

Here are a few tricks to get your students into the spirit of this fun book!

- Bring in a few yo-yo trick books from your local library (or order a few for your school library). Create a display with a variety of yo-yo themed books. Promote a yo-yo tournament for the end of the month.
- Host a Variety Show! Encourage the students to bring in the props for a special talent or skill that they have, and set aside some time at the end of the month for a special variety show in which students demonstrate magic tricks, yo-yo tricks, and other silly talents! Create award certificates, enough for each participant.
- Yo-yo craft: order wooden yo-yos from craft catalogs and have the students paint and decorate their own special yo-yos. Teach them a quick and easy yo-yo trick to show their families.
- Yo-yo marathon: Challenge your students to see who can flick their yo-yo up and down in the most consecutive counts! Tie in math concepts by graphing (with yo-yo shapes, of course) the number of students who reached 5 flicks, 5–10, etc.

Mystery Pictures

In honor of Pinkwater's first book (and its subsequent re-illustrated edition), *Bear's Picture*, have the children create their own mystery pictures. Give them time to paint an abstract picture with a variety of colors. On a separate paper, have the student write down what they see in their own pictures, and attach it to the

artwork. Remember, the picture doesn't have to look like what others might think, because it is THEIR picture!

Hats with Personality

Help the students to make paper hats, shaped like pirate hats, or like top hats. After reading *The Big Orange Splot*, talk with the students about the importance of being themselves. Challenge them to decorate their hats, like Mr. Plumbean decorated his house: with personality! Lay out the following art supplies for the students to use: colored tissue paper streamers, pom-poms, colored and patterned papers, sequins, foam shapes, glitter markers, stickers, magazine pictures/photographs, etc. Have the students think about their own personalities (they could do a pre-art project step and list words that describe themselves first). Next, have them peruse the display of art objects and decide on which items to use to decorate their hats. They must choose items that reflect their own personalities. Once all the hats are completed, have the students parade around the room and show off their beautiful hats with personality!

Alter Egos

After reading Pinkwater's *I Was a Second Grade Werewolf*, ask the class if they believe that the boy in the book really turned into a werewolf, or if he just dreamt that he did. Next, ask what creature or animal they'd want to turn into if they had the chance. Distribute brown paper grocery bags and have them make the bags into masks of the creatures they've chosen to become. Once their masks are complete, have them write a brief story of their adventures as that creature. Glue the stories to the back of the paper bag masks. Students can wear their masks and tell their stories, then put them on display for all to see and read about.

Polar Bear Larry

Larry is a recurring character in a small series of books by Pinkwater. Incorporate the following activities into your celebration, or into various content lessons throughout the month.

- Polar Bear Math: Photocopy the image of a polar bear, one per student, and glue onto a piece of blue construction paper. Draw or cut out an ice floe, and place it beneath the polar bear, as if it is sitting or laying on it. Distribute these story cards to each student, along with a snack bag of fish-shaped crackers. Instruct the students to listen to you as you tell stories about Larry's attempts at catching a fish, or two, for lunch. They are to use the fish crackers to "act out" the story. Sample story problem might be: "Five fish swam near Larry while floating on a chunk of ice. Larry reached down and grabbed three. How many are left in the water?" Continue the stories, manipulating the fish as the math problems are told. Create math problems based on their current unit of study in their textbooks. The teacher could write the math problem on the board for students to use as a reference point.
- Polar Bear Float: Conduct a science experiment on whether a variety of objects will sink or float. Have students make predictions/form hypotheses for the items and complete a graph about their predictions. Conduct the experiment and discuss the results. Lead the children toward a logical conclusion as to why certain items float while others sink.

- Polar Bear Ice Cream Treats: Larry the Polar Bear loves to eat ice cream! Have students enjoy the celebration by making their own ice cream sundaes! Set up the various sauces and toppings along a tabletop, and allow students to proceed through the line, adding their desired toppings to their bowls of ice cream.

Party Favors

Small stuffed polar bears (available through party catalogs); art and writing supplies, such as: colored chalk, small sketchbooks, writing pad, pens (because Pinkwater is both an author and illustrator, and in honor of *Bear's Picture* and *Return of the Moose*); magnifying lenses (in honor of his series, The Werewolf Club).

Party Food

Polar Bear Ice Cream Sundaes (see aforementioned Polar Bear Ice Cream Treats), cupcakes decorated to resemble werewolf faces, chocolate mousse, big orange splot cupcakes (decorate with orange frosting and orange sprinkles).

Happy Birthday, Daniel Pinkwater!

Born November 15, 1941

Picture Books

- *At The Hotel Larry*
- *Aunt Lulu*
- *Author's Day*
- *Bad Bear Detectives: An Irving and Muktuk Story*
- *Bad Bears and a Bunny: An Irving & Muktuk Story*
- *Bear's Picture*
- *The Big Orange Splot*
- *Bongo Larry*
- *Dancing Larry*
- *Ice Cream Larry*
- *Guys From Space*
- *I Was a Second Grade Werewolf*
- *Irving and Muktuk: 2 Bad Bears*
- *The Picture of Morty and Ray*
- *Rainy Morning*
- *Yo-Yo Man*

Beginning Chapter Books

- *Cone Kong: The Scary Ice Cream Giant*
- *Ned Feldman, Space Pirate*
- *Second-Grade Ape*
- *Young Larry*

Series

- **The Werewolf Club Series**
  - *The Lunchroom of Doom*
  - *The Magic Pretzel*
  - *The Werewolf Club Meets Dorkula*
  - *The Werewolf Club Meets the Hound of the Basketballs*
  - *The Werewolf Club Meets Oliver Twit*

- **Big Bob and Gloria**
  - *Big Bob and the Magic Valentine's Day Potatoes*
  - *Big Bob and the Thanksgiving Potatoes*
  - *Big Bob and the Winter Holiday Potatoes*
- **Hoboken Chicken**
  - *The Artsy-Smartsy Club*
  - *The Hoboken Chicken Emergency*
  - *Looking For Bobowicz: A Hoboken Chicken Story*
- **Mush**
  - *Mush's Space Adventures*
- **The Blue Moose Series**
  - *The Blue Moose*
  - *Return of the Moose*
  - *Moosepire*
- **Fat Camp Commandos**
  - *Fat Camp Commandos*
  - *Fat Camp Commandos Go West*

Daniel Pinkwater Reading Log

Read 5 books by **November _____**.

On each line, write the title you've read and have your parent/guardian sign that you read it.

Bring this completed reading log to me by **November _____** and receive your invitation to attend our birthday celebration on

_____.

Date/Time

_____

Title   Parent/Guardian Signature

_____

Title   Parent/Guardian Signature

_____

Title   Parent/Guardian Signature

_____

Title   Parent/Guardian Signature

_____

Title   Parent/Guardian Signature

Happy Birthday, Dear Lois Ehlert!

About Lois Ehlert

- Born November 9, 1934
- Lifelong resident of Beaver Dam, Wisconsin
- Taught art classes for children in Milwaukee
- Has been a designer of toys and games
- Won the 1989 Caldecott Honor Award for *Color Zoo*
- Ehlert feels that her books offer children the opportunity to learn to look around and truly see the natural beauty of our world.
- Ehlert's book, *Hands* (1997), is a memoir of her childhood with two creative parents. See a video interview about it at: www.readingrockets.org/books/interviews/ehlert.

Celebration Ideas

Author's Story

Before the celebration, tape a large piece of butcher paper onto the front chalkboard. Collect a variety of objects that represent key events from Lois Ehlert's life. Have students tape or glue these objects to the paper as you tell the students her story. When you finish your story, you will have a collage mural that you've created in honor of Lois Ehlert.

Write to Lois Ehlert

Have students create their own geometric creatures/animals based on *Color Farm* and *Color Zoo*. Provide pre-cut shapes made from a variety of colors of construction paper. Instruct the students to use the shapes to make an animal and glue their animal onto a 9" x 12" piece of construction paper. Have the students each write a birthday greeting on their projects and mail them to the author.

Hobby Box Craft

Use found objects to make a hobby box based on the concept behind the book, *Hands.* Provide students with a school box and a variety of pictures, photos, and small objects (buttons, beads, ribbons, fabric scraps, stamps, ephemera). Instruct the students to think about a hobby that they enjoy and to look over the objects in order to select those items that might relate to their hobbies. Have them glue the items to the outside of the box (craft glue works best for ephemera). Provide foam or felt letters for their names. Have them take their boxes home to use as storage for their hobby materials.

"My World" Banners

Distribute 9" x 12" felt pieces to each student and read aloud *In My World.* As they listen, students should consider the items in the world that they love. After the book, discuss these items together and instruct the students to use various felt pieces to make their own banners that show items from the world that they love. Fold over the top inch and pin it down, allowing space for a ¼-inch dowel rod to slip through so that each banner can be hung up in the classroom.

Fishing for Fun

Cut a large piece of blue butcher paper to look like a pond. Make a variety of colorful construction paper fish. On the back of each fish, write a math problem, vocabulary word, or other content-area concept that the students could review. Insert a metal paper clip into the mouth of each fish and lay each on the blue paper pond. Using a dowel with a string and magnet tied to it (i.e., a fishing pole), have students take turns fishing in the pond. After a student catches a fish, turn it over and have the student solve the problem. Help all of the children to successfully participate in this activity and reward them with a bag of fish-shaped crackers or candy! This activity is based on *Fish Eyes*.

Birthday Pie!

In honor of Ehlert's *Pie in the Sky*, serve cherry tarts or a cherry pie as you sing "Happy Birthday, Dear Lois Ehlert!" While the children enjoy the treat, read this book aloud and play "I Spy." On each page, Ehlert has a list of birds and insects that she "sees." Read it aloud, and have the students point to the items as they are mentioned.

Bird-Brained Activities

Ehlert has created several books in which birds are featured, such as: *Pie in the Sky, Feathers for Lunch,* and *Red Leaf, Yellow Leaf.* Create a bird observatory center in your classroom or school library. Throughout the month, students could draw a bird to resemble those seen outside the classroom window. Keep reference books on display to help label their drawings.

Make bird feeders with bread, peanut butter, and birdseed by following the directions on the end flap of the book, *Red Leaf, Yellow Leaf.* Hang the bird feeders outside the window to attract birds to the observation station.

Leaf Me Alone!

Bring in a variety of fall leaves. Divide students into pairs. Give each pair three lengths of yarn and tie each length to make a total of three circles. Use the circles to place leaves into categories by sorting them. These yarn circles can be arranged into a Venn diagram for interesting sorting projects. Discuss the categories and the students' thought processes.

Brainstorm a list of leafy creatures that they could make. Have each student make his/her own leaf creature, based on *Leaf Man.*

Silent Sculptures

Divide the students into groups of three or four. Using gourds, pumpkins, squash, and other items from nature (nuts, pine cones, sticks, seeds, etc.), challenge each group to create a sculpture to scare a cat—but they must do this without talking, like the mice in Ehlert's *Boo to You!* Use craft glue, twine, and thumb tacks (with teacher's help) to attach items.

Outdoor Fun for Nature Lovers

Several of Ehlert's books emphasize nature, such as *Waiting for Wings; Nuts to You!; Red Leaf, Yellow Leaf;* and *Growing Vegetable Soup.* Try the following activities in honor of these books:

- Outdoor Read-Aloud Time: Gather in a circle on a grassy part of the playground and read aloud one of Ehlert's nature-themed books.
- Nature Detectives: Have pairs of students tie together the ends of a length of yarn to create a circle, and place the circle on the ground, preferably on a grassy part of the playground. Using a magnifying lens, have each student stoop down and look closely at their circle of land. Give them paper and pencil (attach paper to corrugated cardboard rectangles using a large rubberband; an instant clip board). Have students make a list of the discoveries they've made while looking closely at their small plot of land!
- Nature Scavenger Hunt: Give each small group of students a list of items from nature that are featured in Ehlert's books. Students try to be the first to find all items. They could collect them in a paper bag and use them to make nature collages, or they could be items that they must use their senses to notice (i.e., the sound of a cardinal, the rustle of leaves in the tree, a squirrel's bushy tail, etc.). Vary this activity by challenging each student to create a nature acrostic of Lois Ehlert's name. Do they notice things in nature that start with each letter of her name?

Circus!

In honor of Lois Ehlert's book, *Circus*, have students participate in the following activities. These would be fun to incorporate into their gym class on the celebration day.

- Tightrope Walk: Lay a jumprope on the floor, and have students take turns walking on it without stepping off of the rope.
- Juggling Act: Give each student a set of three facial tissues and have them try to juggle the tissues, in the air. Bring in a book about circus acts to help them learn the technique involved in this feat.
- Gymnastics Routine: Place several gym mats on the floor, and have students line up and take turns doing a gymnastic stunt, such as two somersaults in a row, one cartwheel followed with a hop and a clap, etc.
- Clown Puppets: Children could make puppets out of shapes cut out of construction paper and glued onto white paper lunch bags. They could act out clown routines with a partner for the class to enjoy!

Party Favors

Foam clown noses, plastic magnifying lenses (for nature discoveries), miniature pumpkins, small bird whistles.

Happy Birthday, Lois Ehlert!

Born November 9, 1934

Picture Books

- *Boo To You!*
- *Circus*
- *Color Farm*
- *Color Zoo*
- *Eating the Alphabet: Fruits & Vegetables From A to Z*
- *Feathers for Lunch*
- *Fish Eyes: A Book You Can Count On*
- *Growing Vegetable Soup*
- *Hands*
- *In My World*
- *Leaf Man*
- *Market Day*
- *Mole's Hill*
- *Moon Rope/ Un lazo a la luna*
- *Nuts to You!*
- *Oodles of Animals*
- *Pie in The Sky*
- *Planting a Rainbow*
- *Red Leaf, Yellow Leaf*
- *Snowballs*
- *Top Cat*
- *Waiting for Wings*

Lois Ehlert Reading Log

Read 5 books by **November** ____.

On each line, write the title you've read and have your parent/guardian sign that you read it.

Bring this completed reading log to me by **November** ____ and receive your invitation to attend our birthday celebration on

_____.

Date/Time

_____

Title   Parent/Guardian Signature

_____

Title   Parent/Guardian Signature

_____

Title   Parent/Guardian Signature

_____

Title   Parent/Guardian Signature

_____

Title   Parent/Guardian Signature

Happy Birthday, Dear Ed Young!

About Ed Young

- Born November 28, 1931 in Tientsin, China
- He and his parents moved often to avoid the various invasions into China by Japan.
- While in high school, the Chinese communists took over the city of Shanghai, where he lived with his parents.
- He finished school in Hong Kong and came to the United States in 1951.
- He originally studied architecture at the University of Illinois, Urbana-Champaign.
- After taking an art class at the Art Center College of Design, Young realized he truly wanted to be a full-time artist.
- Young moved to New York to become an artist.
- He often spent his lunch breaks at the Central Park Zoo, sketching animals. These sketches provided him with the opportunity to obtain his first children's book illustration contract for *The Mean Mouse and Other Mean Stories* (Udry, 1962). He won an award from the American Institute of Graphic Arts for these illustrations.
- He won the Caldecott Honor for his illustrations of Jane Yolen's *The Emperor and the Kite.*
- He won the Caldecott Award for his retelling and illustrating of *Lon Po Po* in 1990.

Celebration Ideas

Ed Young's Story

Talk about Ed Young's life by focusing on the years that key events occurred. Locate the Chinese Zodiac symbols for each of those years and paste them onto a poster as you share each year and its event with the students (websites such as www.apples4theteacher.com/holidays/chinese-new-year/chinese-zodiac.html can be helpful). Decorate the poster by writing "Happy Birthday, Ed Young" along the top, and put a photograph of the author in the center. Arrange each zodiac picture in a circle around his photograph. Chinese Zodiac images are available on the placemats of most Chinese restaurants, or through a Google image search.

Ed Young's Story:
Ed was born on November 28, 1931, in Tientsin, China.
(Tape up the Chinese Zodiac image of the Goat, because 1931 was the year of the Goat.)

He immigrated to the United States in 1951.
(Tape up the image of the Rabbit for 1951.)

In 1957, he earned his Bachelor of Arts degree from the Art Center College of Design.
(Tape up the image of the Rooster for 1957.)

He illustrated his first children's book in 1962. It was titled *The Mean Mouse and Other Mean Stories.* He won an award for this book from the American Institute of Graphic Arts!
(Tape up the image of the Tiger for 1962.)

In 1990, he won the Caldecott Award for *Lon Po Po.* This award goes to the illustrator for the best-illustrated book published in the United States.
(Tape up the image of the Horse for 1990.)

Birthday Greetings

The students can each create a birthday card in which they draw a picture of an animal from the Chinese Zodiac for the year in which they were born. Encourage them to write about their favorite book by Ed Young in their cards.

Games Based on *Seven Blind Mice*

* Feely Boxes: Place parts of one large object into three different boxes, such as parts of a bicycle. Children feel inside the box without peeking and guess what each is, and then try to determine what object they are part of (i.e., kick stand, horn, seat).

* Trust Walk: One partner is blindfolded, the other leads her around the room or library to three different locations. The blindfolded child uses her senses to figure out each location. The children should switch roles so they each have a turn to experience this trust walk.

Scavenger Hunt Based on *What About Me?*

Have the students find various objects hidden around the classroom or library, just as the boy had to do in this book.

Before the Celebration

Create a set of five clues, one per small group of students at the party. For each clue, describe an object they need, and tell where to go to get to the next clue and object. The objects described for each group will be the same: they will describe materials needed to construct paper fortune cookies: 3" x 3" construction paper envelope, double-sided tape, markers, small strip of white paper. However, the locations of the objects will be different, so each group has a different quest. For example:

> GROUP 1
> Clue 1: What about me? I need some paper so I can write down all of my good ideas! Go to the picture book section and look near the books by Ed Young. You'll find some paper here for me to use!
> Clue 2: What about me? I need some tape to hold my papers together. Go to the music CD display and find me some tape!

> Clue 3: What about me? I need an envelope to keep all of my precious papers safe in one place! Go to the fiction section and check near the books by Jean Fritz to find envelopes for me to use!
> Clue 4: What about me? I need a marker so I can write down all of my creative ideas! Go to the fish tank and find some markers!
> Clue 5: What about me? I need some good ideas to tell other people! Go to the writing center and brainstorm some good ideas about life with your teammates!

During the Celebration

Divide students into small groups, give each group its first clue, and send them off on their quests. When they have finished, they will meet back in a central location, such as the writing center, and brainstorm good ideas (i.e., fortunes) to write on the small paper strip.

To Make the Fortune Cookie

1. Fold the 3" x 3" paper in half diagonally.
2. Seal edges with tape.
3. Leave small opening on one side.
4. Insert paper fortune into open side of cookie, leaving part of the strip hanging out.
5. Mix all cookies in a bowl and have each child pick one for himself! Prizes: real fortune cookies!

Puppet Show Based on *The Rooster's Horns: A Chinese Puppet Play to Make and Perform*

This book is a guide to creating a shadow puppet play, and Ed Young provides detailed directions on how to do so at the end of this book. Have the students work in groups of three (for the three main characters: Rooster, Dragon, and Worm). They can create their own shadow puppets and act out the story, or create a new adventure for the three characters. Teachers or librarians could use their overhead projectors to recreate the shadow puppet show, too!

Hook Activity

In *Hook*, Ed Young's double-spread chalk drawings and brief text convey the story of an abandoned eaglet who is raised by a hen, and who ultimately learns to soar. To reinforce the book's theme, teach the students how to make a paper wing and have them stand along a line of tape to see whose wing will fly the farthest. This paper wing toy is also described in *Steven Caney's Toy Book* (Caney, 1972), on page 139.

To Make a Wing

1. Cut a 8½" x 11" piece of paper in half so you have a 5½" x 8½" piece of paper.
2. Fold the paper in half, crease it to make a center line, and unfold.
3. Fold one end to the center line and crease this second fold.
4. Keeping this end folded, fold it once more to the center line and crease it.
5. Fold the end once more and crease it (this time it should fold *over* the center line).
6. Curve the folded paper into a wing by running it back-and-forth along the edge of a table, with the folded side facing down.
7. Place the finished wing in one hand, with the folded part facing up and positioned forward. The wing can be released with a slight nudge.
8. Connect this activity to measurement by having the students each measure the distance their wings flew using connecting cubes. Graph the results, too!

Words of Wisdom

Many of Ed Young's picture books have morals or other wise anecdotes. Here are a few ways to incorporate these statements into your celebration.

• Book Display—List the morals on a worksheet and keep the worksheet near a display of Young's picture books. Challenge the students to go on a scavenger hunt for these words of wisdom. Students must read

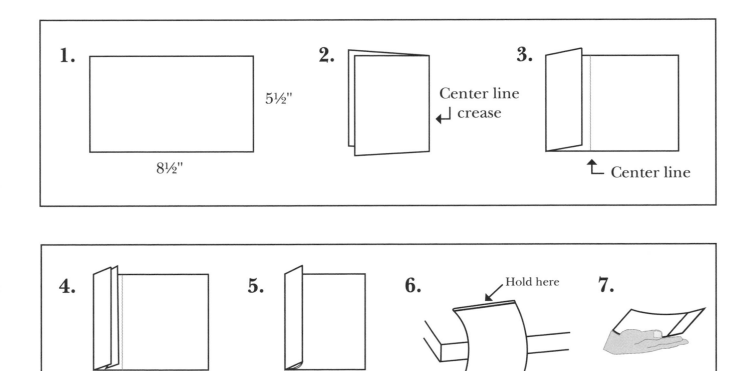

through the picture books to match the statements to their books. Leave this display up during the entire month of November, and have students put their completed worksheets into a box wrapped in birthday gift paper. Draw out several worksheets during the celebration and award prizes. Be sure to distribute a bookmark or other small prize to all the students who completed a worksheet, too!

- Art Project—Type up the moral statements on a sheet of paper, and cut out each statement. Place them in a shoebox, and have students pick a statement from the box. Provide a variety of art supplies, and have the students create a visual image that best represents the lesson of their statement. Hang these up for a colorful display during the month.
- Creative Writing Activity—Have the students choose one of the morals, and rewrite it to reflect the same principles but with a modern twist. Brainstorm ideas, such as names of modern people, current events, fashion trends, music, etc. The students would use the brainstorm ideas to help them create a modern version of these wise sayings.

Sample Words of Wisdom from
Ed Young's Books

- "Knowing in part may make a fine tale, but wisdom comes from seeing the whole" (*Seven Blind Mice*).
- "Be open to work. It is in the willingness to labor that we mature and find excellence" (*Beyond the Great Mountains*).
- ". . . to prosper, they must follow their own hearts" (*Donkey Trouble*).
- ". . . there is strength in admitting to weakness" (*Monkey King*).

Lon Po Po Game

Bring the students to the gym, and have them play this fun chase game. One child is selected to be Lon Po Po, the Wolf. He will stand in the middle of the gym, and the rest of the students will stand along one of the gym walls. Lon Po Po will yell, "Little Children, come and see I am your Grandma visiting for tea!" All the children should respond with, "No, no, you won't catch me!" Then the children all run to the opposite gym wall and must avoid being "caught" (tagged) by the wolf. If they are tagged, they stand in the middle with Lon Po Po and chant the refrain with him. The game continues until all of the children are caught and then a new Lon Po Po is selected for another round.

Party Foods

Sing "Happy Birthday" while you present the students with a platter filled with frosted cupcakes. Create small drawings of animals from Ed Young's books, such as a donkey, monkey, mouse, wolf, rooster, dragon, and eagle. Simply print out clip art images of these animals, in a small size. Cut each out and tape it to a toothpick. Insert the toothpicks into the cupcakes and let the children enjoy recalling the various stories in which each animal was a character.

Party Favors

Fill small party bags with fortune cookies, rice candy, and a small sketch book that you can make by stapling 3" x 5" sheets of blank paper together, with card stock for the sketchbook's covers. Encourage them to keep their booklets with them so they can develop the habit of drawing images of the natural world around them!

Happy Birthday, Ed Young!

Born November 28, 1931

Picture Books Written & Illustrated by Ed Young

- *Beyond the Great Mountains: A Visual Poem About China*
- *Donkey Trouble*
- *Hook*
- *I, Doko: The Tale of a Basket*
- *Lon Po Po: A Red-Riding Hood Story From China*
- *The Lost Horse*
- *Monkey King*
- *Moon Mother: A Native American Creation Tale*
- *My Mei Mei*
- *Seven Blind Mice*

Picture Books Illustrated by Ed Young

- *Birches*
  (by Robert Frost)
- *Dreamcatcher*
  (by Audrey Osofsky)
- *Foolish Rabbit's Big Mistake*
  (by Rafe Martin)
- *I Wish I Were A Butterfly*
  (by James Howe)
- *Moon Bear*
  (by Brenda C. Guiberson)
- *A Pup Just For Me/ A Boy Just For Me*
  (by Dorothea P. Seeber)
- *Tsunami!*
  (by Kimiko Kajikawa)
- *Twenty Heartbeats*
  (by Dennis Haseley)
- *Wabi Sabi*
  (by Mark Reibstein)

Folktales Retold & Illustrated by Ed Young

- *Cat and Rat: The Legend of the Chinese Zodiac*
- *Mouse Match*
- *The Rooster's Horns: A Chinese Puppet Play to Make and Perform*
  (with Hilary Beckett)
- *The Sons of the Dragon King*
- *What About Me?*

Folktales Illustrated by Ed Young

- *Chinese Mother Goose Rhymes*
  (by Robert Wyndham)
- *The Emperor and the Kite*
  (by Jane Yolen)
- *The Hunter: A Chinese Folktale*
  (by Mary Casanova)
- *The Turkey Girl: A Zuni Cinderella Story*
  (by Penny Pollock)
- *White Wave: A Chinese Tale*
  (by Diane Wolkstein)
- *Yeh-Shen: A Cinderella Story From China*
  (by Ai-Ling Louie)

Biography Illustrated by Ed Young

- *Sadako*
  (by Eleanor Coerr)

Ed Young Reading Log

Read 5 books by **November** _____.

On each line, write the title you've read and have your parent/guardian sign that you read it.

Bring this completed reading log to me by **November** _____ and receive your invitation to attend our birthday celebration on

_____.

Date/Time

_____
Title   Parent/Guardian Signature

_____
Title   Parent/Guardian Signature

_____
Title   Parent/Guardian Signature

_____
Title   Parent/Guardian Signature

_____
Title   Parent/Guardian Signature

Happy Birthday, Dear Authors Born in December!

December 1	**Jan Brett***	December 19	Eve Bunting
December 2	David Macaulay		Eleanor H. Porter
	William Wegman	December 20	Lulu Delacre
December 4	George Ancona	December 21	Susan Pearson
December 5	Jim Kjelgaard	December 22	Jarrett J. Krosoczka
December 6	John Reynolds Gardiner		**Jerry Pinkney***
	Elizabeth Yates	December 23	Avi
December 7	Anne Fine		Keiko Kasza
December 9	Joan W. Blos	December 25	Pam Muñoz Ryan
December 10	Douglas Wood	December 26	Jean Van Leeuwen
December 11	William Joyce	December 27	Ted Rand
December 12	Barbara Emberley		**Diane Stanley***
December 13	Lucia Gonzalez	December 28	Cynthia De Felice
	Tamora Pierce		Emily Neville
December 14	Marilyn Hafner	December 29	Molly Bang
	Rosemary Sutcliff		Janet Greenberg
December 15	Ann Nolan Clark		Ruth Robbins
December 16	Quentin Blake	December 30	Mercer Mayer
December 18	Marilyn Sachs		Mary Rayner
		December 31	Cynthia Leitich Smith
			Margery Cuyler

*Author featured in this chapter

Happy Birthday, Dear Jan Brett!

About Jan Brett

- Jan Brett was born on December 1, 1949, in Massachusetts. She continues to live in that state.
- She attended Colby Junior College from 1968–1969, and Boston Museum of Fine Arts School in 1970.
- Her daughter, Lia, was the inspiration for the main character in *Annie and the Wild Animals.*
- Her husband, Joseph Hearne, is a musician and was the inspiration behind *Berlioz the Bear.*
- Jan Brett loves to retreat into the mountains near her summer home in Massachusetts. Many of her books contain images of nature that she drew from this setting.
- Two of her favorite subjects are Christmas and winter; both of these subjects are very common topics in her picture books.
- She has two very unique trademarks: Her use of borders to provide additional story details, and her inclusion of hedgehogs in her illustrations.
- Horses are one of her favorite animals.

Celebration Activities

Tell Jan Brett's Story

Create a mural by placing a large sheet of white butcher paper on a wall. This will be a winter landscape. Add items to the landscape that relate to her life story, such as a bear for her husband, who is a bass player and was the inspiration for the main character in her book, *Berlioz the Bear.* Other objects to add to the mural include a hedgehog, for her pet hedgehog named Buffy (short for Buffalo Gal); a horse, for her own Horse named Hans; four dogs, for her pets, Polly, Naisy, Gretchen, Kylie; four hens, her pets who inspired her book, *Daisy Comes Home;* a stack of books by a fireplace, to show that her hobby is reading; a compass to show her love of travel; and snowflakes to show her love of winter. The final item to add is an outline around the perimeter of the mural, to show her signature feature: her use of borders to provide clues to the readers about what will happen next in her stories.

Craft

Many of Jan Brett's illustrations are populated with birch trees. If you have access to these trees in your community, saw 1-inch thick discs from several branches (approximately 2–3" diameter). Insert a small eye-screw into the side of each disc. This will serve as the hanger. Provide the students with sprigs of evergreens, holly, ribbon, buttons, pine cones, etc. Have the students glue the objects onto the birch tree disc to create a window plaque. Encourage them to hang their completed projects on a window.

Gingerbread Decorating

In honor of Brett's *Gingerbread Baby,* have the students decorate gingerbread people cookies. You can special order a batch of undecorated gingerbread people cookies from your local bakeries. Provide the students with white frosting and set up a station that is filled with a wide variety of decoration supplies: cinnamon red hots, string licorice, raisins, miniature chocolate chips, etc. Give each child a sandwich-size re-sealable plastic bag filled with frosting. Cut a small hole in one corner for students to pipe out frosting onto the cookies. Do this at the beginning of the celebration so the frosting will have time to harden before wrapping them for the children to bring home.

Hide and Seek with Jan Brett's Books

Jan Brett is an artist that enjoys hiding small animals and objects in the illustrations of her books. Give small groups of students an object that Jan Brett hid in one of her books. The group that is first to find their hidden object wins a prize! Once all groups have found their objects, they could trade them with each other to find more objects and continue the fun! Here are a few ideas to get you started:

- *Comet's Nine Lives*—find a yellow lab with a rope bracelet.
- *Daisy Comes Home*—find 15 animals in the mountains.
- *The Mitten*—find the upside-down milk jug and stork's nest.
- *Gingerbread Baby*—find as many hedgehogs as you can in the spingerle cookies.
- *Berlioz the Bear*—look closely at the mule. What is his name?
- *The Hat*—Besides Hedgie, where did Jan Brett hide another small hedgehog in her illustrations?
- *Armadillo Rodeo*—Where did Jan Brett hide a hedgehog in this book?
- *Trouble with Trolls*—What scuttled by Tuffi?
- *Fritz and the Beautiful Horses*—What is missing from all the illustrations? How is this book different from Brett's other books?
- *Honey . . . Honey . . . Lion!*—Find the hedgehog!

This activity could also serve as a scavenger hunt book display. During the month, have all the books on display and provide an activity sheet for the students to work on individually throughout the month. The activity sheet should provide directions and scavenger hunt clues. This is an effective way to get your students into the books—they won't be able to keep from reading them while searching for the hidden objects!

Game: Mitten Race!

In honor of Brett's most popular picture book, *The Mitten*, play this fun party game. Have the students assemble their mittens and gloves into a pile. Divide the class into two teams. At your signal, have the first person from each team run to the pile, find their mittens (or any matching pair), put them on, and then open up a stick of gum and begin to chew it! (If gum is not advisable, consider a wrapped piece of candy, a small packet of gummi bears, etc.) The first team finished gets to pick a prize, then the runners-up pick. The prizes could be a free book to take home, small party bags filled with candy, and a bookmark (Jan Brett has several designs free for downloading on her website *www.janbrett.com*).

Honey . . . Honey . . . Lion!

This story about an African legend is reminiscent of the popular story chant, "Going on a Bear Hunt." Assemble the students in a circle, and have them sit down before you read this book aloud. As you read the section in which the badger begins to follow the honeyguide through the bush, have the students mimic the animal movements by making the sounds with their hands. For example, when you read that Badger ran after the Honeyguide, "pitter, patter," slap your thighs with alternating hands in a soft, quick rhythm and chant, "pitter, patter, pitter, patter," as you do so. The students should join in. Continue until Badger runs into Lion, and then have the students follow your movements as Badger runs frantically away from the lion, similar to how they would move after running into the bear in the traditional story chant.

Geo-Jan!

As you read aloud to the students from Jan Brett's books, share the end pages with them, too. On these pages, Jan tells about the places she visited to do her research for the book. Create a bulletin board of a world map, and place a pushpin on each country that was visited by Jan. Do this as each book is shared with the class, so that by the time of the celebration, you will have shared in traveling vicariously to all of these places with Jan Brett! Highlight each place with a scanned copy of its corresponding book cover.

Winter Warmers

In honor of Jan Brett's collection of winter stories (*The Mitten, Trouble With Trolls, The Three Snow Bears*, etc.), have the students follow directions to make a cocoa mix. Have students research online to find a cocoa mix recipe that they would like to try. This can be a learning center in which young readers must follow the recipe to make the mix and take it home; or it can be a whole-class activity. Gift jars filled with cocoa mix make wonderful presents to give to parents during the month of December!

Blindman's Bluff

In Jan Brett's book, *Armadillo Rodeo*, readers learn that armadillos do not have a strong sense of sight. Help the students to understand this problem by playing a few games, such as the traditional game of Blind Man's Bluff.

Another activity related to this is a trust walk. Pair up students, and have them take turns leading their blindfolded partners to a secret place in the classroom or library. Instruct partners to be tricky by leading their blindfolded friends around chairs that aren't really there, etc. Once they've reached the destination, the blindfolded partner feels the area, then is led back to the starting point. Once the blindfold is removed, the partner must find the secret place, having

only experienced it by his/her sense of touch. Can they meet the challenge? Partners switch roles and play again.

Birthday Cards for Jan Brett

Have students draw their own winter scenes on the front of a folded paper. Obtain a small stamp of a hedgehog and have students stamp the hedgehog into their drawings. Tell them to try to hide the hedgehog for Jan Brett to find when she reads their cards! Write about this in the cover letter that you send to Jan Brett so that she'll know what to do when she reads the students' cards.

Party Favors

Visit Jan Brett's website at janbrett.com and download her activity pages. Create an activity packet for each student and include a small box of crayons or a colorful pencil. Other party favor ideas: wintergreen mints, small felt mittens sewn together to make a pocket that holds peppermint sticks, bookmarks, stickers, etc.

Happy Birthday, Jan Brett!

Born December 1, 1949

Book List

- *Annie and the Wild Animals*
- *Armadillo Rodeo*
- *Beauty and the Beast*
- *Berlioz the Bear*
- *Christmas Trolls*
- *Comet's Nine Lives*
- *Daisy Comes Home*
- *The Easter Egg*
- *The First Dog*
- *Fritz and the Beautiful Horses*
- *Gingerbread Baby*
- *Gingerbread Friends*
- *Goldilocks and the 3 Bears*
- *The Hat*
- *Hedgie Blasts Off!*
- *Hedgie Loves to Read*
- *Hedgie's Surprise*
- *Home for Christmas*
- *Honey, Honey, Lion!*
- *The Mitten*
- *On Noah's Ark*
- *The 3 Little Dassies*
- *The Three Snow Bears*
- *Town Mouse, Country Mouse*
- *Trouble With Trolls*
- *The Twelve Days of Christmas*
- *The Umbrella*

Jan Brett Reading Log

Read 5 books by **December** ____.

On each line, write the title you've read and have your parent/guardian sign that you read it.

Bring this completed reading log to me by **December** ____ and receive your invitation to attend our birthday celebration on

_____.

Date/Time

_____

Title   Parent/Guardian Signature

_____

Title   Parent/Guardian Signature

_____

Title   Parent/Guardian Signature

_____

Title   Parent/Guardian Signature

_____

Title   Parent/Guardian Signature

Happy Birthday, Dear Diane Stanley!

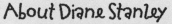

About Diane Stanley

- Diane Stanley was born on December 27, 1943 in Texas.
- After her parents divorce, Diane Stanley and her mother lived in New York City.
- Diane also lived in Texas with an aunt while her mother recuperated from tuberculosis, and later lived in California with her mother.
- Diane was the president of the theater club during high school.
- Although she was always interested in drawing and painting, and made a lot of creative crafts as a child, Diane did not discover her passion for art until she took drawing classes during her senior year in college!
- She graduated in 1970 from Johns Hopkins University College of Medicine with a master's degree.
- She has two daughters and a son.

Celebration Ideas

Tropical Celebration!

In honor of *Moe the Dog in Tropical Paradise*, tell the students to bring in a beach toy for the day of the author party. Play calypso music, bring in seashells for students to sort and later use in a craft, and play beach games, such as limbo, jump the waves (use a long jump rope for the waves), and volleyball (use beach balls and play in the gymnasium). Provide fruit juice and ice cream bars for refreshments. This is a great way to spend a cold December day together!

What Would Sweetness Do?

After reading *Saving Sweetness*, discuss what Sweetness did and why she is the real hero in this story.

Before the Celebration

Type up a list of various sticky situations, similar to those found in the book, *The Worst-Case Scenario Survival Handbook* (Piven, 1999). For example: "You are riding your bike on a trail in the woods and you get a flat tire. What would Sweetness do?"

During the Celebration

Divide the students into teams of three or four, and have them draw a scenario from a box. Give each group time to brainstorm their ideas and create a quick "how-to" demonstration for the class. They need to pantomime their scenario and their survival idea. Vote on most unique survival idea! Make small ribbons that say, "Sweetness saves the day!"

Time-Traveling Twins Scrapbooks

Diane Stanley has written several books about Lenny and Liz, the Time-Traveling Twins. The titles include *Roughing it on the Oregon Trail* and *Thanksgiving on Plymouth Plantation*. Tell the students to imagine that they are the Time-Traveling Twins. Have the students choose an event, such as the signing of the Declaration of Independence, or landing on the moon, and give them a list of items that they should find to include in a scrapbook to remind them of their time-traveling adventures with Grandma. They should include five of the following items: sheet music of a popular song from that era; price list of common grocery items; newspaper headlines; quotes from famous people of that era (authors, artists, musicians, presidents, etc.); fashion from the era; new inventions from that time period; World Series Winners (if appropriate to the era); Academy-Award Winners (as appropriate); recipes for popular meals; etc. This is a great activity for the third grade students and it provides a unique alternative to the common history project.

Scrapbook for Diane Stanley

In honor of her Time-Traveling series, have the students each submit a scrapbook page that tells something interesting about 1943, the year Diane Stanley was born. Each student should also include a letter to the author to wish her a happy birthday! Collate the pages into a paper-bound scrapbook and mail to the author for her birthday!

Project HOPE: Helping Other People Everywhere

Diane Stanley's book, *Rumpelstiltskin's Daughter* tells about Hope, the daughter of Rumpelstiltskin, who taught the greedy king to help his people out of poverty. In honor of Hope, create a class project using the acronym HOPE and identify a service project for your students to participate in together. Scholastic Books often promotes several community service projects, such as Bedtime Stories (students donate pajamas and Scholastic matches each new pajama outfit with a book to donate to children/adults in shelters). On the day of the party, the students could bring in the items that you've decided to collect! Celebrate their contributions by distributing certificates of appreciation.

Goldie and the Three Bears

This fun, updated version of the classic folktale can be highlighted during the author party in several ways.

- For younger students: have a teddy bear picnic. Play a recording of the classic song, have the students make teddy bear headbands, complete with brown bear ears. Provide cupcakes with teddy bear-shaped graham crackers on them. Students could bring in their own stuffed animals (teddy bears, etc.) to use as props in a parade.
- For older students: have them brainstorm the qualities of a perfect friend, such as Goldie's quest to find a friend that "she could love with all her heart" (unpaged). The students could create acrostic poems, with the word "friend" written vertically along the left side of a teddy bear-shaped paper.
- For all students: have them use teddy bear graham crackers to manipulate on story cards as they act out word problems. The story cards could be background scenes related to the book, such as the bears' home, a neighborhood park, etc. Dictate various stories or math problems to the students and have them use the graham crackers to act them out. For example, "Goldie went into the Bears' house and saw one bear. (*Students place one graham cracker bear on the story card.*) Then she laid down to rest, and, when she awoke, she saw that three of the bears' friends had come over. How many bears are in the house now?" Change the problems to reflect the skill level of the students.

Tell the Author's Story!

Diane Stanley has created numerous picture book biographies with her husband, Peter Vennema. Capitalize on her use of this genre to present her biography to the students using pictures that you can tape to the board as you tell her story. Tell the students you are sharing with them a picture biography of Diane Stanley. Be sure to include the following interesting events and pictures:

- Tape up a large map of the United States. Use the map to show the various places that Diane Stanley has lived: born in Abilene, Texas; moved to New York, New York; moved back to Texas while her mother was sick; moved to La Jolla, California, with her mom during her high school years; Baltimore, Maryland, while working on her Master's Degree at Johns Hopkins.
- Tape up a large drama mask to tell about her involvement in the theater productions in her high school.
- Hobbies: reading, drawing, painting (use pictures for each hobby)
- Mom of three children (include a picture of her with her children, or a generic image of a mom and children)

- Awards: Orbis Pictus Award for Outstanding Nonfiction for Children—1996, Leonardo da Vinci; Golden Kite Award Honor Book—1997, Saving Sweetness; and numerous honor awards for many other books.
- Daughter of a flying ace Navy Pilot from WWII

*Visit her website and explore her scrapbook biography with the students at www.dianestanley.com.

Biography Bingo

Stanley has written a variety of biographies, mostly geared toward students in grades 3–6. However, these biographies could also prove to be great resources in primary classrooms as read alouds. For example, several biographies cover famous artists. These books could provide interesting anecdotes to compliment a unit study on renaissance artists. Or, perhaps you could create a bulletin board that is titled, "Diane Stanley's Favorite Famous People." Read aloud some interesting vignettes throughout the month from her books and add a few fun facts to the bulletin board, along with a photograph of the famous person.

If these books have been shared with the students in such a way, a fun party game would be to play bingo. Distribute blank 3 x 3 grids and place a list of biography characters on the board. Tell the students to copy down the characters, one per empty box, in any order they'd like. Before the celebration, search Stanley's biographies for clues about each famous person that you've shared with the students during the month. During the game, read the clues to the class. The students must determine which famous person matches the clue before they can mark their bingo cards. The first to get three in a row wins! They could pick a prize from a box, such as paperback books, boxes of crayons, or other school supplies. These items are all on sale for very inexpensive prices during department stores' back-to-school sales, or from catalogs geared to children's books.

Sculpture Wishes

In honor of Stanley's book, *The Trouble with Wishes*, provide the students with some modeling clay, and challenge them to create a sculpture of someone or something that they would wish to come alive. After creating their sculptures, they could list 3–5 reasons why they'd want it to come to life. Put these on display in the classroom.

You could even have the students make their own salt dough clay. When students follow a recipe, they are practicing their beginning reading skills with a real-world purpose. Try this recipe from *Crafts from Salt Dough* by Audrey Gessat (Bridgestone Books, 2003):

Salt Dough Recipe

Ingredients:	¾ cup flour
	¾ cup cornstarch
	⅔ cup salt
	⅔ cup water
Directions:	1. Mix the flour, cornstarch, and salt in a bowl.
	2. Mix in water, a little at a time.
	3. Knead dough for 10 minutes
	4. Crate a sculpture with a handful of dough.
	5. Let it air-dry overnight.

Party Foods

Here are some fun foods to serve while singing, "Happy Birthday, Dear Diane Stanley!"

- Ice cream sandwiches or popsicles (in honor of *Moe the Dog in Tropical Paradise*)
- Artistic sugar cookies: Since many of Stanley's books revolve around art and artists, have the students try their hand at their own creativity with this treat. Provide a large, round, unfrosted sugar cookie for each student. Create a "decorations bar" in the

middle of the room. This "bar" will hold bowls of edible decorative items, such as gum drops, colored licorice laces, sprinkles, chocolate chips, cinnamon imperials, etc. Have children frost their cookies with white frosting, then go to the bar to collect decorative items and create their artistic cookies at their desks. These works of art will be good enough to eat!

- Apples for the Gentleman: Help students make this tasty treat using fresh apples, just like those held by the Kitchen Maid in Stanley's *The Gentleman and the Kitchen Maid.* In this creative picture book, Diane Stanley challenges her readers to look deeply into famous paintings and imagine a story, such as the romance between the Gentleman and the Kitchen Maid.

The Kitchen Maid's Walking Apple Snacks

Ingredients: 1 apple for each student

peanut butter or cream cheese (depending on allergies)

chocolate chips

raisins

Directions:
1. Core each apple.
2. Mix together peanut butter or cream cheese and the chocolate chips and raisins.
3. Fill the core with the peanut butter mixture.
4. Eat and enjoy!

*These are called "walking apples" because they are excellent snacks to carry while on a hike!

Party Favors

Art supplies, chocolate gold coins (for *Rumpelstiltskin's Daughter* and *Goldie and the Three Bears*), USA maps (for Diane Stanley's love of travel), bookmarks.

Happy Birthday, Diane Stanley!

Born December 27, 1943

Biographies

- *Joan of Arc*
- *Leonardo daVinci*
- *Michelangelo*
- *Mozart, the Wonder Child: A Puppet Play in 3 Acts*
- *Peter the Great*
- *Saladin: Noble Prince of Islam*

Collaborations with Peter Vennema

- *Bard of Avon: The Story of William Shakespeare*
- *Charles Dickens: The Man Who Had Great Expectations*
- *Cleopatra*
- *Good Queen Bess: The Story of Elizabeth 1 of England*
- *Shaka, King of the Zulus*

Picture Books

- *The Gentleman and the Kitchen Maid*
- *The Giant and the Beanstalk*
- *Goldie and the Three Bears*
- *Moe the Dog in Tropical Paradise*
- *Raising Sweetness*
- *Rumpelstiltskin's Daughter*
- *Saving Sweetness*
- *The Trouble with Wishes*
- *Woe is Moe*

Fiction/Novella

- *Elena*

Time-Traveling Twins Series (with Holly Berry)

- *Joining the Boston Tea Party*
- *Roughing it on the Oregon Trail*
- *Thanksgiving on Plymouth Plantation*

Diane Stanley Reading Log

Read 5 books by **December** ____.

On each line, write the title you've read and have your parent/guardian sign that you read it.

Bring this completed reading log to me by **December** ____ and receive your invitation to attend our birthday celebration on

_____.

Date/Time

_____

Title   Parent/Guardian Signature

_____

Title   Parent/Guardian Signature

_____

Title   Parent/Guardian Signature

_____

Title   Parent/Guardian Signature

_____

Title   Parent/Guardian Signature

Happy Birthday, Dear Jerry Pinkney!

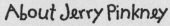

About Jerry Pinkney

- Jerry Pinkney was born on December 22, 1939 in Philadelphia, Pennsylvania.
- He is one of six children: three boys and three girls.
- He was the first child in his family to go to college. He went to the Philadelphia College of Art after attending Dobbins Vocational Art School.
- He met his wife, Gloria Jean, during his third year at Dobbins.
- Jerry and Gloria Jean have four children: Troy Bernadette, Jerry Brian, Scott, and Myles.
- He created a variety of commemorative stamps for the United States Postal Service during the 1980s.
- He has received a Caldecott Honor Award for the following books: *Mirandy and Brother Wind*, *The Talking Eggs: A Folktale from the American South*, and *John Henry*.
- He has received the Caldecott Award for his wordless picture book, *The Lion and the Mouse* (2009).
- Jerry Pinkney suffered from dyslexia, and learned to compensate for his difficulties in reading by drawing. Despite his learning disability, he graduated elementary school with top honors.

Celebration Ideas

The Colorful Life of Jerry Pinkney

Tell the students the story of Jerry Pinkney's life by associating key life events with colors on a painter's palette.

Before the Celebration

Cut out "blobs" of paint from each color of construction paper: red, blue, yellow, orange, green, purple, white, black. Lay these pieces down on your desk, in the order that you will refer to them for the story. Cut out a large palette shape from brown construction paper and place it on the chalkboard. As you tell the following story, tape the corresponding colored paint blob to the palette.

- **Red** (cut into a heart shape): Jerry Pinkney was born on December 22, 1939, in Philadelphia, Pennsylvania, the city of brotherly love. He shares his love with his wife, Gloria Jean (another author), and his four children.
- **Yellow** (cut into the shape of the sun): Jerry went to elementary school in the 1940s, a time when learning difficulties were not always known about. Jerry struggled with learning to read because he has what we now know as dyslexia. However, he did not give up! In fact, he worked even more diligently to overcome his struggles, and he used his excellent drawing skills to pull him through his difficulties. He let his true self shine through, just like the sun. Listen to what he has to say to us all:

  ". . . Never forget there are many different ways to learn. Be curious. Do not be afraid to try. Do not be disappointed when making mistakes. You will discover your own unique way of understanding the things being taught. Learn from mistakes. Everything that happens to you will frame who you are, and who you will become. Your path to success will follow." (www.jerrypinkneystudio.com/frameset.html).

- **Green** (cut into the shape of a leaf): Although he is best known for his illustrations of picture books, which he has done since 1964, he has also worked as an artist for our National Park Service.
- **Blue** (cut into a circle): He used his artistic talent to journey into the depths of our blue skies when he created a painting for the NASA Art Collection of the John F. Kennedy Space Center.
- **White** (cut into the shape of a postage stamp): Jerry Pinkney filled the white canvas of United States postage stamps with several designs. He even served on the U.S. Postal Service's Stamp Advisory Committee from 1982 to 1992.
- **Silver** (cut into a circle): Jerry Pinkney has won five Caldecott Honor Awards. These books have a silver medal on their cover.
- **Gold** (cut into a circle): Jerry won a Caldecott Award in 2009! It was awarded to him for his picture book, *The Lion and the Mouse*. This book has a gold medal on its cover.
- **Purple** (cut into a circle): Jerry Pinkney is still working on new books. He is a king-like figure in the world of picture books, so I am adding a purple circle because this color symbolizes royalty!

Welcome to Folktale Island!

Since most of Pinkney's picture books are illustrated versions of popular folktales, have the students pick the title of one of his illustrated folktales from a container. They must create their own illustration of the main character from the folktale. Have them sign their names on their characters and glue them onto a large sheet of butcher paper that the students have colored to resemble an island. Add a sign, such as "Welcome to Folktale Island!", and write a happy birthday message to Jerry Pinkney on it. All the students' signatures will be found on their folktale characters that they've attached to the island mural. Include a cover letter that explains your author program, and ask the students if they have any questions they'd like to ask Mr. Pinkney to include in the letter. Mail this to Mr. Pinkney for his birthday!

Family Memories

Jerry Pinkney illustrated two books about family memories that were written by his wife, Gloria Jean Pinkney. The first book is titled *Back Home*, and the second is a prequel, titled *The Sunday Outing*. Both books provide readers with insights into the powerful connections all children have with their grandparents and great aunts/uncles. Capitalize on this topic by sharing an object with the students that is meaningful to your own family, such as an old blanket, an antique camera, a locket, etc. Encourage the children to bring in a similar object for the special birthday celebration.

On the day of the author party, have the children form small groups of 4–6 students and give time for each student to tell the story behind the object that he/she brought to school. Allow time for the students to participate in a gallery walk, in which they would walk around to the other groups and view their objects. Finally, create a memory game by placing the objects on a serving tray. Tell the students to get a good look at the items, and then place the tray out of sight. Give students a paper, and have them try to list as many objects on the tray as possible during a specified period of time. Give a small prize to all the students, such as small plastic train whistles (available through toy and party catalogs). The trains would remind the students of how Ernestine, the main character in both books, traveled by train to her great aunt's home.

The Lion and the Mouse

This Caldecott winner is perfect for storytelling! Jerry Pinkney chose to illustrate this fable as a wordless picture book, making this the perfect format for storytelling activities. Here are a few suggestions:

- Rhythmic Instruments: Discuss the differences between the lion and the mouse, and have the students listen to a variety of rhythmic instruments in order to determine which would best compliment the lion, and which would best compliment the mouse. They could vote by filling out a picture graph, a great way to tie in math concepts.

Once the top two instruments have been determined, divide the class in half and give one half the instrument for the mouse, and the other an instrument for the lion. Hold up the book, and turn each page slowly, without filling in any dialogue. Point to the mouse group when the mouse is pictured so they can play their instruments. Do the same for the lion group. Teach them how to play their instruments quietly, loudly, slowly, quickly, etc., depending on the action in the illustration.

- Snap and Clap: Do the same technique described above, using the students' hands to create the appropriate sound for each animal. Teach the students to create snap-and-clap patterns that they could clap out during their assigned animal's escapades. For example, the lion group might clap out the following rhythm: clap hands twice, then slap both thighs once (clap, clap, slap). They could do this slowly while the lion is shown walking through the jungle.
- Paper Plate Puppets: Divide the class in half, assigning lion to one half and mouse to the other. The lion group will use a paper plate to create a lion mask, while the mouse group creates a mouse mask. Once the masks are complete, have the students wear their masks and silently move like their assigned animal. Brainstorm appropriate movements, and help the students to mimic the animals for each scene's actions.
- Background Music: Jerry Pinkney created a realistic setting for this fable by placing it in the Serengeti of Tanzania and Kenya. Download music that is from this region of Africa, and play it while sharing this book with the students.

Listen to Your Heart!

This is the command of *The Nightingale*, the famous Hans Christian Andersen tale retold by Jerry Pinkney. The small bird with the beautiful song told the king to "Listen to your heart and always live in peace" (unpaged). With this important message in mind, brainstorm with your students ideas for living out this command in our modern society. Students could either focus on the concept of listening to their hearts (being true to themselves, loving one another, etc.), or of living in peace (anti-bullying efforts, cooperation with their peers, etc.). Have them work on social justice posters to hang throughout the school. Each student should write one idea for living out the command on a heart-shaped paper. Write the command in large letters along the tops of the posters and adhere the paper hearts in a collage format on the poster boards. This is an effective way to enable younger students to think about their roles in society.

Video Chat

Jerry Pinkney has created several brief videos in which he shares his process of creating his books. Go to Youtube™ and search: "Jerry Pinkney talks about the Lion and the Mouse." This will link you to several brief videos of Jerry Pinkney that your students will enjoy watching during your author celebration.

Pinkney Pictures

Jerry Pinkney's distinctive artistic style is one that the students will enjoy imitating. Line up a variety of picture books by Mr. Pinkney, and help the students to become acquainted with this use of perspective (Pinkney often places the reader on the same level as the main character), his realistic portraits of people and animals, and his use of watercolors to create shades of light on faces and objects. This will help young readers to become empowered in their ability to independently select books by Jerry Pinkney.

Using a document camera, place one of Pinkney's illustrated classics on the screen for all to see how he used colored pencils and watercolors to create his pictures. This is especially evident in *The Lion and the Mouse, The Sunday Outing, Back Home, The Talking Eggs* (San Souci, 1989), and *The Patchwork Quilt* (Flournoy, 1985).

Have the students draw a picture from a scene in their favorite folktale, using pencils and colored pencils to outline the images. Next, have the students use watercolors to fill in the images. Encourage them to experiment with the shading of the watercolors to add light and dimension to the images. Have them fill in details, once the watercolors have dried, with colored pencils. Hang up the completed pictures for a colorful display of Pinkney-inspired artwork!

Party Food

Serve raisin muffins (*Little Red Riding Hood*) with hot chocolate (*The Patchwork Quilt*), while singing "Happy Birthday" to Jerry Pinkney!

Also consider providing bread and jam treats in honor of Pinkney's retelling of *The Little Red Hen*. Bring in some refrigerator bread rolls, enough for each student to have one. Give the uncooked rolls out to the children and instruct them to knead it and shape it into his/her own unique bread roll. Sprinkle them with cinnamon and sugar and place in an oven (according to the directions on the label). Once the rolls have cooked and cooled, allow the students to add jam to them and enjoy! Since they each worked hard on their own rolls, they've earned the right to eat them; just like the Little Red Hen!

The Talking Eggs Treasure Hunt

Before the celebration, use plastic Easter eggs and fill each egg with a clue. Hide the eggs throughout the classroom or library. Make sure that you have 4–5 eggs for each small group of 3–4 students. During the celebration: Divide the students into small groups, and give each group a "talking egg." The groups must open their egg and read its message aloud to their group mates. The message could simply tell the students where to look for the next egg, or it could have a question inside that is related to Pinkney's books. If you use questions, write the answer on the next egg they must find. Have them search for the egg with the correct answer, then open it to read the next question/clue. Younger students could simply hunt for eggs that are the same color (all yellow eggs for group 1, green eggs for group 2, etc.). The last egg will lead them to a treat, such as eggs filled with small candies.

Party Favors

Small watercolor sets, colored pencils, small candies.

Happy Birthday, Jerry Pinkney!

Born December 22, 1939

Folktales Retold and Illustrated by Jerry Pinkney

- *Aesop's Fables*
- *The Lion and the Mouse*
- *The Little Red Hen*
- *Little Red Riding Hood*
- *Noah's Ark*
- *The Three Little Kittens*

Hans Christian Andersen Tales

- *The Little Match Girl*
- *The Nightingale*
- *The Ugly Duckling*

Collaborations with Julius Lester

- *Black Cowboy, Wild Horses*
- *The Complete Tales of Uncle Remus*
- *John Henry*
- *The Old African*
- *Sam and the Tigers: A Retelling of Little Black Sambo*

Collaborations with Victoria Flournoy

- *The Patchwork Quilt*
- *Tanya's Reunion*

Collaborations with Gloria Jean Pinkney

- *Back Home*
- *The Sunday Outing*

Collaborations with Patricia McKissack

- *The All-I'll-Ever-Want Christmas Doll*
- *Goin' Someplace Special*
- *Mirandy and Brother Wind*

Collaborations with Robert D. San Souci

- *The Hired Hand*
- *The Talking Eggs: A Folktale from the American South*

Books by Rudyard Kipling

- *The Jungle Book*
- *Rikki-Tikki-Tavi*

Miscellaneous Authors

- *Minty: A Story of Young Harriet Tubman* by Alan Schroeder
- *The Moon Over Star* by Dianna Hutts Aston
- *Rabbit Makes a Monkey of Lion* by Verna Aardema
- *Undersea Animals: A Dramatic Dimensional Visit to Strange Underwater Realms* by Jane Buxton

Jerry Pinkney Reading Log

Read 5 books by **December** _____.

On each line, write the title you've read and have your parent/guardian sign that you read it.

Bring this completed reading log to me by **December** _____ and receive your invitation to attend our birthday celebration on

_____.

Date/Time

_____

Title   Parent/Guardian Signature

_____

Title   Parent/Guardian Signature

_____

Title   Parent/Guardian Signature

_____

Title   Parent/Guardian Signature

_____

Title   Parent/Guardian Signature

Happy Birthday, Dear Authors Born in January!

January 1	Lauren Child	January 17	Shari Lewis
	Barbara Williams		**Janet Stevens***
January 2	Jean Little	January 18	Catherine Anholt
January 3	Alma Flor Ada		Alan Schroeder
	Patricia lee Gauch	January 19	Nina Bawden
	Carolyn Haywood		**Pat Mora***
January 4	Robert Burleigh	January 20	Tedd Arnold
January 5	Lynne Cherry	January 22	Sheila Gordon
	Betsy Maestro		Rafe Martin
January 7	Kay Chorao		Brian Wildsmith
	Mingfong Ho	January 25	Debbi Chocolate
January 8	Floyd Cooper		James Flora
	Marjorie Priceman	January 26	Ashley Wolff
January 9	Clyde Robert Bulla	January 27	Harry Allard
January 10	Sook Nyul Choi		Julius Lester
January 11	Robert C. O'Brien		Janice VanCleave
	Mary Rodgers	January 28	Ann Jonas
	Ann Tompert		Vera B. Williams
January 12	William Muñoz	January 29	Rosemary Wells
	Margaret Rostkowski	January 30	Tony Johnston
January 13	N. M. Bodecker	January 31	Denise Fleming
	Michael Bond		**Gerald McDermott***
January 14	Hugh Lofting		
January 16	Robert Lipsyte	*Author featured in this chapter	
	Kate McMullan		

Happy Birthday, Dear Janet Stevens!

About Janet Stevens

- Janet Stevens was born on January 17, 1953, in Dallas, Texas.
- Her father was in the Navy, so she moved around a lot as a child. She has lived in 14 different cities across the United States!
- Janet Stevens is the youngest of three children. Her sister, Susie Stevens Crummel, has collaborated with her on many picture books!
- As a child, Janet loved to doodle on her homework, but never felt like she was good at anything.
- Janet was in the lowest reading group in her classroom.
- Janet started creating artwork after high school graduation, while living in Hawaii. She painted animals in clothing and people's pets on surfboards and other odd objects.
- When she moved to New York to pursue a career in art in 1977, publishers saw her imaginative animals and encouraged her to illustrate children's books.

Celebration Ideas

Tell the Author's Story

Trickster Tale! Since Janet Stevens has illustrated Eric Kimmel's *Anansi* folktale retellings, use the trickster theme prevalent in these tales as the basis for the following "Tricky Number Tale."

Before the Celebration

Write the following 7 numerals on 2-inch squares of paper: 1, 2, 3, 5, 7, 14, 24. Next, create the following "Tricky Number Squares" on large poster board, or project them on a document camera.

Tricky Number Squares (show all five to the entire class):

| 1 3 5 7 9 |
| 11 13 15 17 |
| 19 21 23 25 |

| 2 3 6 7 |
| 10 11 14 15 |
| 18 19 22 23 |

| 4 5 6 7 |
| 12 13 14 15 |
| 20 21 22 23 |

| 8 9 10 11 |
| 12 13 14 15 |
| 24 25 |

| 16 17 18 19 |
| 20 21 22 23 |
| 24 25 |

During the Celebration

Walk through the room and have random children each pick a numeral card from a party bag. Tell them to make sure that they hide it so no one can see what they've picked.

Once the 7 children have each picked 1 of the 7 numeral cards, explain that in honor of Janet Stevens' illustrations for Eric Kimmel's trickster tales about Anansi the Spider, you are going to tell them about her using these Tricky Number Squares. Call on the first child and ask her if the numeral on the card is located in the first Tricky Number Square. If she answers yes, look at the first numeral in that square (1) and remember it. Continue with the second square. If she answers yes, look at its first numeral (2), and add it to 1, from the first square. Keep a running total in your mind. So far, your total is 3. Go to square 3, if the answer is yes, look at its first numeral (4). Add them up, and now your running total is 7. Continue with the fourth square. This time the child answers no, so you do not add any numerals. Your total is still 7. On the fifth square, the child answers no. Therefore, her tricky number is 7. After you announce this number to the class, have the child show her numeral card. It will be 7.

After the students have all gasped in amazement, tell them how this numeral relates to Janet Stevens. Here are the numerals and their relationship to her:

1—Janet Stevens has illustrated one Caldecott Honor book so far. That book is titled, *Tops and Bottoms.*

2—Janet and her husband, Ted, have two grown children: Lindsey and Blake.

3—Janet grew up in a family of five, and she was the youngest of three children. Her big sister, Susan, has collaborated with her on several books.

5—Janet Stevens has illustrated five Anansi stories for Eric Kimmel!

7—This is the number of books, as of now, that Janet and Susan have co-authored!

14—Janet's dad was in the Navy, so they moved around a lot! She has lived in 14 different cities, including Honolulu, Hawaii!

24—In 1977, Janet moved to New York to try to sell some of her paintings and drawings. Because of her whimsical animal drawings, she was encouraged to work in the field of children's picture books. At the time, she was only 24 years old!

Write to the Author

Stevens enjoys embellishing her realistic paintings of animals with unrealistic accessories, such as clothing, jewelry, hats, etc. Use a document camera to show students examples from her book, *From Pictures to Words: A Book About Making a Book.* Have your students create birthday cards in which they each draw their favorite animal in a realistic pose and add clothing or other accessories to it. These animals could go on the cover of the card, leaving room for a brief note and birthday wish on the inside of the card.

Follow the Map

Using the same idea from Stevens' and Crummel's *And the DISH Ran Away with the SPOON,* create a map of one of the following venues: your classroom, your library, or your school's playground. The map's setting will depend on where you decide to conduct this activity. Do not label everything; create a map key. During the celebration, divide the students into 3–4 small groups. Give each group the same map and their own set of clues. The clues should relate to well-known Mother Goose rhymes (like the book). These clues will guide the groups to the hiding place of the dish and the spoon. For example, if you decide to use your classroom as the venue, give the first group a clue to get them started that tells them to head north to a certain location where they would most likely find the three kittens' missing mittens (the coat rack). When they get to that spot, there will be another clue that tells them to go to the place on the map where Little Jack Horner sat (the corner). Give each group a set of four clues. The final clue will lead to a paper plate and plastic spoon taped together with the message, "Hooray, you've found us!" Give each group a small prize, such as white plastic spoons with a round lollipop taped to it. Draw a face on the convex side of the spoon. Tie a colorful ribbon over the taped section.

High-Tech Art

Janet Stevens creates collages in many of her illustrations by laying real objects on her scanner and scanning them into her computer. Next, she manipulates the images' sizes and places them into her artwork. When she is happy with the layout of the illustration, she prints it out and then paints over it to create more texture.

Challenge your students to do this, too. Have them create collages by either gluing photos and magazine pictures onto paper and painting details around them, or, if you have access to similar computer equipment, set up time in the computer lab for students to scan in found objects and manipulate them into their own artwork.

Plaidypus Obstacle Course

The little girl in *Plaidypus Lost* went to a variety of places and ended up leaving her stuffed toy at each place. Have your students imagine that they are the main character in this story. Tell them that they must carry a stuffed animal through the obstacle course that you've set up in the gymnasium or playground. The object of the game is to complete the course without dropping the stuffed animal. Divide the class into two teams, and give each team a stuffed animal. Line up the teams by a starting line, and have them run through the course while holding the stuffed animal. They must return to their team and hand off the stuffed animal to the next teammate in line. The first team to make it through the course with the stuffed animal is the winner!

The Great Fuzz Frenzy Game!

Divide the students into two teams. Line them up so they are facing each other with approximately 10 yards between them. Place a handful of pulled cotton on the floor at the halfway point between the two teams. At the whistle, the first member of both teams runs to the cotton ("fuzz") and tries to grab it before the other member. Whoever successfully grabs the fuzz must run back to his team before the other player tags him. Return the fuzz to the middle of the floor and continue play until all students have had a chance to steal the fuzz!

Use the gymnasium for other race-related games based on books by Janet Stevens, such as *Coyote Steals the Blanket: A Ute Tale,* or *The Tortoise and the Hare.*

Wish Upon a Star

In Stevens' and Crummel's story, *Jackalope,* the Jackrabbit wishes on an evening star to become "anything but me!" (unpaged). Use a die cut machine to cut stars from card stock or cardboard. Have the students think about a wish that they'd make on a star to make them the best person they could be, and have them write their wish on the back of the star. Provide small objects, such as buttons, foam shapes, etc., and glitter glue, metallic markers, and other bright writing/decorating utensils for the students to use to decorate the front of their stars. Hang these in varying lengths from the ceiling to provide a magical learning environment!

Recipe Books

In *Cook-A-Doodle-Doo!,* Stevens and Crummel refer to Rooster's use of his great-grandmother's (a.k.a., The Little Red Hen) cookbook, "The Joy of Cooking Alone." Throughout the month of your author study, have the students bring in their favorite family recipes and create a class/library club cookbook. Allow each student to illustrate his own recipe. Collate the books and hand them out at the party as a fun party favor, or have the students give them to their parents for a Valentine's Day Gift (accompanied with some homemade chocolate candies, of course!).

Party Food

- In *Cook-A-Doodle-Doo!,* Stevens and Crummel provide the recipe for the strawberry shortcake that the rooster and his animal friends baked. If you have access to the school kitchen, bring the students to the lunchroom and have them follow along and help to make strawberry shortcake. A quicker way to provide this snack is to purchase the prepared shortcake shells and fill them with fresh or frozen (thawed) strawberries and whipped cream.
- In *Tops and Bottoms,* Rabbit outsmarts Bear and eats most of the vegetables that they grow on the farm. One of the vegetables eaten by Rabbit is corn; therefore, make a popcorn snack mix, mixing in raisins, cereal, chocolate chips, etc., and serve it at the party.

Party Favors

Recipe books (see above), small stuffed animals (available through party catalogs or Dollar Stores), spider rings (Anansi stories), small candies.

Happy Birthday, Janet Stevens!

Born January 17, 1953

Anansi Tales: Illustrated by Janet Stevens, retold by Eric Kimmel

- *Anansi and the Magic Stick*
- *Anansi and the Moss-Covered Rock*
- *Anansi and the Talking Melon*
- *Anansi Goes Fishing*
- *Anansi's Party Time*

Epossumondas Tales: Illustrated by Janet Stevens, written by Coleen Salley

- *Epossumondas*
- *Epossumondas Plays Possum*
- *Epossumondas Saves the Day*
- *Why Epossumondas Has No Hair on his Tail*

Collaborations with Susan Stevens Crummel

- *And the Dish Ran Away with the Spoon*
- *Cock-A-Doodle-Doo!*
- *The Great Fuzz Frenzy*
- *Help Me, Mr. Mutt!*
- *Jackalope*
- *My Big Dog*
- *Plaidypus Lost*

Collaborations with other Authors

- *The Dog Who Had Kittens* (by Polly M. Robertus)
- *Gates of the Wind* (by Kathryn Lasky)
- *To Market, To Market* (by Anne Miranda)

Adapted and Illustrated by Janet Stevens

- *Coyote Steals the Blanket*
- *How the Manx Cat Lost its Tail*
- *Old Bag of Bones: A Coyote Tale*
- *The Princess and the Pea*
- *The Three Billy Goats Gruff*
- *Tops and Bottoms*
- *The Tortoise and the Hare*

Autobiographical Narrative

- *From Pictures to Words: A Book About Making a Book*

Janet Stevens Reading Log

Read 5 books by **January** _____.

On each line, write the title you've read and have your parent/guardian sign that you read it.

Bring this completed reading log to me by **January** _____ and receive your invitation to attend our birthday celebration on

_____.

Date/Time

_____

Title   Parent/Guardian Signature

_____

Title   Parent/Guardian Signature

_____

Title   Parent/Guardian Signature

_____

Title   Parent/Guardian Signature

_____

Title   Parent/Guardian Signature

Happy Birthday, Dear Pat Mora!

About Pat Mora

- Pat Mora was born on January 19, 1942, in El Paso, Texas.
- Pat Mora founded the El día de los niños/El día de los libros (Children's Day/Book Day) during National Poetry Month, 1996. This special day is held on April 30 and emphasizes childhood and bilingual literacy. It is now known simply as "Día."
- Mora is bilingual; she speaks Spanish and English.
- An avid reader, Mora grew up hiding her Spanish-speaking skills and wished her elementary school had provided books and activities that included her Mexican culture.
- Mora earned her B.A. in education from Texas Western College (currently the University of Texas—El Paso) in 1963.
- She earned her M.A. in 1967.
- She has three children, William, Elizabeth, and Cecilia.
- She is married to Vernon Lee Scarborough, an archeologist and professor.
- She taught English and Spanish in elementary and secondary schools during the 1960s.
- Several of her early picture books were inspired by her own family's experiences.
- Pat Mora has always loved books and poetry. Her poetry anthologies celebrate the Hispanic culture and the southwestern region of the United States.
- Pat Mora coined the term, "bookjoy."
- She and her siblings created the Estela and Raúl Mora Award in honor of her parents. This award goes to the libraries that have most effectively promoted "Día." The award focuses on the work of public libraries with Hispanic communities.

Celebration Ideas

Tell the Author's Story

Use the idea behind *A Birthday Basket for Tía* as the inspiration for this storytelling activity. In the book, young Cecilia collects various items that represent special moments shared with her aunt. She places the items in a basket as a 90th birthday present for Tía.

Collect the following objects to place in a basket, decorated to resemble a birthday present. Tell the students that, like Cecilia, you've collected objects that you would give to Pat Mora for her birthday. Use the objects to tell the story of Pat Mora's life.

- Picture books: To show Pat Mora's love of reading as a child.
- Mexican flag: To honor her Mexican heritage.
- Notebook: To provide her with a place to record her ideas for new poems or stories.
- Spanish-English dictionary: To honor her bilingual skills.
- Measuring cups: To emphasize her love of cooking.
- Pack of seeds: To tell the students about her interest in gardening.
- Picture frame: To give her a place to put a recent family photo, because family is very important to her.
- Be creative, and think of other objects that would enhance your storytelling activity!

Find Someone Who . . .

Pat Mora has written several books that focus on libraries and reading: *Book Fiesta, A Library for Juana: The World of Sor Juana Inés*, and *Tomás and the Library Lady*. Use these books as the inspiration behind this fun opening activity on the day of the celebration.

Before the Celebration

Create a chart or list with ten different statements on it. The statements should encourage students to find a classmate/friend that fits the statement's criteria. After each statement, leave a space for students to autograph those for which they qualify. Here are a few sample statements, all relating to reading books and the love of libraries.

- Find someone who has read at least five books by Pat Mora.
- Find someone who has read a book in Spanish.
- Find someone who loves poetry.
- Find someone who has a library card.
- Find someone who has been to the public library twice this month.
- Find someone who can name a favorite book written by Pat Mora.
- Find someone who has been to Pat Mora's home state of Texas.
- Find someone who has checked out three books from the school library this month.
- Find someone who has learned a new Spanish word after reading Pat Mora's books.
- Find someone who would like to read one of Pat Mora's poems aloud to the class.

During the Celebration

Challenge students to be the first to find five friends that fit the statements—and remind them that they may sign many statements, but only *one* statement per classmate. Increase the challenge as appropriate. Allow time for students who have signed off on statements such as naming a favorite book or reading aloud a poem to share their answers with the class.

Provide small prizes for students who found at least five friends during the given time limit. The prizes could be library coupons, such as "Good for one extra book checked out during your library period" or, "Good for one overdue fine waiver." Think of other creative coupons that the children would enjoy using at the school library!

Pablo's Tree

In this story, young Pablo turns five and cannot wait until he sees the tree that his Abuelito (Grandfather) has decorated in honor of his birthday. Each year, his Abuelito has decorated the tree with different objects, such as streamers, balloons, and bird cages.

In honor of this tradition, bring in a tree branch with several off-shoots, and plant it in an empty coffee can. Fill the can with pea gravel to anchor the branch. Decorate the coffee can with a copy of the book's cover or other colorful pictures. Before the celebration, decorate the tree with an item that relates to Pat Mora, such as bookmarks (to recognize her love of reading), paper flowers (for her love of gardening), etc. Have students fill out a graph in which they try to guess what object you've used to decorate the "tree," and unveil it at the party. Keep the tree on display throughout the school year, changing the decorations to reflect the seasons and/or holidays.

As a quick craft during the party, distribute snowflakes cut from card stock using a die-cut machine. Provide sequins, buttons, ribbons, foam shapes, etc., for student to use to decorate their snowflakes. Add them to the tree after the party for a winter wonderland theme!

Help Doña Flor find the Puma!

Create a treasure hunt activity related to the events in Mora's book, *Doña Flor*. Before the celebration: Create five sets of hunt clues which will steer the students to various landmarks in the classroom, or book collections in the library, until they reach the final clue that tells them where their group's puma is hidden. Use a small plastic animal figure, available in packages in most dollar stores. The clues should convey elements of the book, too.

Sample Clues:
1. Help! The villagers hear a loud "Rroarrrr!" It seems to be coming from the winter book display. Go to this display quietly, walking on tiptoe, and see if you can find the puma there!

2. Oh, the puma seems to have moved on already. See if it is near the writing center, trying to use his paw prints to write a note! Doña Flor loved to sing, so everyone in the group must hum the tune, "Twinkle, Twinkle Little Star" as you walk to the writing center.

3. (*Use a paw print stamp on the borders of this next clue.*) See, the puma was here! He is too quick for you to catch. Think like an animal . . . hop like the rabbits that helped Doña Flor over to the alphabet books, and see if the puma is lingering on the book shelf.

4. You are so close! Did you hear that? Listen carefully. Walk with your hand cupped over your ear to listen for his roar while you walk over to the science center.

5. Congratulations! You've found the little pumito! (*Place the clue around the body of the plastic puma/animal.*)

Award small prizes, such as a small plastic animal for each student, or party blow horns (to resemble the hollow tree trunk used by the puma in the story to amplify his roar).

Join Hands!

Join Hands! The Ways We Celebrate Life is a lively, engaging picture book by George Ancona filled with photographs of children and adults celebrating life. It is a great motivator for a dance party! Here are a few ways to integrate dance into your author celebration.

- Free Dance: Play a variety of party music, and have the students dance in a way that reflects the rhythm and mood of the songs.
- Simon Says: Play some ethnic music, and tell the students that they need to follow your moves as you lead them in a variety of rhythmic movements. If they don't follow you accurately, they should sit down; or just have them try their best without consequences if they have difficulty.
- If your school has access to interactive video dance games, get permission to use these games during your party time. Have the students work in stations, or project the game on a large screen, and have the students try to follow along as a whole group.
- Consult the Kimbo™ catalog or website for a variety of DVDs and CDs that offer dance instructional materials for all ages of children, in all varieties of musical genres. Go to www.kimboed.com.
- Freeze Dance: Play music and have the children dance along. Stop the music at random moments. When the music stops, the children must stop immediately. Anyone still dancing must sit down. The last child left standing wins!
- Share *¡Marimba! Animales from A to Z* and play marimba music while students dance along to the book's beat.

Letter to the Author

In her book, *Join Hands! The Ways We Celebrate Life*, Mora tells her readers about the style of poetry called a *pantoum* (pan-TOOM) that she used in it. This four-line stanza format uses a unique system of repetition: the second line of the first stanza is used as the first line of the next stanza. The fourth line of stanza one becomes the third line of the next stanza. Use a document camera to show Mora's colorful layout of this format, included at the end of her book. Encourage pairs of students to write one sentence about Pat Mora and/or her books. Give each group a sentence strip to write on and then tape the strips to the chalkboard. The class will then work together, selecting four sentence strips as the first stanza of a poetic letter to the author. Next, go to stanza 1, copy sentence 2, and place it in the first line for stanza 2. Copy sentence 4 from stanza 1 and place it in the third line space for stanza 2. Continue on, adding new sentence strips to complete each four-sentence stanza. Read over the completed pantoum before copying it onto large chart paper. Once it is copied (or typed with a large font, printed, and taped into place on chart paper), have the students each decorate their own handprints to tape around the border of the poem, as if they, too, are joining hands. Mail this to Pat Mora, using her contact information at www.patmora. com. Include a cover letter to explain your poem to her!

This Big Sky

Steve Jenkins' collage images of southwestern animals enhances each poem written by Pat Mora in this beautiful tribute to the sights and sounds of the southwest region of the United States. Use Jenkins' illustrations to inspire the children to create their own animal collages. Place the names of all the animals from the book into a hat, and have each child pick an animal. The children will then use a variety of papers, magazines, wallpapers, etc., to create a collage in the image of their animal. Once the collages are complete, read the poems aloud to the class, calling on the child(ren) whose collages match the animals in the poem to move their animal pictures in a way that their real animal would move across the desert. This dramatic reading of Mora's poetry will be a great homage to the power of poetry to inspire and delight.

Pat's Poetry Power

Throughout the month, take time to read aloud a poem each day from one of Pat Mora's books. This is a great way to expose the students to her poetry and prepare them for the author celebration. Librarians could be sure to feature one of her poems during the students' weekly library visits, or create a "Pat's Poetry Power" bulletin board display to entice students to join this fun author program and participate in the party later in the month. An excellent book that lends itself well to the overall party atmosphere is Mora's *Confetti: Poems for Children.* This collection features poems on such a wide variety of topics that all children will relate to, such as colors, dragons, sunshine, music, bakeries, grandmothers, etc.

Enrique O. Sanchez's illustrations are acrylic on paper, but they have a batik quality to them. This could serve as a model for students in creating crayon resist artwork to accompany their favor-

ite poems by Mora. Crayon resist is a technique similar to batik. To create the effect, students would use a white crayon (or any light color) to make the outlines of their drawings. When they are finished with their crayon outlines, they fill in the drawings with watercolors. The crayon will resist the watercolor, allowing it to show through the paint. The harder they press down with the crayon, the more the crayon will show through the paint.

General Party Activities

Bring in a piñata for the students to break open during the celebration. Piñatas are featured in the illustrations of Mora's *Uno, Dos, Tres: One, Two, Three.* Students could also make individual piñatas using balloons and newspaper strips that they dip into a flour-and-water paste. Teachers/ Librarians could make these ahead of time and fill them with party favors, such as: miniature writing notebooks, candies, and small stickers or custom-made buttons that say "Bookjoy!"

Party Food

Serve cupcakes with hidden trinkets inside, in honor of *The Bakery Lady/La señora de la panadería.* This book also featured lemon cookies, which would be a great treat, too!

In *The Rainbow Tulip*, Estelita and her mother eat lime sherbet. This would be fun to serve to the students, or, in honor of the rainbow tulip costume that Estelita wears in this story, serve rainbow sherbet! Don't forget to sing happy birthday to Pat Mora!

Happy Birthday, Pat Mora!

Born January 19, 1942

Picture Books

- *Abuelos*
- *Agua, Agua, Agua*
- *The Bakery Lady/La señora de la panadería*
- *A Birthday Basket for Tía*
- *Book Fiesta*
- *Delicious Hullabaloo/Pachana deliciosa*
- *Doña Flor: A Tall Tale About a Giant Woman with a Great Big Heart*
- *The Gift of the Poinsettia, with Charles Ramirez Berg*
- *Gracias~Thanks*
- *Here, Kitty, Kitty!/¡Ven gatita, ven!*
- *Join Hands! The Ways We Celebrate Life*
- *Let's Eat!/¡A comer!*
- *A Library for Juana: The World of Sor Juana Inés*
- *Listen to the Desert/Oye al desierto*
- *Maria Paints the Hills*
- *The Night the Moon Fell*
- *Pablo's Tree*
- *A Piñata in a Pine Tree!*
- *The Race of Toad and Deer*
- *The Rainbow Tulip*
- *The Song of Francis and the Animals*
- *Sweet Dreams/Dulces sueños*
- *Tomás and the Library Lady*
- *Wiggling Pockets/Tus bolsillos se mueven*

Poetry for Children

- *This Big Sky*
- *Confetti: Poems for Children*
- *The Desert is My Mother/El desierto es mí madre*
- *Love to Mamá: A Tribute to Mothers*
- *¡Marimba! Animales from A toZ*
- *My Own True Name: New and Selected Poems for Young Adults*
- *Uno, Dos, Tres: One, Two, Three*
- *Yum! ¡Mmm! ¡Qué Rico! Americas' Sproutings*

Pat Mora Reading Log

Read 5 books by **January** ____.

On each line, write the title you've read and have your parent/guardian sign that you read it.

Bring this completed reading log to me by **January** ____ and receive your invitation to attend our birthday celebration on

_____.

Date/Time

_____

Title   Parent/Guardian Signature

_____

Title   Parent/Guardian Signature

_____

Title   Parent/Guardian Signature

_____

Title   Parent/Guardian Signature

_____

Title   Parent/Guardian Signature

Happy Birthday, Dear Gerald McDermott!

About Gerald McDermott

- Gerald McDermott was born on January 31, 1941, in Detroit, Michigan.
- His parents enrolled him in art classes at the Detroit Institute of Arts when he was four years old!
- As a child, McDermott acted on a local television station for a "Storytime" program.
- During his years at Pratt Institute in New York, McDermott worked as a graphic designer for New York's PBS station and worked on animated films. Folktales became his prime source of material.
- By the end of the 1960s, McDermott was asked to transform his film techniques for folktales into picture books.
- The first folktale that McDermott transformed into picture book format was *Anansi the Spider*, which earned him a Caldecott Honor Award.
- He followed up with a simultaneous rendering of both film and book versions of *Arrow to the Sun*. This book earned him the Caldecott Medal!

Celebration Ideas

Tell the Author's Story

McDermott's artistic style involves the use of bright colors and geometric shapes.

Before the Celebration

Make a sun shape with geometric format by using brightly colored paper and making a large (12" diameter) circle. Then cut the circle into six equal-size wedges. Next, cut out six smaller triangle shapes from the paper. It should look like this:

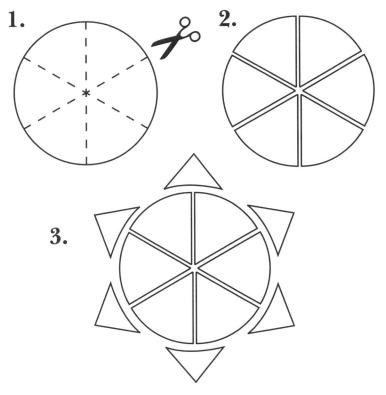

During the Celebration

Add a wedge of sun as you share the following statements below about McDermott:

- Gerald McDermott was born on January 31, 1941.
- His first art class was at the Detroit Museum of Art when he was only four years old!
- He went to a gifted vocational high school in Detroit, where he focused on art.
- He was awarded a national scholarship to Pratt Institute in New York.
- He worked in film and directed his first animated movie called *The Stonecutter* during a leave of absence from Pratt Institute after his junior year.
- He was the first graphic designer for Channel 13, New York's educational television station.
- He produced and directed a series of animated films about folktales.

- In 1973, he created his first picture book, *Anansi the Spider*. It won a Caldecott Honor Award.
- In 1974, *Arrow to the Sun* won a Caldecott Medal!
- His goal is to combine the spiritual, cultural, and emotional elements of art with the true nature of each folktale that he retells and illustrates.
- Recently, *Raven* won a Caldecott Honor Award, too!
- Now he is a leader of an annual retreat held in California that guides people in understanding the influence of mythology on their lives.

*Once the wedges are all in place and the shape of a sun is evident, say, "All the parts of Gerald McDermott's life have come together, like this sun, to shed light on the folklore of many cultures."

Letters to Gerald McDermott

Have the children each create their own geometric-style birthday cards by gluing precut shapes onto paper in an arrangement that resembles an animal or book character.

Trickster Trail Treasure Hunt

Many of the folktales that McDermott has selected to retell and illustrate are trickster animal tales. In honor of these books, have the students use clues to find geometric shapes (tangram pieces) that will fit together to make a specific animal: fox, rabbit, bear, snake, owl. Give each group a template and their first clue to the first tangram shape they'll need to find (for a tangram template and shape guide, see page 107). The animal shapes don't have to take up an entire page—in fact, if you can fit all five onto one repro page with a label for each one, that would be great.

Sample clues: Group 1—You must crack the code to find where your shapes are hidden. Be sure to use your code key and work together to solve each clue!

- Code Key for Group 1:

A = 1	B = 2	C = 3	D = 4
E = 5	F = 6	G = 26	H = 25
I = 24	J = 23	K = 22	L = 21
M = 7	N = 8	O = 9	P = 10
Q = 11	R = 12	S = 20	T =19
U = 18	V = 17	W = 16	X = 15
Y =14	Z = 13		

- They will go to the first place in the classroom/library to find the first tangram piece for their assigned animal, as well as the new puzzle for the location of the next tangram piece.

Puzzle #1

‾‾ ‾‾ ‾‾ ‾‾ ‾‾   ‾‾ ‾‾ ‾‾ ‾‾ ‾‾ ‾‾ ‾‾
1 18 4 24 9   20 5 3 19 24 9 8

[AUDIO SECTION]

Here the group will find their first Tangram piece and their next puzzle clue.

Puzzle #2

‾‾ ‾‾ ‾‾ ‾‾ ‾‾ ‾‾ ‾‾ ‾‾ ‾‾
7 1 26 1 13 24 8 5 20

[MAGAZINES]

Puzzle #3

‾‾ ‾‾ ‾‾ ‾‾ ‾‾ ‾‾ ‾‾ ‾‾
2 5 1 12 2 9 9 22

‾‾ ‾‾ ‾‾ ‾‾ ‾‾ ‾‾ ‾‾
4 24 20 10 21 1 14

[BEAR BOOK DISPLAY]

Puzzle #4

‾‾ ‾‾ ‾‾ ‾‾ ‾‾ ‾‾ ‾‾ ‾‾
6 24 20 25 19 1 8 22

[FISH TANK]

Puzzle #5

_____ _____ _____ _____ _____ _____ _____ _____ _____
20   3   9   9   2   14   4   9   9

_____ _____ _____ _____ _____
2   9   9   24 20

[SCOOBY DOO BOOKS]

*Once the groups have found all of their tangram shapes, they must use the template of their animal to manipulate the pieces into that shape.

Journey Bags

Purchase plain white fabric bags or backpacks from a craft store or a catalog supply company. Provide paints and have the students paint their bags with bright colors and geometric designs, similar to McDermott's style. The bags are a reminder of the imaginative journeys that McDermott's folktale heroes must take as they learn about the world around them.

Jabutí the Tortoise: A Trickster Tale from the Amazon

In this folktale, Jabutí's smooth tortoise shell cracks across its surface, creating a mosaic of colors. This happened because he was tricked by Vulture, who offered to carry him up to the King of Heaven so he could play his beautiful flute music for him. Distribute outlines of a tortoise, printed on card stock. Instruct the students to design their own shell designs on their tortoise. Play flute music to inspire them in their creative process. They can cut them out and hang them around the classroom, as if Jabutí is actually flying up to Heaven!

Who Is the Lord of the Sun?

Play this game in honor of McDermott's Caldecott book, *Arrow to the Sun*. Arrange all the students in a circle, and have them sit on the floor. Select one person to be a villager from the pueblo, and have him/her leave the room. While the student is gone, choose one seated child to be the "Lord of the Sun." This child will lead the rest of the students through various motions, such as clapping, tapping knees, snapping, etc. All remaining students must follow the "Lord of the Sun's" movements without always looking straight at him/her. The child playing the villager returns to the room and stands in the center of the circle of children. He/She watches as the movements change, trying to figure out who is initiating the new movements as the "Lord of the Sun." The villager has three guesses before he/she must quit. Play continues, having the child that was the "Lord of the Sun" become the new villager.

Mystery Present

In McDermott's tale, *Raven: A Trickster Tale from the Pacific Northwest*, Raven tricks a young woman so that he can open a box that contains the sun. Use this book as the impetus for playing this guessing game.

Before the Celebration

Decide on an object that fits into a medium-sized box, such as the newest book by McDermott, a stuffed animal from one of his books, party food (cupcakes or cookies), etc. Place the object into the box, and cover the box with birthday wrapping paper.

During the Celebration

Tell the students that they will try to guess what is in the box by only asking questions with a yes or no answer. Integrate this activity into reading practice by writing each answer, in a complete sentence, on the board and reading through the answers/clues in language-experience style. For example, if a student asks if the object is round, and you've placed a book inside the box, the answer would be no and you would write, "It is not a round object." Play continues until they guess what is in the box. Then unwrap the present, and share it with the class!

Spider Art

In honor of *Anansi the Spider: A Tale from the Ashanti*, tell the students to think about a special quality/talent that they have, just as Anansi's six spider sons each have a special quality.

<u>Before the Celebration</u>

Cut out spider shapes from black construction paper, or use the reproducible on page 108. Distribute one shape to each student and have the student use sketch paper to create a design using McDermott's geometric style that depicts their special quality. Once they are happy with their designs, they then will create the design on their spiders using brightly colored paper. Display the spiders on a bulletin board with a large web on it that reads, "Get Caught in the Web of McDermott's Books!"

Party Food

Provide a buffet of small candies, popcorn, cereal, etc., and give each student an ice cream cone. Allow time for the students to go to the buffet and fill their cones with their favorite "pig-out" foods, in honor of *Pig-Boy: A Trickster Tale from Hawai'i.*

Party Favors

Pocket puzzles, as mementos of McDermott's many trickster tales; flashlight key chains (available from party catalogs), as mementos of the sun in *Raven* and *Arrow to the Sun.*

Tangram Template

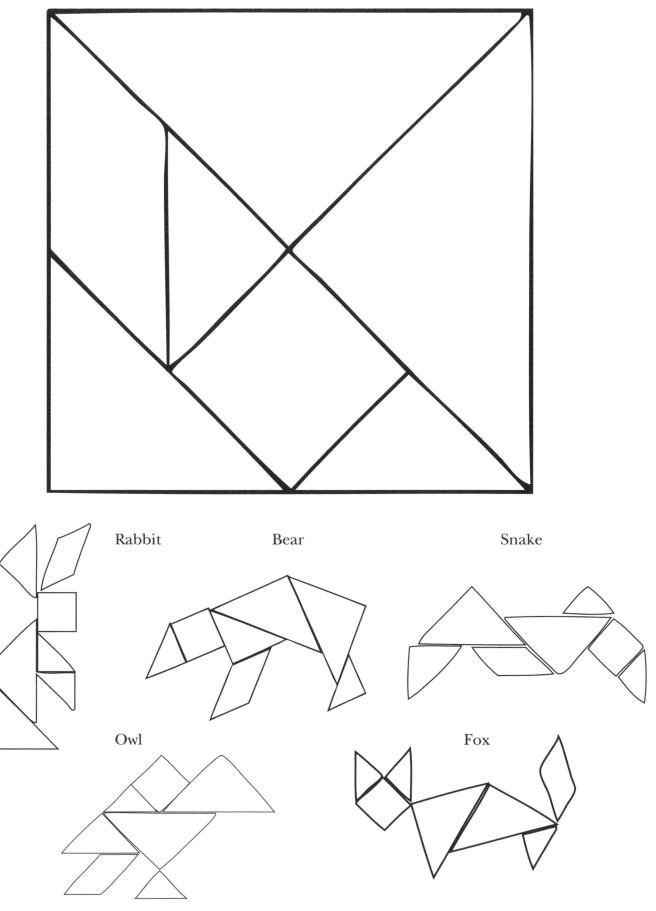

Rabbit   Bear   Snake

Owl   Fox

Spider

Happy Birthday, Gerald McDermott!

Born January 31, 1941

Folktales

- *Anansi the Spider: A Tale From the Ashanti*
- *Arrow to the Sun: A Pueblo Indian Tale*
- *Coyote: A Trickster Tale From the American Southwest*
- *Daniel O'Rourke: An Irish Tale*
- *Jabutí the Tortoise: A Trickster Tale from the Amazon Rain Forest*
- *The Magic Tree: A Tale from the Congo*
- *Monkey: A Trickster Tale from India*
- *Musicians of the Sun*
- *Papagayo: The Mischief Maker*
- *Pig Boy: A Trickster Tale from Hawai'i*
- *Raven: A Trickster Tale From the Pacific Northwest*

- *The Stonecutter: A Japanese Folktale*
- *Sun Flight*
- *Tim O'Toole and the Wee Folk: An Irish Tale*
- *Zomo the Rabbit: A Trickster Tale From West Africa*

Miscellaneous

- *Creation*
- *The Fox and the Stork*

Gerald McDermott Reading Log

Read 5 books by **January** ____.

On each line, write the title you've read and have your parent/guardian sign that you read it.

Bring this completed reading log to me by **January** ____ and receive your invitation to attend our birthday celebration on

_____.

Date/Time

_____

Title   Parent/Guardian Signature

_____

Title   Parent/Guardian Signature

_____

Title   Parent/Guardian Signature

_____

Title   Parent/Guardian Signature

_____

Title   Parent/Guardian Signature

Happy Birthday, Dear Authors Born in February!

February 1	Jerry Spinelli	February 15	Norman Bridwell
February 2	Eve Rice	February 17	Dorothy Canfield Fisher
	Judith Viorst	February 18	Barbara Joosse
February 4	Barbara Shook Hazen		Toni Morrison
February 5	Patricia Lauber	February 21	Jim Aylesworth
	David Wiesner		Virginia Driving Hawk Sneve
February 6	Betsy Duffey	February 22	Edward Gorey
February 8	Anne Rockwell	February 23	C. S. Adler
February 9	Stephen Roos		Walter Wick
	Alice Walker	February 24	Mary Ellen Chase
February 10	Lucy Cousins		Matthew Holm
	Stephen Gammell		Uri Orlev
	Mark Teague	February 25	Cynthia Voigt
February 11	**Jane Yolen***	February 26	Colby Rodowsky
	Mo Willems*		Judith St. George
February 12	Judy Blume		Bernard Wolf
	David Small	February 27	Uri Shulevitz
February 13	Simms Taback	February 28	Dee Brown
	Judy Young		Megan McDonald
February 14	Jamake Highwater	February 29	Susan L. Roth
	George Shannon		
	Paul O. Zelinsky*		

*Author featured in this chapter

Happy Birthday, Dear Jane Yolen!

About Jane Yolen

- Jane Yolen was born on February 11, 1939, in New York.
- Her full name is Jane Hyatt Yolen. All the children, boys and girls, in her family were given Hyatt as a middle name because it was her grandmother's last name, and she did not have any boys to pass on the name!
- Jane was a "gold star girl" in elementary school! She wrote stories, sang in the school chorus, and took piano and ballet lessons, all while earning excellent grades.
- Jane graduated from high school 7th in her class and went on to Smith College.
- At Smith College, Jane wrote poetry, won many campus poetry awards, and wrote songs for the school musical.
- After college, Jane became an editor and continued to write poetry, and also began to write nonfiction.
- She soon became interested in writing children's books and had her first book published on her 22nd birthday! The book was titled *Pirates in Petticoats*.
- Jane Yolen married David Stemple and had three children: Heidi, Adam, and Jason.
- Jane's daughter, Heidi, was the girl in her award-winning book, *Owl Moon*. David, her husband, was "Pa."
- Jane Yolen has written over 300 books for children and young adults!

Celebration Ideas

An Owling Adventure

Create clues for the children to follow in order to find their owl, in honor of *Owl Moon*. Divide the students into small groups. Assign one owl to each group: barn owl, snowy owl, spotted owl, etc.

<u>Before the Celebration</u>

Prepare 4–5 clue cards per small group of students by making several copies of the owl images from page 116 onto card stock and cutting them out. Write a set of clues for each set of owls (so for instance, if you have 16 students, make 4 groups of 4 students, and assign each group a type of owl. Reproduce and cut out those four owls several times, depending on how many clues you write). Print labels with the clues, and stick them on the back of the owls; or hand write them.

You should now have a set of owls for each group—the same owl on one side, with a different clue on the back. The clues will lead the students around the school library or your classroom.

Here is a sample set of clues for the "Snowy Owl" Group:

- The Snowy Owl is in the picture book section! Look at the books by Eve Bunting (Call # BUN).
- She already flew away! Go to the books by Ezra Jack Keats (Call # KEA).
- You must be very quiet when you go owling! She's already taken off. Check the books by Paul Zelinsky (Call # ZEL).
- Congratulations, you've found the Snowy Owl! Be very quiet so you don't scare her away, and bring your clues to the teacher/librarian for your prize.

During the Celebration

Pass out the first owl clue to each group and set them soaring around the library or classroom! When each group has found its last clue, hand out prizes, such as a cardboard tube "owl pellet" filled with small candies.

Piggins Solves the Mystery!

In honor of Yolen's series of Piggins picture books, play this fun game. Go to www.highlight-steachers.com and click on the link to teachers' toolbox, hidden pictures. This website provides free printable versions of their popular hidden picture worksheets. Each worksheet has a list of the items hidden in the picture. Once you've selected the hidden picture worksheet for this activity, look through the hidden objects and choose one object to be the mystery item for which Piggins is looking. Next, think of a clue for the remaining objects. During the celebration, distribute the hidden picture worksheet, and tell the students that Piggins must solve the mystery of finding one particular object hidden in this picture. You will give them clues, and they will need to find the objects until only the mystery object is left for them to find.

For example, if one of the hidden objects is a crayon, tell the students, "Piggins must find an important object in this picture. The problem is that there are a lot of objects hidden, and only one of them is the mystery object. We'll have to use the powers of deduction to see which object is left after all the other objects have been found. The last object is the mystery object that Piggins needs! The mystery object is NOT something you use to color pictures." The children will look at the list of hidden objects and realize that they must find the crayon so that they can cross that off their list. Continue in this manner until the final mystery object is left. The first child to raise her hand indicating that she found it, is the winner! Award all students with a prize, such as a packet of hidden picture puzzles that you've downloaded from this website.

Dinosaur Drama

Pair up the children during the party. Have each pair take a turn and draw a slip of paper from a party bag. Each slip will contain a possible title for a new book in Yolen's and Teague's series, *How Do Dinosaurs Say Goodnight?*. After each pair has picked a title from the bag, give them time to decide on 3–5 answers for "How do dinosaurs . . . ?" Use the same question/answer framework as used in the picture books. One child will read aloud their questions, while the partner acts out the possible answers. The children in the audience respond to each action and answer with, "No!"

Sample titles/questions:

- How do dinosaurs eat their dinner?
- How do dinosaurs play a game?
- How do dinosaurs behave at parties?
- How do dinosaurs fly on an airplane?

Raising Yoder's Barn

This wonderful tribute to the Amish community's way of life can inspire several activities that focus on friendship and teamwork.

- Partners by heart: In honor of Valentine's Day and teamwork, play this fun matchmaking game. Before the celebration, cut red construction paper hearts for half of the students that will be at the party. Cut each heart in half using a variety of cutting patterns, like a puzzle. During the party, the students will pick a half-heart from a box and try to find the matching half. The two students whose hearts match will become partners for the next activity.
- Building Buddies: Give each pair of students a box of toothpicks and some clay. Instruct them to work together to build their own barn structure out of toothpicks. Show them how to roll the clay into small balls (approximately ½ cm wide) and use them as connectors between the toothpicks. Set a time limit, and then provide time for the students to walk around the room and admire their classmates' barns.
- Amish Friendship Bread: Provide partners with a recipe card and supplies for making a starter for Amish Friendship Bread. Use the

recipe below. When they have completed the recipe, give them two resealable plastic bags to divide the starter between them. When the bags are sealed, tape the directions for next steps (page 117) to the bags. Instruct students to finish the process at home with their families.

Amish Friendship Bread

Ingredients:
- 1 pkg. active dry yeast
- 1/4 cup warm water (110°F)
- 1 cup all-purpose flour
- 1 cup white sugar
- 1 cup warm milk (110°F)

Directions:

1. In a small bowl, dissolve the yeast in warm water for about 10 minutes. Stir well. [You could do this a few minutes before the party and pass it out to the students for their recipes.]

2. In a 2-quart glass or plastic container, combine 1 cup sifted flour and 1 cup sugar.

3. Slowly stir in warm milk [You can bring a thermos of warm milk to expedite this process], and dissolved yeast mixture. Loosely cover the mixture with a lid or plastic wrap. The mixture will get bubbly. Consider this Day 1 of the cycle, or the day you receive the starter.

Honker Race

This game is based on the book, *Honkers*. In this story, three young geese "followed the compass of their hearts home" (unpaged) and flew south for the winter. Give each child a 9" square piece of cardboard, and tell them to draw a goose with its head, neck, and wings outstretched as if flying. After they color their picture, they need to cut it out and use a 1/4" hole punch to make a hole at the base of the neck. Tie 2 10-foot lengths of string to two chairs. Divide the group into two teams, and line them up opposite their chair. The first child in each line holds the string, pulls it tight, and threads the goose on the end near their hands. They must move the string to enable their goose to "fly" home, which is located at the end tied to the chair. The first team to get all of their geese home wins!

Nature Poems

Jane Yolen and her son, Jason Stemple, have coauthored several poetry anthologies based on nature. Give the students small clipboards made by cutting corrugated cardboard into letter-sized rectangles. Use thick rubberbands as the clips. Slide a paper under the rubberband. The papers should have one of the following words written vertically along the left margin: "NATURE," "WINTER," "MY WORLD," etc. Instruct the students to go outside with the group for a set period of time, and use their five senses to find items outside that start with each letter in their word, thereby creating acrostic poems. They will write the ideas down and come inside to illustrate their poems. These could be collated into a book of nature poems. Include this book in the classroom book corner, or as a special "reference" book in the school library.

Party Food

- Tea party foods, such as iced tea and small cupcakes in honor of *Piggins*
- Flower-shaped cookies that the children decorate themselves, in honor of *An Invitation to the Butterfly Ball* and her more recent book, *Come to the Fairies Ball*

- Serve up a creation from *Fairy Tale Feasts*, coauthored with her daughter, Heidi Yolen Stemple.

Party Favors

- Butterfly nets, plastic insects
- Blank books for writing their own stories (include stickers to decorate their books, too), writing utensils (because Yolen is such a prolific author)
- Magnifying lens (variety of mysteries written by Yolen)

Read Aloud Fun

Jane Yolen has written many novels. Select one to read aloud, a chapter each day, for the month of her birthday. One particularly fun read aloud for primary-level students is *Twelve Impossible Things Before Breakfast: Stories*. In this book, Yolen has written a dozen short stories, which will be wonderful to share all through the month of February!

Helpful Hint

Be sure to visit Jane Yolen's wonderful website for a complete list of books, a thorough biography with photographs, and many other links. Her website is: www.janeyolen.com.

Owls

Spotted Owl

Screech Owl

Barn Owl

Snowy Owl

Horned Owl

Amish Friendship Bread Starter Kit

Parents, use this starter kit to make a loaf of Amish friendship bread with your children.

DAY 1: Place the starter in a plastic bowl and stir.

DAYS 2–4: Stir the starter.

DAY 5: Add one cup each: flour, sugar, milk. Stir.

DAYS 6–9: Stir

DAY 10: Add one more cup each: flour, sugar, milk. Stir and divide mixture into 4 1-cup portions. Give 3 portions to 3 friends. Keep one portion and make the bread by adding the following ingredients:

⅔ cup oil

 3 eggs

½ tsp. salt

1 tsp. vanilla

1 to 1 ½ tsp. cinnamon

1 cup sugar

2 cups flour

1 ¼ tsp. baking powder

½ tsp. baking soda

Beat by hand; add raisins or nuts if desired. Pour into two greased bread pans and sprinkle sugar on top. Bake at 325°F for 45 minutes. Makes two loaves.

Happy Birthday, Jane Yolen!

Born February 11, 1939

Picture Books

- *A Sip of Aesop*
- *All Those Secrets of the World*
- *An Invitation to the Butterfly Ball*
- *Creepy Monsters, Sleeping Monsters*
- *The Day Tiger Rose Said Good-bye*
- *Dinosaur Dances*
- *Elfabet: An ABC of Elves*
- *Elsie's Bird*
- *The Girl in the Golden Bower*
- *Granddad Bill's Song*
- *Greyling*
- *Honkers*
- *Hoptoad*
- *How Do Dinosaurs Get Well Soon?*
- *How Do Dinosaurs Laugh Out Loud?*
- *How Do Dinosaurs Say Good Night?*
- *How Do Dinosaurs Say I Love You?*
- *Hush Little Horsie*
- *King Long Shanks*
- *Letting Swift River Go*
- *Lost Boy*
- *Miz Berlin Walks*
- *Mouse's Birthday*
- *My Father Knows the Names of Things*
- *Nocturne*
- *Not All Princesses Dress in Pink*
- *Off We Go!*
- *Old Dame Counterpane*
- *Owl Moon*
- *Picnic With Piggins*
- *Piggins*
- *Piggins and the Royal Wedding*
- *Pretty Princess Pig*
- *Raining Cats & Dogs*
- *Raising Yoder's Barn*
- *The Seeing Stick*
- *Welcome to the Green House*
- *Welcome to the Ice House*
- *Welcome to the Sea of Sand*

Fiction

- *And Twelve Chinese Acrobats*
- *The Ballad of the Pirate Queens*
- *Encounter*
- *The Flying Witch*
- *The Mary Celeste*
- *Merlin and the Dragons*

Folktales

- *Mightier Than the Sword*
- *Not One Damsel in Distress*
- *Wings*

Poetry

- *Birds of a Feather*
- *Color Me A Rhyme*
- *Horizons: Poems As Far As the Eye Can See*
- *Least Things: Poems About Small Natures*
- *The Originals: Animals That Time Forgot*
- *Sea Watch: A Book of Poetry*
- *Snow, Snow: Winter Poems*
- *Switching on the Moon*
- *Wild Wings: Poems for Young People*

Autobiography

- *A Letter From Phoenix Farm*
- *My Brothers' Flying Machine*

Easy Readers

- *Commander Toad and the Dis-asteroid*
- *Commander Toad and the Voyage Home*
- *Commander Toad in Space*

Jane Yolen Reading Log

Read 5 books by **February** ____.

On each line, write the title you've read and have your parent/guardian sign that you read it.

Bring this completed reading log to me by **February** ____ and receive your invitation to attend our birthday celebration on

_____.

Date/Time

_____

Title   Parent/Guardian Signature

_____

Title   Parent/Guardian Signature

_____

Title   Parent/Guardian Signature

_____

Title   Parent/Guardian Signature

_____

Title   Parent/Guardian Signature

Happy Birthday, Dear Paul Zelinsky!

About Paul Zelinsky

- Paul Zelinsky was born on February 14, 1953, in Wilmette, Illinois.
- He went to Yale University and graduated in 1974.
- He earned an M.F.A. in painting.
- He took a class on children's book illustration. Maurice Sendak was his teacher!
- He won a Caldecott Award for *Rapunzel* (1997).
- His daughter, Anna, inspired him to create his pop-up board book, The Wheels on the Bus (1990).
- His hobbies are cooking and eating.
- He has always loved to doodle and draw, even during nursery school! In elementary and high school, he was often known as the "class artist."
- He lives in New York with his wife and two daughters.

Celebration Ideas

Tell the Author's Story

In honor of Zelinsky's two pop-up books (*The Wheels on the Bus*; *Knick-Knack Paddywhack*), tell his biography in the same style. Before the celebration, do an image search of key events from Zelinsky's life, such as: a photo of the author, an image of the Caldecott Medal, a photo of Maurice Sendak, graduation cap, map of New York, etc. Next, make a simple pop-up book by following these instructions:

a. Gather 12" x 18" construction paper, enough for one sheet per photo/image.
b. Fold each sheet in half.
c. Make a cut into the folded edge about 1–2 inches long. Make a parallel cut, the same length, about 1–2 inches away from the first cut. Try to center these cuts.
d. Unfold the paper to a 90°-angle, and push out the section of paper between the cuts, forming a bench-like shape.
e. Glue one image onto the bench shape.
f. Assemble all the pages into a book in the order that they will be presented to the class. Hold the book flat, with the open end facing the students. As each event is shared with the class, open the book to reveal the corresponding photo orimage. The images will "pop" out at the students like a pop-up book!

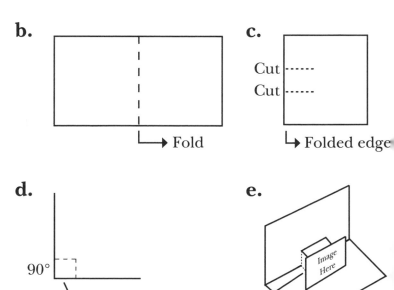

Write to the Author

Teach the students how to make the same pop-up format. Use 9" x 12" construction paper. Have the students fold their paper in half and make the pop-up benches in the creases. Give them a second piece of paper to create a birthday image, such as a cake, cupcake, party hats, presents, etc. They will glue the images onto their pop-up benches and then write birthday greetings inside their card.

* Paul Zelinsky illustrated several Beverly Cleary books, such as *Dear Mr. Henshaw* (Scholastic, 1983). Throughout the month, read a section of this chapter book aloud to the students. This book tells the story of a boy who writes to a favorite author, so this will lend itself well as a discussion piece while the students create their own letters to Paul Zelinsky!

Hansel & Gretel: Search for Home

Students will work in small groups to use clues in order to find their way home. Tell the class, "Imagine you were Hansel and Gretel and you had to find your way back to your home. Use these clues to find your way through the forest of book shelves!" The clues should involve the students in finding materials in the library. This fun activity will help them develop their skills in finding items in the library. Here is a sample list of clues:

Group 1:

- Go to the fiction section. You left some breadcrumbs by *Mr. Popper's Penguins*, written by Richard Atwater.
- So far, so good! Now go to the nonfiction section and look for the book, *Field Trios*, by Jim Arnosky, call #_____.
- You are very clever! Next go to the picture book section and find the book, *Owl Moon*, by Jane Yolen. Owls love to hoot in the woods!
- You are very brave! You're almost home. Go to the DVD section and find the movie, *Harry Potter and the Sorcerer's Stone*.
- You did it! Bring all your clues to the librarian. He/She is at her home headquarters waiting for you!

*Print the clues on paper cut into house shapes. Provide small prizes, such as baggies of old-fashioned candy (for the witch's candy house), lollipops, etc.

Dust Devil's Great Escape

Play the following game in honor of Zelinsky's and Isaacs' newest picture book, *Dust Devil*. This companion to *Swamp Angel* is a tall tale about Angelica Longhorn's new life in Montana and how she finds her trusty sidekick horse, Dust Devil. To play the game, have all the children stand in a circle and join hands. Select one child to play "Dust Devil." This child must stand in the middle of the circle. Place a chair or desk about 7 yards away from the children's circle. This will be Dust Devil's barn.

Tell Dust Devil that he/she wants to escape this corral (the children holding hands in a circle). If the corral breaks, Dust Devil tries to escape and run to his barn. Dust Devil can push through the corral, he/she can try to crawl under the corral, etc. The goal is for Dust Devil to reach the barn before being tagged by the children. Play continues by having Dust Devil select the next horse. Set a time limit to ensure that most children have a chance to be the Dust Devil.

Valentine Ornament Craft

Since Paul Zelinsky often creates his classical illustrations by painting on wood (see *Swamp Angel* and *Dust Devil*), AND his birthday falls on Valentine's Day, this craft is a natural for Zelinsky's birthday celebration. Purchase a package of thin wooden heart shapes, approximately 4–5 inches tall. Make sure they have a hole in the top for hanging. Most craft and/or dollar stores have wooden ornaments.

Discuss Zelinsky's style of painting with the students, and have them use colorful paints to create a picture on their heart shapes. These hearts will be colorful party decorations!

Shivering Spelling Contest

Play this fun game, based on Zelinsky's colorful illustrations for Fran Manushkin's *The Shivers in the Fridge*. Before the celebration, obtain enough refrigerator magnets so that each child (or pair of children) has 7–10 magnets, with a balance of consonants and vowels. Use the magnets for a variety of spelling games, such as:

- Making Words: This excellent word recognition activity based on concepts from Patricia Cunningham, et al's *Making Words* (Good Apple, 2001) can serve the purpose of a party game. Give each student a pack of magnetic letters, set the timer, and tell the students to arrange their letters into as many words as possible within the time limit. Since students will have different combinations of letters, simply have them raise their hands if they made more than 5 words, 7 words, 10 words. When you get up to 10 words, only a few children will likely raise their hands. Call on them to read out the letters they worked with, write them on the board, then have them read off their word lists. The rest of the class will listen and read the words from the board to check that the words use only the letters from the child's packet. The child (or children) with the longest list of acceptable words, wins! Give a small prize to all the students, such as a pack of their own magnetic letters (made by running copies of letters through a laminator that has a magnetic laminate cartridge).
- Making Words in Partners: Play the game with a partner. Give one set of refrigerator magnet letters to a pair of students. Have each pair place the letters in the middle of the table, set the timer, and have them compete against their partners to see who can make the most words.
- Hangman: If the whiteboard in your room is magnetic, use the magnetic letters to set up small hangman games. Divide the students into groups of three students to play hangman against each other. They should use the magnetic letters to fill in the missing words.

- Spelling Challenge: Give each child or pair of children a set of magnetic letters, containing all the letters from the weekly spelling list. Read a word from the spelling list and have the students use their magnetic letters to spell out the word.

There are many other word games to play! Be creative!

Doodle Journals

Use Zelinsky's illustrations for Gelman's *Doodler Doodling* as an inspiration for your students to keep their own doodle journals. If this book is shared with students early in the month, they could be given a doodle prompt each day of the month to get them going on their new journals! Sample prompts could be extensions of the doodles in the book, or they could be new ideas, such as: "Doodle your backpack's contents," "Doodle your view through the classroom's windows," "Doodle Rapunzel's room in the tower as you imagine it to be," etc. A great resource for doodle prompts is *Doodle Diary: Art Journaling for Girls* (Sokol, 2010).

Rapunzel Climbing Tower

If your gymnasium has a climbing wall, schedule time for the students to use it during your celebration. Provide students with the opportunity to climb "Rapunzel's Tower" in honor of Zelinsky's Caldecott Medal picture book of this famous fairy tale.

If a climbing wall isn't available, create an obstacle course and connect it to each of Zelinsky's illustrated fairy tales: *Hansel and Gretel*, *Rumpelstiltskin*, and *Rapunzel*. In each tale, the main characters had important obstacles to overcome, so the obstacle course will be a natural connection! Set up a basic course in the gymnasium, with balance beams, hula hoops, floor mats (for forward rolls), etc.

Ogre Body Puppets

In honor of Zelinsky's illustrations for Prelutsky's book of poems titled, *Awful Ogre's Awful Day*, help the students participate in this art activity. Gather one paper shopping bag per student.

Before the Celebration

Prepare the bags for the activity. The bag will become a vest/costume. First, cut down the front center section of the bag, toward the bottom. Next, cut halfway through the bottom section, then cut a round opening. Hold the bag upside down. The bottom, with the round opening, will fit around a child's neck. Cut two armholes, one on each side, near the bottom of the bag.

During the Celebration

Distribute the bags/vests to each student and instruct him/her to color or paint the bag to look like an ogre's clothing (torn, patched up, etc.). Give each child a paper plate taped to a popsicle stick. The students will use these plates to make ogre masks. Once they have finished their ogre body puppets, read several poems aloud, and encourage the students to move around and act like the ogre in the poems. This is a very creative way to integrate visual art with creative movement!

Party Food

Serve "magic wands" in honor of Zelinsky's magical fairy tale picture books. Use large pretzel rods, and dip one end into melted chocolate. Add colorful sprinkles to the chocolate, then refrigerate to harden the chocolate.

Party Favors

Candy conversation hearts, small artist sketchbooks, bookmarks.

Happy Birthday, Paul Zelinsky!

Born February 14, 1953

Picture Books

- *Doodler Doodling*
  (by Rita Golden Gelman)
- *Dust Devil*
  (by Anne Isaacs)
- *The Shivers in the Fridge*
  (by Fran Manushkin)
- *The Story of Mrs. Loveright and Her Purrless Cat*
  (by Lore Segal)
- *Swamp Angel*
  (by Anne Isaacs)
- *Toy Dance Party*
  (by Emily Jenkins)
- *Toys Go Out*
  (by Emily Jenkins)

Folktales

- *Hansel and Gretel*
  (retold by Rika Lesser)
- *Rapunzel*
  (retold by Paul O. Zelinsky)
- *Rumpelstiltskin*
  (retold by Paul O. Zelinsky)

Pop-Up Folksong Books

- *Knick Knack Paddywhack*
  (adapted by Paul O. Zelinsky)
- *The Wheels on the Bus*
  (adapted by Paul O. Zelinsky)

Illustrated Poetry

- *Awful Ogre's Awful Day*
  (by Jack Prelutsky)
- *Awful Ogre Running Wild*
  (by Jack Prelutsky)
- *Zoo Doings: Animal Poems*
  (by Jack Prelutsky)

Paul Zelinsky Reading Log

Read 5 books by **February** ____.

On each line, write the title you've read and have your parent/guardian sign that you read it.

Bring this completed reading log to me by **February** ____ and receive your invitation to attend our birthday celebration on

_____.

Date/Time

_____

Title   Parent/Guardian Signature

_____

Title   Parent/Guardian Signature

_____

Title   Parent/Guardian Signature

_____

Title   Parent/Guardian Signature

_____

Title   Parent/Guardian Signature

Happy Birthday, Dear Mo Willems!

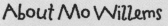

About Mo Willems

- Mo Willems was born on February 11, 1968.
- He was raised in New Orleans, Louisiana.
- His parents were immigrants, and he relied on the illustrations in picture books to help him understand the words in the stories he read as a child.
- His real name is Maurice.
- He was a writer and filmmaker for Sesame Street™ and he earned six Emmy Awards during his tenure there!
- He has won three Caldecott Honor Awards and two Theodore Seuss Geisel Awards for his children's books.
- Mo Willems hides an illustration of the pigeon in every book! He does this because the pigeon is very jealous when Mo writes a book that isn't about the pigeon.
- Mo Willems has provided entertaining and insightful videos of himself and his creative process on his website at www.mowillems.com. Show these to the students during the celebration.

Celebration Ideas

Tell the Author's Story: "Get on the Bus of Life Before It Pulls Away!"

Tell the story of Mo Willems by drawing a large school bus on the board. Draw or use images to create the following mementos of Mo Willems's life: a photo of Mo Willems, the Sesame Street™ sign, an image of New Orleans, art supplies, several of his famous book characters, and comic strips. As you share facts about his life, place the correlating image in a window of the bus. Show his photo last, and place it in the driver seat. Tell the students that this should serve as a reminder that, just like Mo, when we need to take charge of our lives and try something new, we need to grab hold of the steering wheel and drive the bus!

Write to the Author

Mo Willems purposely creates characters that young children can try to draw on their own. Since he encourages children of all ages to draw and practice their craft as often as possible, have the students draw their favorite pictures to share with him. Tell them to sign their names and to include questions they'd like to ask him about drawing, along with their birthday wishes to him. He encourages teachers/librarians to have their students write to him. Go to his website at www.mowillems.com and click on "F.A.Q.s" to find his instructions on mailing letters to him.

Draw the Pigeon!

Mo Willems has a fun, interactive website at www.mowillems.com that the students will enjoy visiting during class. The site provides step-by-step directions for drawing his popular character, the Pigeon. Click on the picture of his "Pals" and then click on "The Pigeon" for the drawing instructions. Divide the students into groups of 4–5 children. Give each group a printout of the directions below, a large die to roll, and one sheet of paper per child:

Roll 1 = Draw the pigeon's head.
Roll 2 = Draw the pigeon's body.
Roll 3 = Draw the pigeon's neck.
Roll 4 = Draw the pigeon's stick feet.
Roll 5 = Draw the pigeon's eyeball and beak.
Roll 6 = Draw the pigeon's wings.

*The first child in each group to successfully draw all six parts of the pigeon wins the game!

Knuffle Bunny, Where Are You?

Divide the students into small groups and give each group clues to find where their picture of Knuffle Bunny has been hidden! Here are a few sample clues:

- Help! Trixie has lost Knuffle Bunny! She's almost positive that she was holding Knuffle Bunny while she was looking through books about rabbits. Go to the section where the rabbit books are shelved (Dewey section: 636.9).
- Okay, so she was wrong. She must have dragged Knuffle Bunny over to the author's book display. Hop like a Knuffle Bunny over to the Mo Willems book display.
- That is one tricky Knuffle Bunny! Trixie must have held tight to it while reading her favorite Mo Willems book. Then she wandered over to the craft book section. She loves to make a lot of crafty projects! Tip toe over to the craft section (Dewey section: 745) to see if Knuffle Bunny is hiding over there!
- Hmmm. No crafty Knuffle Bunny over here! Wait a minute. Wasn't Trixie trying to figure out what to feed her Knuffle Bunny? Yes, that's it. March over to the cooking section (Dewey section: 641.5).
- (*Place a picture of Knuffle Bunny on the shelf of cookbooks.*)
  Way to go! You've found Trixie's Knuffle Bunny! Bring this picture to your teacher/librarian for a prize!

  Prizes: Mo Willems activity packets (print handouts from his website), bookmarks with images of Knuffle Bunny on them, etc.

Friend Games

In honor of Willems' *City Dog, Country Frog* (illustrated by Jon J. Muth), pair up the students, and lead the whole group in a series of partner games. Here are a few ideas:

- *Miss Mary Mack and Other Children's Street Rhymes* by Joanna Cole et al. (HarperCollins, 1990) has several easy-to-learn hand rhymes to use during the party.
- Connect the Dots: Provide each pair with a paper that has a grid of dots on it. The object of the game is to connect dots to make a box, making only one line between 2 dots for each turn. Once a box is made, that student writes her initial inside of it. Count up the boxes for each student to determine who has made the most boxes.

How Do You Say "Knuffle Bunny"?

Have the students complete a graph in which they vote on whether the /K/ in Knuffle Bunny is silent, or pronounced. Mo Willems has said that he says the word both ways, so there is no right answer! The answer with the most votes wins, which will determine how you pronounce it as you read the latest adventure of Knuffle Bunny aloud to the class.

Naked Mole Rat Gets Dressed

Play this relay race as a reminder of Wilbur, the Mole Rat who dared to wear clothes! Before the celebration, fill two suitcases with a variety of clothes: hats, scarves, sport jackets, large shirts, gloves, etc. Divide the students into two teams. Line them up at a starting line and place a closed suitcase at the other end of the room, one for each team. At the signal, the first two students race to their suitcase, put on three items of clothing, close the suitcase, carry it back to the next teammate in line, take off the three items, put them into the suitcase, and hand it to their teammate. The teammate carries the suitcase back to its original spot, opens it up and puts on three items of clothing, runs back to the next teammate, takes off the three items, puts them back into the suitcase, and hands it off to the next teammate. Play continues until one team finishes through their line of students! Award a prize to all the students, such as a pair of silly socks (available at most dollar stores).

BINGO with Elephant and Piggie!

Mo Willems has written over 13 early readers featuring his delightful duo, Elephant (a.k.a., Gerald), and Piggie (a.k.a., Piggie). If the students have read a wide variety of these books by the date of the celebration, this game will be a fun way to review the books and share some laughs.

Before the Celebration

Make a list of 12–15 words related to the events in this early reader series, and a blank 3 x 3 Bingo grid for each student. Gather marker pieces for each student for a Bingo game.

During the Celebration

To begin the game, write the list of words on the board. Distribute a blank 3 x 3 Bingo grid and instruct the students to copy 9 different words from the list, one per box. Provide game markers (buttons, candy conversation hearts, etc.). Pull a word from the bag, and tell the students a clue about it. For example, if the word is "snake," the clue could be, "This is the new friend who wanted to play catch with Elephant and Piggie." Once the students state the correct answer, those who have chosen that word from the list can mark it on their Bingo cards. The first to get three in a row wins. Play until everyone has had a chance to win. Prizes could be individual boxes of candy conversation hearts, in honor of Valentine's Day and because we all love our friends, Elephant and Piggie!

Party Food

Hot dogs (*The Pigeon Finds a Hot Dog*), ice cream (*Should I Share My Ice Cream?*), bunny-shaped graham crackers (Knuffle Bunny books)

Craft: Fleece Scarves

In honor of Wilbur, the naked mole rat, provide each student with a fleece scarf, cut from bulk fleece purchased at a craft store. Set out an assortment of fleece shapes, cut with a die-cut machine, or allow the students to cut out their own colorful designs. Have the students attach the designs to their scarves with fabric glue. This craft will allow the students to focus on being unique and creative, just like Wilbur.

Party Favors

Award certificates that state a unique characteristic of each student, in honor of Wilbur, the naked mole rat who wasn't afraid to be himself. Use the resources on Mo Willems website (www. mowillems.com) to print out coloring pages and activity sheets. Collate them into a book, and provide an activity book and a new pencil to each student.

Happy Birthday, Mo Willems!

Born February 11, 1968

Picture Books

- *City Dog, Country Frog*
- *Don't Let the Pigeon Drive the Bus*
- *Don't Let the Pigeon Stay Up Late*
- *Edwina, The Dinosaur Who Didn't Know She Was Extinct*
- *Hooray for Amanda and Her Alligator!*
- *Knuffle Bunny: A Cautionary Tale*
- *Knuffle Bunny Free*
- *Knuffle Bunny Too: A Case of Mistaken Identity*
- *Leonardo the Terrible Monster*
- *Naked Mole Rat Gets Dressed*
- *The Pigeon Finds a Hot Dog!*
- *The Pigeon Has Feelings, Too*
- *The Pigeon Loves Things That Go!*
- *The Pigeon Wants a Puppy*
- *Time to Pee!*
- *Time to Say, "Please!"*

Easy Readers Series Elephant and Piggie

- *Are You Ready to Play Outside?*
- *Can I Play, Too?*
- *Cat the Cat*
- *Cat the Cat, Who is That?*
- *Elephants Cannot Dance!*
- *Happy Pig Day!*
- *I Am Going!*
- *I Am Invited to a Party!*
- *I Broke My Trunk!*
- *I Love My New Toy!*

- *I Will Surprise My Friend!*
- *Let's Say Hi to Friends Who Fly!*
- *My Friend is Sad*
- *Pigs Make Me Sneeze!*
- *There is a Bird on Your Head!*
- *Time to Sleep, Sheep the Sheep*
- *Today I Will Fly!*
- *Watch Me Throw the Ball!*
- *We Are In a Book!*
- *What's Your Sound, Hound the Hound?*

Mo Willems Reading Log

Read 5 books by **February** ____.

On each line, write the title you've read and have your parent/guardian sign that you read it.

Bring this completed reading log to me by **February** ____ and receive your invitation to attend our birthday celebration on

_____.

Date/Time

_____

Title   Parent/Guardian Signature

_____

Title   Parent/Guardian Signature

_____

Title   Parent/Guardian Signature

_____

Title   Parent/Guardian Signature

_____

Title   Parent/Guardian Signature

Happy Birthday, Dear Authors Born in March!

March 1	Ruth Gross	March 15	Barbara Cohen
March 2	**Leo Dillon***		Ruth White
	Doug Keith	March 16	Sid Fleischman
	Marjorie Parker	March 17	Keith Baker
March 3	Suse MacDonald		Ralph Fletcher
	Patricia MacLachlan	March 18	**Douglas Florian***
March 4	Helen Frost		Susan Patron
	Dav Pilkey*	March 20	Mitsumasa Anno
	Peggy Rathmann		Lois Lowry
March 5	Mem Fox		Louis Sachar
March 6	Kathleen Hague	March 21	Lisa Desimini
	Chris Raschka		Michael Foreman
March 7	Joanne Rocklin	March 23	Eleanor Cameron
March 8	Robert Sabuda	March 24	Bill Cleaver
March 9	Harry Bliss	March 25	Kate DiCamillo
	Ellen Levine	March 26	T. A. Barron
March 10	Ilene Cooper		Jerry Pallotta
	Jack Kent	March 27	Julia Alvarez
March 12	Daniel Cohen		Patricia C. Wrede
	Naomi Shihab Nye	March 28	Byrd Baylor
March 13	**Diane Dillon**		Doreen Cronin
	Ellen Raskin		Mary Stolz
	Thomas Rockwell	March 29	Sucie Stevenson

*Author featured in this chapter

Happy Birthday, Dear Dav Pilkey!

About Dav Pilkey

- Dav Pilkey was born on March 4, 1966, in Cleveland, Ohio.
- He has an older sister named Cindy, whom he refers to as "a highly skilled, professional tattletale!" (www.pilkey.com/adv-text.php)
- While in elementary school, Dav was often in trouble for talking and making funny noises during class. He was eventually diagnosed with attention deficit hyperactivity disorder.
- His teachers often made him sit in the hallway as punishment. This is where he created cartoon characters, such as "The Amazing Captain Underpants."
- He received encouragement to write from one of his English professors at Kent State University.
- He entered a contest for students who wrote and illustrated their own books, and he won with his first book, *World War Won* (1987).
- In Dav's book, *The Adventures of Captain Underpants*, he chose to have his two main characters (George and Harold) live in Piqua, Ohio. He picked this city because it has an Underwear Festival!

Celebration Ideas

Tell the Author's Story

<u>Before the Celebration</u>

Gather the following supplies: two sheets of newspaper, and card stock cut into 2" x 4" rectangles. Open one sheet of newspaper and cut a 6" square section of text. Use a glue stick and glide the glue over three sides of the square.

Glue it over a similar section in the second sheet of newspaper, making a pocket. Write words on the card stock rectangles that relate to Dav Pilkey (see list of sample words below). Tuck the word cards into the pocket you created.

Sample words:

- Birthday: Dav's birthday is March 4, 1966. He was born in Cleveland, Ohio, and has one older sister, Cindy.
- Hallway: Because Dav liked to joke around a lot during class, his second-grade teacher often sent him out to the hallway as punishment. He was sent there so often, the teacher put a desk out there just for him!
- Artist: Dav loved to draw, so he usually sat in the hallway desk and drew comics. This is where he created his "Captain Underpants" cartoon!
- Contest: By the time he was in college, he decided to major in art, and he entered a picture book contest and won! The prize was the publication of his book, *World War Won* (1987)!
- Oregon: Dav has lived in Oregon since 1993.
- Pets: Dav has several cats and dogs.
- Silly: Dav was a silly kid in school, and he uses his silly sense of humor to make his hilarious books for all of us to enjoy!

<u>During the Celebration</u>

Begin the story by talking about Pilkey's book, *The Paperboy*, and hold up the newspaper. While talking about Pilkey's book, fold newspaper and turn it, letting several word cards fall to the floor, as if by magic! As each word card is retrieved, talk about how that word relates to Dav Pilkey.

Write to Dav Pilkey

In honor of Captain Underpants, bring in a new pair of white underpants and a black marker for the students to sign their names and write "Happy Birthday, Dav Pilkey" on them!

Treasure Hunt: Find a Friend for Ricky Ricotta's Robot!

To celebrate Ricky Ricotta, divide the students into groups of three, and have each group follow clue directions that you create (see sample clues below) to find a picture of a robot. You can create robot images from the reproducible on page 135.

Explain that Ricky Ricotta's robot is happy with Ricky, but he wants his own robot friend, too. Instruct students to find the clues hidden around the room until you find a robot that could be a friend for Ricky's robot!

Sample Clues for Group 1:

- "Can you guess where I am hiding? Go to the chalkboard and take 10 baby steps over to the classroom writing center, and you will find your first clue!"
- "Good job!" Now, walk like a robot over to the Dav Pilkey book display for your next clue."
- "Still haven't found the robot yet? Take five scissor steps over to the teacher's desk and you will find me!"

When each group has found their robot picture, give them each a small prize, such as small robot key chains, candy bags, etc.

Captain Underpants

This series is Pilkey's best-known work by far. Capitalize on students' interest in this irreverent portrayal of a silly super hero through the following games.

- Three-Legged Race: Use a large pair of boxer shorts for each team of students. Divide the teams into partners, line them up behind a starting line, and tell the students to each put one leg into the boxer shorts, race to the finish line, take off the shorts, and run back to the next pair in line. The first team to complete the three-legged race wins!

- Toilet Paper Toss: In honor of the toilet humor found in these books ("Professor Poopy Pants," "Wedgie Woman," etc.), have students work in small groups to see which group can successfully toss the most balls of toilet paper into a training toilet within a given time limit.

- Fly High, Captain Underpants! Lay two jump ropes on the floor, parallel to each other, about 18" apart. Arrange the students in a single-file line, about 10–12' away from the ropes. The students each approach the ropes, one at a time, at a run. They must jump ("fly") across the two ropes. Those who do not make it over the ropes are out. After each student has successfully flown over the ropes, increase the distance between the ropes and have them all try again. Continue to increase the distance until one student is able to fly across the ropes. For added fun, have each student yell, "Tra La La!" as he/she flies over the ropes, just like Captain Underpants would!

Craft: "Flip-O-Rama" Books

Dav Pilkey uses an old-fashioned cartoon technique in most of his series books, which he refers to as "flip-o-rama." Share these cartoons from his books with the students, and talk about his technique of drawing a simple picture and then drawing a second picture of the same object in a new position. Next, show how to lay one picture over the other and pull the corner of the top picture up and down quickly so that the image appears to be moving. Give each student a small booklet of blank paper stapled together. The students will draw a picture of a person or animal for their own flip-o-rama books. If time permits, have them exchange their booklets with friends to try out each other's books.

Name Tags

Begin the celebration by having students create a new name for themselves using "Professor Poopypants' Name Change-O-Chart." Give the students a copy of the name-changing chart and tell them to use the chart to figure out their new names. Provide nametags and markers so they can write their new names down and introduce themselves to their classmates. This will help to break the ice and make everyone laugh!

Dav Pilkey Online

Visit Dav Pilkey's website at www.pilkey.com to find a variety of reproducible sheets, such as word finds, mazes, coloring pages, jokes, and much more! Download these pages and create an activity packet for each student. Use the packets as independent activities during the beginning or end of the celebration. The packet could also be used as a game prize.

Surreal Artwork

After reading *When Cats Dream*, page through the illustrations, and point out some of the famous paintings that Pilkey imitated in this book. Discuss his use of unusual objects in the illustrations, as well as the variety of cat activities that he portrays. Have the students think about a surreal picture of an animal in which it would be placed in an unfamiliar setting, with unusual objects. Provide time for them to create their own illustrations of what cats (or an animal of their choice) might dream about. Have them use oil pastels for bold colors.

Party Food

Serve blue cupcakes, in honor of Pilkey's blue dragon (*A Friend for Dragon*) or pink cupcakes with an animal cracker on top (*The Moonglow Roll-O-Rama*).

Party Favors

Ring pops (Captain Underpants' decoder ring), activity packet.

Robots

Happy Birthday, Dav Pilkey!

Born March 4, 1966

Picture Books

- *Dog Breath*
- *Dogzilla*
- *Dragon Gets By*
- *Dragon's Fat Cat*
- *Dragon's Halloween*
- *Dragon's Merry Christmas*
- *A Friend For Dragon*
- *God Bless the Gargoyles*
- *The Hallo-wiener*
- *Juliius*
- *Kat Kong*
- *The Moonglow Roll-O-Rama*
- *The Paperboy*
- *The Silly Gooses*
- *'Twas the Night Before Thanksgiving*
- *When Cats Dream*
- *World War Won*

Series Books

- *The Adventures of Captain Underpants: An Epic Novel*
- *The Adventures of Super Diaper Baby: The First Graphic Novel*
- *Captain Underpants and the Attack of the Talking Toilets*
- *Captain Underpants and the Big, Bad Battle of the Bionic Booger Boy, Part 1*
- *Captain Underpants and the Big, Bad Battle of the Bionic Booger Boy, Part 2*
- *Captain Underpants and the Invasion of the Incredibly Naughty Cafeteria Ladies From Outer Space*

- *Captain Underpants and the Perilous Plot of Professor Poopypants*
- *Captain Underpants and the Wrath of the Wicked Wedgie Woman*
- *The Dumb Bunnies*
- *The Dumb Bunnies' Easter*
- *The Dumb Bunnies go to the Zoo*
- *Make Way for Dumb Bunnies*
- *Ook and Gluk: Kung-Fu Cavemen from the Future*
- *Ricky Ricotta's Mighty Robot*
- *Ricky Ricotta's Mighty Robot vs. the Jurassic Jack Rabbits from Jupiter*
- *Ricky Ricotta's Mighty Robot vs. the Mecha Monkeys from Mars*
- *Ricky Ricotta's Mighty Robot vs. The Mutant Mosquitoes . . .*
- *Ricky Ricotta's Mighty Robot vs. the Stupid Stinkbugs from Saturn*
- *Ricky Ricotta's Mighty Robot vs. The Voodoo Vultures . . .*

Dav Pilkey Reading Log

Read 5 books by **March** _____.

On each line, write the title you've read and have your parent/guardian sign that you read it.

Bring this completed reading log to me by **March** _____ and receive your invitation to attend our birthday celebration on

_____.

Date/Time

_____
Title   Parent/Guardian Signature

_____
Title   Parent/Guardian Signature

_____
Title   Parent/Guardian Signature

_____
Title   Parent/Guardian Signature

_____
Title   Parent/Guardian Signature

Happy Birthday, Dear Leo and Diane Dillon!

About Leo and Diane Dillon

- Leo Dillon was born on March 2, 1933, in New York.
- Diane Dillon was born on March 13, 1933, in California.
- Leo Dillon met Diane Sorber while they were students at Parsons School of Design in New York.
- They graduated from Parsons in 1956 and married in 1957.
- They have collaborated on illustrations for science fiction, children's novels, and children's picture books for over 50 years!
- They won two consecutive Caldecott Medals: *Why Mosquitoes Buzz in People's Ears* (Aardema, 1975) and *Ashanti to Zulu: African Traditions* (Musgrove, 1976).
- Leo Dillon was the first African American to win the Caldecott Medal.

Celebration Ideas

Tell the Authors' Story

Since Leo and Diane Dillon are renowned American artists, tell their life stories in a Draw-and-Tell format. Use the following story and diagrams for the drawing, which will eventually be a picture of a painter's palette.

1. On March 2, 1933, Lionel John Dillon, Jr., was born. His nickname is Leo. He was raised in Brooklyn, New York. *(Draw one large black dot, positioning it on the right side of the (eventual) palette.)*
2. On March 13, 1933, Diane Claire Sorber was born. She was raised in California. *(Draw one large black dot, positioning it on the left side of the [eventual] palette.)*
3. Leo never traveled to California. He stayed in New York to attend Parsons School of Design. *(Draw a curving line from the right dot to the left dot, sweeping in an upward circle and then concaving down to the left dot. This will form the top side of the palette.)*
4. In 1953, Diane left her home in California to attend Parsons School of Design in New York City. *(Draw a curving line from the left dot to the right dot, sweeping in a downward circle to form the bottom of the palette.)*
5. In 1956, they both graduated from Parsons School of Design, and, in 1957, they married each other. *(Draw a small circle to resemble a wedding band. This circle should be drawn on the lower-right side of the palette, like an oval hole.)*
6. Their lives have been filled with many joys. *(For each statement that follows, use a different color marker to make paint "blobs" on the palette. Add the blobs of color as each statement is shared with the children.)*
   a. In 1959 they began illustrating book covers for science fiction stories.
   b. In 1965 their son, Lionel John Dillon III (Lee) was born. He, too, became an artist and helped them illustrate *Pish, Posh, Said Hieronymous Bosch* (by Nancy Willard).
   c. In 1975 they won the Caldecott Award for their illustrations of *Why Mosquitoes Buzz in People's Ears*. Leo was the first African American to win this award!
   d. In 1976 they won their second Caldecott Award for *Ashanti to Zulu: African Traditions*. They are the only artists to have won back-to-back Caldecott Awards!
7. Perhaps what is most amazing about Leo and Diane Dillon is that each illustration is a unique creation of both of them work-

ing together! They call this the "third artist" because none of their illustrations are created by one or the other, but by both of them immersing themselves into their work simultaneously. *(While sharing this fact, draw a paintbrush: draw the top line of the handle when emphasizing one artist, the bottom line for the other, and the brush tip for the merging of both artists.)*

Letters to Leo and Diane Dillon

Have the students write birthday greetings on palette shapes made with a die-cut on white card stock. They can use colorful markers to decorate their palettes when they've finished writing their letters.

Game: What's in Rabbit's Hole?

This game is based on *Who's in Rabbit's House?*, which the Dillons illustrated. Before the celebration, gather (or make) three "feely boxes" using old shoeboxes. Cover each box with colorful birthday paper and scan an image of the rabbit from the book. Number each box, cut a hole in each for the children's hands to fit inside as they feel around the box for an object. Tape the image of the rabbit next to the hole. Tell the students that they will each get a turn to feel inside each box. Distribute paper with blank lines for each box and its corresponding number. The children will feel inside the box and write down their guess as to what is in each of rabbit's "houses." Once everyone has had a chance to guess, reveal the items and award prizes, such as small candy bags.

Turn, Turn, Turn Game

The Dillons' book, *To Every Thing There is a Season*, is based on verses from the Bible. These same verses were used in a popular song by The Byrds, called "Turn, Turn, Turn."

Before the Celebration

Gather together small prizes, such as party bags filled with bookmarks, stickers, pencils, flower seeds, etc. Place these bags, one for each child, in a small box, and wrap it with birthday gift wrap. Place the box inside a larger box, and

wrap it in birthday paper. Find a third, larger box, and place everything inside it. Wrap it up, and place a bow on it.

During the Celebration

Have the children sit in a circle while the song by The Byrds is played aloud. The children must begin the game by passing the large gift box around the circle in the same direction until the music stops. When the music stops, the child holding the box opens it up, revealing another wrapped box. Play continues, passing the box in the opposite direction until the music stops, until the smallest box is opened to reveal the party bags for everyone!

Estimation Activity

Since the Dillons illustrated *The Hundred Penny Box*, a short chapter book, capitalize on the idea of saving coins by creating an estimation activity.

Before the Celebration

Fill a few glass jars of varying size and shape with pennies. Count them and record how many are in each jar.

During the Celebration

Give the students a guessing form for them to write their estimations for each jar. The winners can keep the jar of pennies, or you could give out a small bag of pennies to each child and use the pennies for other activities.

Pin the Mosquito on the Ear!

Enlarge the mosquito image from *Why Mosquitoes Buzz in People's Ears*, and copy it so that each student has one. Have them write their names on their mosquitoes. Before the celebration, draw the outline of a large ear on chart paper or the front board. Have the students take turns being blindfolded and brought to the front board to try to place the mosquito closest to the ear's center.

Craft: African Pendants

Use modeling clay and bring in reference books that show traditional African pendants. Have the students manipulate their clay to create similar designs. Make a hole near the top of the pendant, place on a foil-lined baking sheet, and bake in a 275°F oven for 15 minutes (for ¼-inch thick pendants). Provide leather strips for students to string on their pendants and wear after the party.

Artist Palette Color Search

Divide the students into small groups. Give each group a palette made from a die-cut pattern. Make color blobs by cutting out one "blob" of the following colors for each group: red, blue, yellow, green. Each group's task will be to find one of each of the four colors of blobs that have an answer to their clue written on them. Before the celebration, write the answers on the color blobs, and scatter them around the room. The trick lies in finding the colors with the correct answers for each group's palette, not in finding hidden colors around the room. Use the following clues:

Group 1: You must find four color blobs that name jungle animals found in the Dillons' folktale illustrations.
Answers: Lion, Snake, Iguana, Rabbit

Group 2: You must find four color blobs that name folktale titles.
Answers: *Rumpelstiltskin, Why Mosquitoes Buzz in People's Ears, Who's In Rabbit's House?, The People Could Fly*

Group 3: You must find four color blobs that name an object that is found on a penny.
Answers: President Lincoln, "Liberty," "one cent," a building

Group 4: You must find four color blobs that name the four seasons.
Answers: Fall, Winter, Spring, Summer

Musical Chairs

In honor of their picture books, *Rap A Tap Tap: Here's Bojangles—Think of That!* and *Jazz on a Saturday Night*, play some jazz music while the students participate in musical chairs! Play music by the same jazz musicians that they wrote about. In addition to sound recordings, go to youtube.com™ and search for "Bill Bojangles Robinson." A variety of videos with original footage can be viewed with the students.

Party Favors
- Papier mache boxes for the students to decorate. Provide each student with 10 pennies to start their own Hundred Penny Box.
- Art supplies
- Pencil top erasers in the shape of jungle animals

Party Food

Sugar cookies cut with music note cookie cutters, animal crackers.

Happy Birthday, Leo and Diane Dillon

Leo born March 2, 1933 * Diane born March 13, 1933

Picture Books (including collaborations with other authors)

- *Northern Lullaby*
  (by Nancy White Carlstrom)
- *Jazz on a Saturday Night*
  (by Leo & Diane Dillon)
- *Mother Goose: Numbers on the Loose*
  (by Leo & Diane Dillon)
- *Never Forgotten*
  (by Patricia McKissack)
- *One Winter's Night*
  (by John Herman)
- *Earth Mother* (by Ellen Jackson)
- *The People Could Fly: The Picture Book*
  (by Virginia Hamilton)
- *Rap a Tap Tap: Here's Bojangles—Think of That!*
  (by Leo & Diane Dillon)
- *The Secret River*
  (by Marjorie Kinnan Rawlings)
- *Switch on the Night*
  (by Ray Bradbury)
- *Tale of the Mandarin Ducks*
  (by Katherine Paterson)
- *To Every Thing There is a Season*
  (by Leo & Diane Dillon)
- *Two Little Trains*
  (by Margaret Wise Brown)
- *Two Pairs of Shoes*
  (by P. L. Travers)
- *Mama Says: A Book of Love for Mothers and Sons*
  (by Rob D. Walker)
- *Pish, Posh, Said Hieronymous Bosch*
  (by Nancy Willard)
- *Where Have You Been?*
  (by Margaret Wise Brown)
- *Who's In Rabbit's House*
  (by Verna Aardema)
- *Why Mosquitoes Buzz in People's Ears*
  (by Verna Aardema)
- *Wind Child*
  (by Shirley Rousseau Murphy)

Fiction

- *The Hundred Penny Box*
  (by Sharon Bell Mathis)
- *Mansa Musa*
  (by Khephra Burns)

Nonfiction: Folktales & Poetry

- *Aida* (by Leontyne Price)
- *Ashanti to Zulu: African Traditions*
  (by Margaret Musgrove)
- *Behind the Back of the Mountain*
  (by Verna Aardema)
- *The Girl Who Dreamed Only Geese*
  (by Howard Norman)
- *The Girl Who Spun Gold*
  (by Virginia Hamilton)
- *Her Stories* (by Virginia Hamilton)
- *Honey, I Love and Other Love Poems*
  (by Eloise Greenfield)
- *Many Thousand Gone*
  (by Virginia Hamilton)

Leo and Diane Dillon Reading Log

Read 5 books by **March** _____.

On each line, write the title you've read and have your parent/guardian sign that you read it.

Bring this completed reading log to me by **March** _____ and receive your invitation to attend our birthday celebration on

_____.

Date/Time

_____

Title   Parent/Guardian Signature

_____

Title   Parent/Guardian Signature

_____

Title   Parent/Guardian Signature

_____

Title   Parent/Guardian Signature

_____

Title   Parent/Guardian Signature

Happy Birthday, Dear Douglas Florian!

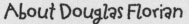

About Douglas Florian

- Douglas Florian was born on March 18, 1950, in New York, New York.
- He and his wife, Edith, have five children.
- Douglas Florian is known outside of the children's books arena as an abstract artist (see www.douglasflorian.com).
- When Florian first started illustrating children's books in the 1970s and 1980s, he worked mostly on nonfiction.
- While working for Greenwillow Books, he asked about illustrating Jack Prelutsky's poetry anthologies. He was told there was a long waiting list for this, so he decided to write his own poetry to illustrate, and that's how Douglas Florian began his career as a children's poet and book illustrator.
- His first book of poetry was published in 1992, titled *Monster Motel: Poems and Paintings.*
- He won the Lee Bennett Hopkins Award for poetry in 1995 for *Beast Feast.*
- Florian refers to his use of alliteration, puns, invented words, and unconventional structures as his "poetic license."
- His father, Harold Florian, was an artist who shared artwork and the spellbinding effects of the natural world with him. This has inspired his emphasis on nature in his poetry collections.

Celebration Ideas

Tell the Author's Story

Many of Douglas Florian's poems are written in the form of concrete poetry. Convey this poetic form by creating concrete poems that relate to Florian's life story. Following are some sample concrete poems to pull from your "poetry suitcase" (bring in an old suitcase for this purpose).

- Use an outline of the state of New York and put words around its perimeter that relate to Florian's life in this state, such as: "born and raised here," "has not moved from this state," "raises his own children in this state," "college," etc. As you read the phrases, elaborate on their facts. For example, after reading, "born and raised here," tell the students his birthdate, his parents' names and occupations, etc.
- Use an outline of a heart to tell about his family: "husband to Edith since 1985," "father of five children," "loves nature," "passionate about his artwork," etc.
- Use an outline of a tree to tell about his use of nature in his poetry. For example:
  - "four seasons" (mention his four poetry books on the seasons)
  - "animals on land" (*Beast Feast, Omnibeasts, bow wow meow meow, Zoo's Who,* etc.)
  - "animals in the sea" (*In the Swim*)
  - "tiny creatures" (*Insectlopedia; Lizards, Frogs, and Polliwogs*)
  - "animals in the air" (*On the Wing*)
- Use an outline of a paintbrush to tell about his artwork: "watercolors," "collage technique," "abstract artist," "art college" (*he attended the School of the Visual Arts in NY in 1976*), "observant" (*he takes the time to notice the world around him*), "creative," etc.
- Use a picture of a pen to emphasize his writing talents: "author" (*note his extensive list of nonfiction and poetry*), "poetic license" (*discuss his use of new words and puns in his poems*), "vocabulary," "play on words," "alliteration," "rhythm and rhyme," etc.

Write to the Author

Have the students each create a concrete poem in the shape of a heart. Have them write what they love about Florian's poetry books around the perimeter of the heart. In the middle of the heart they could write a brief birthday greeting and sign their name.

Signs of Spring

Since Doug Florian's birthday is near the start of spring, read aloud from his seasonal poetry book, *Handsprings*. Focus on the poems related to the transition between winter and spring. Take the students outside for a "Signs of Spring Scavenger Hunt" and give them paper and pencil to record their findings.

Begin this activity by assembling the students in a circle and telling them to close their eyes. Using their sense of sound, what signs of spring can they hear? Have them write them down on their paper. Next, have them explore the area with their sense of touch, and, finally, focus on the sense of sight. Once the students return to the classroom/library, have them use their signs of spring to create a poetry collage. They will choose several interesting signs of spring and arrange those words on the paper in an artistically appealing way (show them how Florian did this on the cover of the book, *Handsprings*). Next, have them go through magazines or use a search engine to find pictures that relate to those signs of spring and arrange them on the paper, too. Encourage them to use bright crayons to add dimensions to the borders of their pictures, or to emphasize key words. Display these beautiful works of art in your school hallways.

Dog and Cat BINGO!

Play this game after sharing the poems in Florian's book, *bow wow meow meow*. Write the species of the dogs and cats written about in this book on the board in the front of the room. Give each student a page with a blank 5 x 5 grid on it. Instruct the students to choose the names of the dogs and cats from the list and write each name, one time only, in a box. To play the game, open the book and read the poem on that page, without revealing the title (which is the animal's name). Have the students guess which type of dog or cat the poem is about. Students then seek that animal on their BINGO grid and mark it. The first to get five in a row wins the game. Play until all students have made BINGO. Award bookmarks with pictures of cats or dogs on them as prizes.

Craft: Paper Bag Zoo

Many of Florian's illustrations are created by painting watercolors over brown paper bags. Combine this idea with his book, *Zoo's Who*.

Before the Celebration

Write down the names of each animal found in *Zoo's Who*. Put the names in a brown paper lunch bag. Have a brown paper lunch bag on hand for each student.

During the Celebration

Have the students come forward and pick a name from the bag. Tell them to create their own illustration of their animal using tempera paints. They will paint the picture on a brown paper lunch bag. Tell them to paint the head near the lunch bag's opening, and the feet near the bottom (opposite of how the animal would be arranged if the bag were to be used as a puppet). When their paintings are finished, have them open their bags and fill the bag with largely printed words that describe their animal. Challenge them to trade their animal bag with another student and use the word cards in the bag to create their own poems about that animal. The poems could be placed inside the bags, or glued to the back of the bag. This instant classroom zoo makes a wonderful display!

Sharks and Fishes Game

Play this game in honor of Florian's poetry book, *In the Swim*. If possible, reserve the gym, or go outside to the playground to play this game.

Have all the students line up on one side of the playing area; they will be the fishes. Choose one student to be the shark and have her stand in the middle of the play area. At your signal, all the fishes must "swim" (run) over to the opposite end of the play area without being caught by the shark. If the shark tags them, they become a shark, too, and stand in the middle of the play area during the next round of the game. Play continues until one child is left; that child will start the new round of the game as the shark. Start the game by reading aloud Florian's poem, "The Sharks," from this poetry book (page 26).

Poetry Café

Before the Celebration

Tell the students to be ready to select a favorite poem by Douglas Florian during the party. Decorate the room with vases of flowers, and arrange desks so that they convey a sense of coffeehouse atmosphere. Play piano music in the background. Provide hot chocolate and small cakes or brownies.

During the Celebration

Set aside time during the celebration for students to gather together and take turns reading aloud one of his poems, imitating a poetry café format. Model the oral reading of poetry by sharing your favorite poems by Douglas Florian, too. Teach the students to hold up their hands and snap their fingers to show appreciation at the end of each reader's poem!

Rhyme Time

Discuss Florian's creative rhymes, and read aloud a few favorite poems from *Bing Bang Boing*. Seat the students in a circle, and place a stack of word cards face down on the floor in front of you, the leader. Lift a word card and read it aloud. The student seated to your right must supply a rhyming word, followed by the next student, and around the circle. The object of the game is to name a new rhyming word without a pause. If a student hesitates or doesn't say a word right away, he is out. Play continues until one student is left. Start the game with easy rhyming words, such as cat, and progressively move toward more difficult words, such as lizard. Focus on animal words to make this activity connect strongly to Florian's books.

Party Favors

- Pocket notepads to encourage observational skills and collecting ideas on paper
- Small plastic animals (divide a large set of plastic animals into small sets of five for each student
- Inexpensive set of watercolors (available in most party or novelty catalogs)

Party Food

Poetry Stew: Combine sweet ideas (small chocolate candies or chocolate chips), crunchy words (cereal or small pretzels), healthy vocabulary (raisins or other dried fruits), a nutty sense of humor (coconut flakes), and spicy topics (cinnamon candies). "Mix it all together to develop your wonderful talents in writing poetry!"

Happy Birthday, Douglas Florian!

Born March 18, 1950

Poetry About the Seasons

- *Autumnblings*
- *Handsprings*
- *Summersaults*
- *Winter Eyes*

Poetry About Animals

- *Beast Feast*
- *bow wow meow meow: it's rhyming cats and dogs*
- *Dinothesaurus*
- *In the Swim*
- *Insectlopedia*
- *Lizards, Frogs, and Polliwogs*
- *Mammalabilia*
- *Omnibeasts*
- *On the Wing*
- *A Pig is Big*
- *Zoo's Who*

Poetry About Miscellaneous Topics

- *Bing Bang Boing*
- *Comets, Stars, the Moon and Mars: Space Poems & Paintings*
- *Laugheteria*
- *Monster Motel*
- *Poetrees*
- *A Summer Day*
- *A Winter Day*

Nonfiction Picture Books

- *Airplane Ride*
- *An Auto Mechanic: How We Work*
- *At the Zoo*
- *A Beach Day*
- *A Chef (How We Work)*
- *The City*
- *City Street*
- *A Fisher (How We Work)*
- *A Painter (How We Work)*
- *A Potter (How We Work)*
- *See For Yourself (Meet the Author)*
- *Vegetable Garden*
- *A Year in the Country*

Douglas Florian Reading Log

Read 5 books by **March** _____.

On each line, write the title you've read and have your parent/guardian sign that you read it.

Bring this completed reading log to me by **March** _____ and receive your invitation to attend our birthday celebration on

_____.

Date/Time

_____

Title   Parent/Guardian Signature

_____

Title   Parent/Guardian Signature

_____

Title   Parent/Guardian Signature

_____

Title   Parent/Guardian Signature

_____

Title   Parent/Guardian Signature

Happy Birthday, Dear Authors Born in April!

April 1	Anne McCaffrey	April 13	Erik Haugaard
	Tad Hills		**Lee Bennett Hopkins***
	Jan Wahl	April 15	Jacqueline Briggs Martin
April 2	Ruth Heller	April 16	John Christopher
	Anne Mazer		Eva Moore
	Amy Schwartz	April 17	Roy A. Gallant
April 3	Sandra Boynton		Dayal Kaur Khalsa
	Virginia B. Silverstein		Jane Kurtz
April 4	Elizabeth Levy	April 18	Mitchell Sharmat
	Glen Rounds	April 19	Jon Agee
April 5	Lurlene McDaniel		Javaka Steptoe
	Richard Peck	April 21	Jane Breskin Zalben
April 6	Graeme Base	April 22	Eileen Christelow
	Douglas Hill		Ron Koertge
April 7	Donald Carrick	April 25	George Ella Lyon
	Alice Schertle		Stuart J. Murphy
April 8	Susan Bonners		Alvin Schwartz
	Harold Keith	April 26	Patricia Reilly Giff
	Steven Schnur		Marilyn Nelson
April 10	David A. Adler	April 27	John Burningham
	Wendy Halperin		Barbara Park
	Martin Waddell		Nancy Shaw
April 11	Graham Salisbury	April 28	Brett Harvey
	April Pulley Sayre*		Amy Hest
April 12	Beverly Cleary	April 29	Jill Paton Walsh
	Gary Soto*	April 30	Dorothy Hinshaw Patent

*Author featured in this chapter

Happy Birthday, Dear April Pulley Sayre!

About April Pulley Sayre

- April Pulley Sayre was born in Greenville, South Carolina, on April 11, 1966.
- She has written over 55 informational picture books!
- April has traveled around the world, most often to Latin American countries, where she has been inspired to write many of her books.
- She met her husband in college. Together, they share a love of nature and forest conservation.
- Some of her favorite childhood memories involve riding her pony bareback with her best friend through the Appalachian Mountain region, and picking wildflowers with her mom.
- She graduated from Duke University with a Bachelor's Degree in Biology.
- Her favorite Latin American country is Panama. She and her husband have led tours through this country.
- She dedicated her book, *Dig, Wait, Listen: A Desert Toad's Tale* to her grandfather, "Who taught [her] that truth has a story too." Use this to set the tone for the reading of her books throughout the month.

Celebration Ideas

Tell a Story about the Author:

April Pulley Sayre has written so many informational books about animals that it seems natural to use this theme in the story about her life. Print and cut out the animals from pages 153–156.

Tape the animals on the whiteboard/chalkboard and write "April Pulley Sayre's Zoo" in bold letters across the top. Tell the students,

"April Sayre has spent her entire life surrounded by animals and has always been fascinated by wildlife. In honor of that, today's story will focus on her life with animals. To learn more about her life, we'll take an imaginary trip to the zoo!"

- Horse—April grew up in South Carolina. One of her favorite memories is of breaking in her pony with her best friend. She and her friend each rode their ponies bareback along the roads of rural South Carolina!
- Hawk—By the time April was a teenager, she worked at a raptor center. She spent a lot of time with rehabilitating hawks and owls!
- Bird house—April loves birds! As a child, her mother taught her all about the birds and wildflowers that lived and grew near their home. She still loves to go bird watching with her husband, Jeff. They often visit Whitefish Point in the upper peninsula of Michigan and watch hawks, eagles, and cranes as they migrate.
- Deer—While earning her bachelor of arts degree from Duke University (in biology), she met her husband, Jeff Sayre, a forest conservationist. They spend a lot of time in the forest, and have seen many deer through the years!
- Toad—April wrote the book, *Dig, Wait, Listen: A Desert Toad's Tale*, because she loves all animals of nature. She dedicated this book to her grandpa, who told her, "Truth has a story, too." April has dedicated her life to making sure that she tells the true story of animals to her readers!
- Vulture—This animal is the subject of her book, *Vulture View*. It earned her the Theodore Seuss Geisel Honor Award in 2008!
- Howler Monkey—April and her husband have traveled to 27 different countries, but one of their favorite countries to visit is

Panama. They have even led tour groups in Panama! April's book, *Meet the Howlers*, is set in Panama.

- Rabbit—Her recent book, *If You're Hoppy*, presents a variety of animals that hop in a fun, rhyming book. Thank you, April Pulley Sayre, for making reading about animals such a hopping-good time!

Write to the Author

Visit her website at www.aprilsayre.com to read her blog and find out about her latest adventures in nature. To send her birthday greetings, create a large mural of a natural habitat, such as a forest and lake. Then have the students each choose an animal's name from a hat. They will draw a picture of this animal and cut it out. Have them write a brief birthday greeting to April Pulley Sayre on the animal's body, then glue the animal to the mural. Send the mural to the author along with a cover letter explaining your program.

Noodle Man-ia!

In honor of Pulley Sayre's book, *Noodle Man: The Pasta Superhero*, have the students participate in the following pasta activities.

- Pasta Collages: Provide the students with a variety of uncooked pasta shapes. Have them create an illustration of a pasta emergency for Al Dente to resolve. They will draw a setting on white construction paper. Tell them to use brightly colored crayons and press down hard to make vibrant outlines of buildings, trees, etc. Next, have them glue down their pasta shapes. They could paint the pastas with tempera paints. Finally, have them draw their own version of "Noodle Man," and glue it onto the collage.
- Pasta Party: Provide cooked pasta and set up a buffet of various toppings, such as: shredded cheese, chopped vegetables, tomato sauce, etc. Allow each student time to visit the buffet and enjoy their pasta dish.
- Pasta Pot Relay Race: Divide the students into two teams, and have them line up, single file, behind a line. Place an empty pot a good distance from each team of players. Give each student a plastic spoon and

place a large bowl of uncooked pasta on a desk between the two teams. On signal, the first two players use their spoons to scoop up some pasta and walk quickly to their empty pot, dumping the pasta into the pot. Next, they run to the next teammate in line and tag him so he can fill the spoon and get to the pot. The first team to fill the pot to a pre-determined level is the winner.

Web of Life Activity

After reading *Trout Are Made of Trees*, discuss with the children how everything in nature is connected. Ask the class to make a list of items found in the typical backyard. The list will likely include: soil, worms, grass, ants, bumble bees, trees, bushes, flowers, rabbits, spiders, birds, toys, sunlight, rocks, etc.

List their ideas on the board and then write the words on index cards, one word per card. Distribute the cards to the children. It's best to have one word for each child at the celebration. Arrange the students in a circle. Using a ball of string, talk about how the items are connected and give the string to one child. That child must roll the ball of string to another child whose card names an item connected to the first child's item. That child holds the string and rolls the ball to another child that is connected to the first or second child. This continues until all connections are made and the children have created a complex web. Ask the class a few questions, such as, "What will happen if we remove the ants (for example)?" Have the child holding the ant card drop her string so that the class can see how many items this would affect.

Continue to play, asking a variety of questions such as, "How many different ways can we make a web?" "Are some items more influential than others?" "How do people affect the environment?" "Why do some backyards have more wildlife than others?" Conclude the activity by having the students fill in the blanks: "_____ are made of _____, because _____ eat _____." They could illustrate the pictures and collate the pages to make a group book for either the classroom or school library (see Rockwell, Sherwood, & Williams, 1986).

Nature's Treasure Hunt

So many of April Pulley Sayre's books teach us about natural habitats and animal behaviors. Capitalize on this by having a treasure hunt on the school playground. This can be done in several ways. If the playground is not conducive to finding natural objects, bring them into the room, and have the students find them inside. Talk about where these objects would be found in their natural environments.

- Acrostic Poem Treasure Hunt: Write the letters of April Pulley Sayre's name vertically along the left margin of a paper, and leave a blank line after each name. Challenge the students to find one object on the playground for each letter in her name. If her name is too long for this activity, change the vertical word to "Nature," or "April Findings," or "Spring," etc.

- Create a 3 x 3 grid. In each box, write an item that they could find on the playground. Give each student a paper and a few crayons. Tell them to go outside and find the items. They must use their crayons to make a crayon rubbing of the item when it is found. They make the rubbing in the corresponding box on the grid. The first child to fill in the grid is the winner. Award a small prize to all participants, such as: plastic magnifying glass, plastic click bugs, etc. Here is a sample grid:

Oak tree (list other types of trees to help students learn to identify them)	Wood chips	Grass blades
Pine cone	Free Choice	Rough surface (rocks, gravel)
Leaf	Seed pod (acorn, maple tree pod, etc.)	Weeds (Dandelions, etc.)

- Rainbow Hunt: Divide a paper into seven sections, one for each color in the spectrum (red, orange, yellow, green, blue, purple). Create interesting shapes or outlines of items from nature to create the sections on the paper. Send the children outside to find at least one item for each color.

Who Am I?

This is a fun activity for children to play because it provides a review of various animals that they would have read about in April Pulley Sayre's books. Before the celebration, write the name of one animal (found in Sayre's books) on a sheet of card stock. Make one animal card per child. During the celebration, tape the animal card to the back of each child. Tell the children that their goal is to figure out the name of the animal taped to their back. To do this, they must mingle with their classmates and ask a question that can only be answered with "yes," or "no." Their job is to deduce the name of their animal after gaining clues through the answers to their questions. When they think they know the name of their animal, they must ask, "Am I a _____?" If the answer is "yes!" they have won the game. Conclude the activity by having the children make lunch bag puppets of their animals. They could use the animals to act out a play.

Watercolor Sunset Paintings

In honor of new knowledge about dust after reading *Stars Beneath Your Bed: The Surprising Story of Dust*, talk about the amazing colors of the sunset and how dust plays an integral role in it. Use a search engine to find photographs of sunsets, and project these on a screen for the whole group to view. Talk about the colors and review the information from the book. Give each student a 12" x 18" sheet of white construction paper and a set of watercolor paints. Have the students paint a large, round sun on their paper using a lot of water to moisten the area. Have them use other colors to bleed into the round sun, creating a blurred effect. Show them how to dip their paintbrushes into water and hold it over the sky to drip onto the paint for a unique effect. Challenge them to cover the paper with beautiful colors, just like the dust filters through the sky to reflect the colors while the sun sets at night.

Walk Like an Animal!

Read aloud *If You're Hoppy*, and encourage the children to move like the animals found in this chant based on the folksong, "If You're Happy and You Know It."

Next, go to the gymnasium or playground to play Animal Tag. Divide the students into two teams. Have each team meet at a line drawn at opposite ends of the play area to quietly decide which animal they will imitate. Call both teams back to the center of the area, assigning a line for each team to stand on, facing the other team, approximately five feet apart. One team goes first and begins to move like the animal they've selected. They cannot talk. The other team will have a chance to guess the animal's name. If they are correct, the team who had been imitating that animal must turn and run to their line without being tagged by the other team. All those who are tagged must join the other team. Take turns between teams for imitating and guessing animals. Set up a signal in which the guessing team states its guess. This will keep the guessing/chasing element organized.

Earth Day Connection

April Pulley Sayre's birth month also happens to be the month in which we celebrate Earth Day! Since her books all center on natural habitats and animals, this author is a perfect connection to Earth Day activities. During the celebration of her birthday, have the students make posters that encourage their peers to help the environment by putting litter in garbage cans, or recycling paper, etc. The students could also write letters to the National Park Service, requesting additional conservation information to share with their friends and classmates.

Contact the National Park Service at: www.nps.gov. Students can also become Junior Rangers by going to www.nps.gov/webrangers.

Party Food: Bagel Faces!

Tell the group that they will make animal faces in honor of Pulley Sayre's newest book, *Rah Rah Radishes!*. Provide bagel halves and cream cheese or peanut butter for students to spread over their bagel half. Next, provide a buffet of prepared vegetables that the students will use to create facial features. Possibilities include: grape tomatoes, olives, shredded carrots, celery slices, sliced radishes, shredded zucchini, etc. Encourage them to pick an animal that has been featured in one of Pulley Sayre's books. Have them plan out their animal's face before going to the buffet to select the vegetables. As always, check for allergies beforehand! Once all of the animal faces have been assembled, take a group photo to include in the birthday greeting for April Pulley Sayre, and remember to sing "Happy Birthday!"

Party Favors

Small magnifying glasses, insect boxes (cardboard boxes with metal screening), small plastic insects or animals, animal stickers.

April Pulley Sayre's Zoo Animals

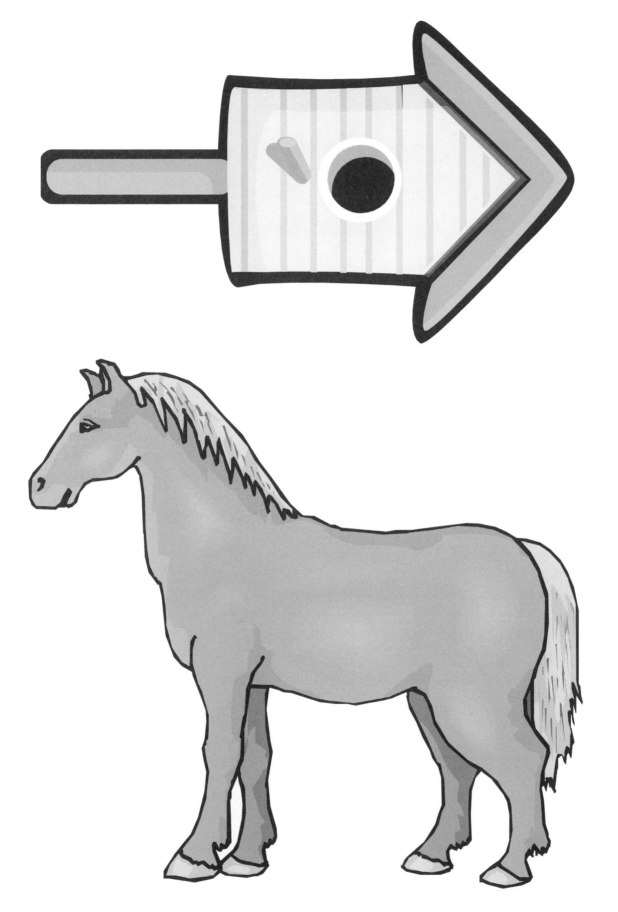

April Pulley Sayre's Zoo Animals

April Pulley Sayre's Zoo Animals

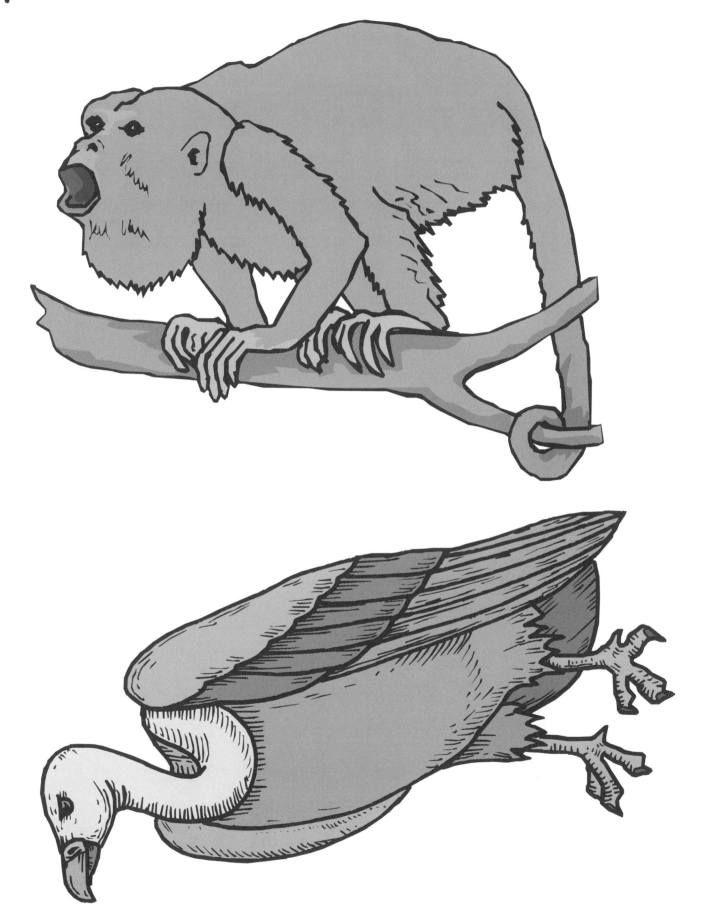

April Pulley Sayre's Zoo Animals

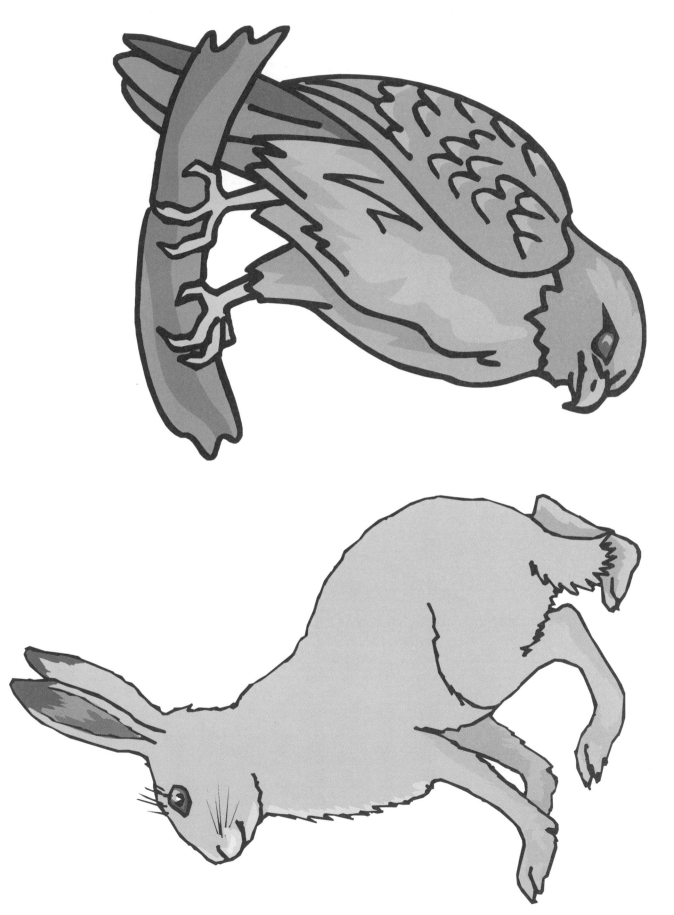

Happy Birthday, April Pulley Sayre!

Born April 11, 1966

Picture Books

- *If You're Hoppy*
- *Noodle Man: The Pasta Superhero*

Nonfiction

- *Ant, Ant, Ant: An Insect Chant*
- *Army Ant Parade*
- *Bird, Bird, Bird: A Chirping Chant*
- *The Bumblebee Queen*
- *Crocodile Listens*
- *Dig, Wait, Listen: A Desert Toad's Tale*
- *Home at Last: A Song of Migration*
- *Honk, Honk, Goose! Canada Geese Start a Family*
- *The Hungry Hummingbird*
- *Hush Little Puppy*
- *If You Should Hear a Honey Guide*
- *It's My City! A Singing Map*
- *Meet the Howlers*
- *One is a Snail, Ten is a Crab*
- *Rah, Rah, Radishes! A Vegetable Chant*
- *Splish, Splash! Animal Baths!*
- *Shadows*
- *Stars Beneath Your Bed: The Surprising Story of Dust*
- *Trout, Trout, Trout: A Fish Chant*
- *Turtle, Turtle, Watch Out!*
- *Vulture View*

April Pulley Sayre Reading Log

Read 5 books by **April** ___.

On each line, write the title you've read and have your parent/guardian sign that you read it.

Bring this completed reading log to me by **April** ___ and receive your invitation to attend our birthday celebration on

_____.

Date/Time

_____
Title   Parent/Guardian Signature

_____
Title   Parent/Guardian Signature

_____
Title   Parent/Guardian Signature

_____
Title   Parent/Guardian Signature

_____
Title   Parent/Guardian Signature

Happy Birthday, Dear Gary Soto!

About Gary Soto

- Gary Soto was born on April 12, 1952, in Fresno, California, where he lived throughout his childhood.
- He is one of three children: brother Rick, sister Debra, and himself!
- He has written poetry for adults, young adults, and children.
- He has also written a variety of picture books and novels geared toward a middle school audience.
- He earned a BA in English at Fresno City College.
- He published his first poem in his college newspaper in 1972.
- He married his wife, Carolyn, in 1975. They have one daughter, Mariko, who is a veterinarian.
- He enjoys reading, writing, gardening, and baking cookies!
- He opened a museum of his work at Fresno City College in 2010.

Celebration Ideas

Tell the Author's Story

Gary Soto's books reflect his Mexican American heritage. In honor of Mexico, tell the story of his life while playing a traditional Mexican party game called La Florón. Before the celebration, type up 5–7 questions that students could ask about Gary Soto. Cut the list of questions into individual strips, one question per strip, and fold each in half. Place the questions into a colorful bowl or cookie jar. During the celebration, arrange the students in a circle and give them a silk white flower to pass around. Begin to tell the story of Gary Soto and then stop after a brief introduction. The child who is left holding the white flower must reach into the bowl and select a question to ask you. Here are some sample questions and answers:

- *How did he become interested in writing books and poetry?*
  Answer: Gary Soto loved to read, and, during high school and college, he discovered some favorite authors like Gabriel Garcia Marquez and Pablo Neruda. They inspired him to write his own stories and poems.
- *Was he a good student in school?*
  Answer: No! He had a very low grade point average in high school, but once he developed a passion for writing, he took his studies more seriously.
- *Does he have a family?*
  Answer: Yes! He and his wife, Carolyn, have a grown daughter, Mariko. He is also the middle of three children: big brother, Rick; and little sister, Debra.
- *What does he like to do when he isn't writing?*
  Answer: He loves to read a lot of books. He also enjoys hanging out in his hometown of Fresno, California, working in his garden, and baking cookies.

(For additional questions and answers, check out his website at www.garysoto.com. Click on the link, FAQs.)

Send Birthday Cards to Gary Soto

Use a die-cut machine to cut card stock into the shape of a cat (in honor of his series of picture books about Chato, the cat). Have the students write their birthday greetings on one side of the cat shape and then decorate the other side.

Craft: Make Maracas!

Gather enough toilet paper tubes for one per child. Cover one end of the tube with paper. Have the children pour dried beans or rice into the tube, then cover the opposite end with paper. Use colorful tempera paints to decorate the "maracas," and have them shake the tubes to the beat of some of their favorite poems by Gary Soto.

Hunt Down the Ingredients

Tell the students that in this activity, they will help each other find the ingredients needed to make a birthday treat called churritos! In honor of Soto's book, *Too Many Tamales*, tell the students that they will make "Too many churritos!"

Divide the students into small groups of 3–4. Give each group the first card with a clue on it to start them on their way. Each clue will lead them to a new clue with one of the necessary ingredients or utensils attached. By the end of the hunt, they will have found all of the ingredients and tools needed to make the churritos.

Here is a sample set of clues for one group:

- Look near the new fiction book display and you will find some tortillas!
- Muy bien! Now walk quietly over to the writing center where you'll find some cooking tools (plastic knives, paper plates).
- Fantástico! Tip toe over to the nature books on display where you'll find a baggie full of cinnamon.
- Magnífico! Skip over to the CDs to find a baggie full of sugar.
- Espléndido! Hop on over to the art station to find the recipe card.
- Muy bien! You are ready to bring your supplies to the tables so you can make your Churritos!

Recipe for Churritos

Ingredients:
- Small flour tortillas
- Teaspoon of cinnamon
- 2 tablespoons of sugar
- vanilla ice cream (you will supply separately)
- cooking spray
- plastic knife
- paper plate
- baking pan

Directions:
1. Preheat the oven to 350°F (you will do this before the celebration begins).
2. Place the tortillas on your paper plate and use the knife to cut tortillas into 4 pieces (one tortilla and knife per student).
3. Coat baking sheet with cooking spray (you will do this before the celebration).
4. Place tortilla pieces on the baking sheet.
5. Sprinkle with cinnamon and sugar (each student can do this for her tortilla).
6. Bake until crispy (5–7 minutes).
7. Serve with vanilla ice cream.

If the Shoe Fits Relay Race

Talk with the students about Rigo's situation in this book, and how he and his family solved the problem. Then, have the students take off their shoes, and put them into one large pile on one end of the room (or gymnasium or playground). Divide the group into two teams, and line them up a good distance from the shoe pile. On your signal, have the first player from each team run to the pile, find both of his shoes, put them on, and run back to tag the next teammate in line. The race continues until one team successfully has all players lined up with their own shoes on their feet!

Chato the Cat

Soto has written three books about a cat named Chato (*Chato's Kitchen*, *Chato and the Party Animals*, and *Chato Goes Cruisin'*). Each book focuses on friendship and parties. Incorporate these books into the celebration through the following activities.

- Cat and Mouse Game: In *Chato's Kitchen*, Chato tries to deceive the neighborhood mice by inviting them over for dinner, but the mice have the last laugh! Act out this scenario by playing this common playground game. Have all the students stand in a circle, holding hands. Choose one student to be Chato, and another to be a mouse. The mouse starts the game inside the circle of students, and the cat (Chato) stays on the outside of the circle. The mouse runs out of the circle and around it, while trying to keep from getting tagged by Chato. Only the mouse is allowed to run inside the circle, as long as students lift up their joined hands to let the mouse into it! The students will act as friends of the mouse and block Chato from entering the circle. Once Chato tags the mouse, the mouse becomes Chato for the next round of the game.

- Chato Chatter: Distribute papers with a 6 x 6 grid on it. Leave the first box (top left) blank, then write one letter per box for Chato's name across the top row. For the boxes on the far-left column, keep the top box blank, and fill in the remaining five boxes with categories based on what the students know about Chato, such as: favorite foods, cruise activities, Chato's personality traits, favorite books, favorite songs, etc. Set a timer for a pre-determined time limit, and have the students fill in as many boxes as possible during that time. They must fill in the category boxes with an item that starts with the letter at the top of that column. Once the timer rings, tell the students to put down their pencils and share their answers. Provide small prizes for everyone, such as bookmarks, stickers, pencils, etc.

Sample Game Grid:

	C	H	A	T	O
Favorite Foods	Chorizo				
Personality Traits	Cunning				
Favorite Games	Cat's Cradle				
Cruise Activities	Climbing chairs				
Favorite Music	Classical				

Door Prizes

In honor of Soto's silly story, *The Old Man and His Door*, have a fun raffle in your room! Gather small prizes (most teachers usually have a plethora of extra fast food meal prizes, small toys from dollar stores, paperbacks from book orders, etc.). Cover the classroom/library door with colorful wrapping paper, and tape the prizes to the door (be sure to have at least one prize per student). Place each child's name on a slip of paper and put the slips into a hat. When each name is drawn from the hat, call out the name, and then ask the child a question about one of Soto's books, or ask the child to tell the English translation of one of the Spanish words used in Soto's books. Once the child answers the question correctly, he/she can go to the door and remove a prize. To add more suspense, wrap the individual prizes before displaying them on the door so that the students will have to wait until everyone has a prize before opening them to see what they've won!

April Read Alouds

Gary Soto's book, *Baseball in April and Other Stories*, is a collection of short stories about growing up in central California. Each story tells about typical experiences for children, such as trying out for Little League, hanging out with friends, and dealing with grandparents. This book lends itself to read alouds throughout the month, especially for third graders because they would relate to the stories more than younger students.

Party Favors

Use a piñata, filled with Mexican candy and small erasers, toys, etc. To ensure that each child gets an equal amount once the piñata is broken open, package the candies and prizes in small resealable baggies, one per student.

Party Food

Churritos (see Hunt Down the Ingredients activity on page 160), chips and guacamole dip and/or salsa, Jarritos™ brand soda.

Happy Birthday, Gary Soto!

Born April 12, 1952

Picture Books

- *Big Bushy Mustache*
- *Chato Goes Cruisin'*
- *Chato's Kitchen*
- *Chato and the Party Animals*
- *If The Shoe Fits*
- *My Little Car*
- *The Old Man and His Door*
- *Snapshots From The Wedding*
- *Too Many Tamales*

Chapter Books

- *Baseball In April and Other Stories*
- *The Cat's Meow*
- *Marisol: An American Girl Story*
- *The Skirt*

Poetry

- *Canto Familiar*
- *A Fire in My Hands*
- *Fearless Fernie*
- *Neighborhood Odes*
- *Partly Cloudy: Poems of Love and Longing*
- *Worlds Apart: Traveling with Fernie and Me*

Gary Soto Reading Log

Read 5 books by **April** ____.

On each line, write the title you've read and have your parent/guardian sign that you read it.

Bring this completed reading log to me by **April** ____ and receive your invitation to attend our birthday celebration on

_____.

Date/Time

_____

Title   Parent/Guardian Signature

_____

Title   Parent/Guardian Signature

_____

Title   Parent/Guardian Signature

_____

Title   Parent/Guardian Signature

_____

Title   Parent/Guardian Signature

Happy Birthday, Dear Lee Bennett Hopkins!

About Lee Bennett Hopkins

- Lee Bennett Hopkins was born in Scranton, Pennsylvania, on April 13, 1938.
- He is the oldest of three children: a brother and a sister.
- When he was 13 years old, his parents divorced and he lived in low-income housing in New Jersey with his mother and siblings.
- Lee's first love of reading came through comic books.
- When he was in high school, one teacher, Ms. McLaughlin, mentored him and inspired him to read plays, and other literature.
- He earned his BA in Education in 1960 from Newark State Teachers College (now Kean University).
- His first teaching job was for a sixth grade classroom in New Jersey.
- During this first teaching position, Lee Bennett Hopkins discovered the power of poetry to inspire his students, and he integrated it into all subjects.
- By 1964 he earned a master's degree from Bank Street College and was hired as a resource teacher for the city's at-risk children, just like he was as a child.
- He used African American poetry to inspire the children.
- He worked for Scholastic Books from 1968–1974 and published many anthologies during that time.
- Since 1974 he has worked full time as a poet and anthologist of poetry for children.
- He created the Lee Bennett Hopkins/International Reading Association Promising Poet Award in 1995.

Celebration Ideas

Tell the Author's Story

<u>Before the Celebration</u>

Think of nine numbers that relate to Lee Bennett Hopkins' life story. Write them down and place them in a birthday party bag.

<u>During the Celebration</u>

List the numbers on the board and distribute a 3 x 3 Bingo grid. Instruct the students to assign one number per box, using all nine numbers. When they have filled in all the boxes on their grids, pull one of the numbers from the party bag and relate a clue about the meaning of the number without telling the number. Have the students raise their hands to guess which number best answers the clue. Here are a few numbers you could use for this activity:

- His age: Tell the students that this number indicates how old Lee Bennett Hopkins will be when he celebrates his birthday this year.
- 3: Number of kids in his family when he was a child.
- Number of years he's worked full time as a poet (1974–today).
- Number of years that he's awarded the Lee Bennett Hopkins/IRA Award to a promising poet (1995–today).
- 98: Number of poetry anthologies that he has compiled since 1969 (as of 2010).
- 21: Number of original poems by Hopkins in his book, *Good Rhymes, Good Times*.
- 365: Number of days in a year that Hopkins is thinking about poetry: "There isn't a day that goes by that I'm not reading poetry or working on a poem of my own" (*The Writing Bug*).

- 6: Number of years that Hopkins taught in the public schools of Fair Lawn, New Jersey.
- 2: Number of autobiographies that he's written (*The Writing Bug; Been to Yesterdays: Poems of a Life*).

Write to the Author

Have the students write a cinquain poem about themselves. This is a five-line poem that is based on syllables. (See Hopkins' book, *Pass the Poetry, Please*, for a discussion about this poetic form.) Most teachers might be familiar with using this poem in connection with grammatical structures, but Hopkins writes that this format actually calls for the use of the following syllable pattern: Line 1 = 2 syllables (you could have the students write their first names here). Line 2 = 4 syllables (this could be 2, 2-syllable words about themselves). Line 3 = 6 syllables, line 4 = 8 syllables, and line 5 = 2 syllables (usually a repetition of their name from line 1). They could make basic birthday cards and put their completed cinquains on the inside of the card, along with a birthday greeting. He'll be very impressed that you had the students write this poem in the traditional syllable format!

Craft: "Keep a Poem in Your Pocket!"

Make locker pockets from old denim jeans pockets.

<u>Before the Celebration</u>

Send a note home to parents requesting a pair of old blue jeans. Cut out the back pockets on each pair of jeans. Use hot glue to adhere four magnetic discs to the back of each pocket.

<u>During the Celebration</u>

Provide buttons, fabric markers, and ribbons for the students to use in decorating their locker pockets. Have the students scour one of Hopkins' poetry anthologies to find a poem that they'd like to copy on an index card and place inside the pocket. Allow the students to put their finished locker pockets in their school lockers. They will serve as poetry collectors, and handy pencil cases, too!

Mystery Word

<u>Before the Celebration</u>

Inflate five balloons and tape them to the board at the front of the room. Choose one balloon to be the mystery balloon. Make an "X" with two strips of tape on the side of this balloon. Select one of the poems in Hopkins' anthology, *Happy Birthday* and choose five words from the poem that you want the children to guess to fill in the blank. Write one word on each of five index cards, and tape the word cards to each balloon. The word card that is taped to the balloon with the "X" on it will be the mystery word.

<u>During the Celebration</u>

Write the poem on the board, leaving out the five words. As you read the poem aloud, have the students raise their hands to tell which of the five words should fill in the blank. Take the word card off the balloon and tape it on the line (blank space) in the poem where the children think it belongs. Then use a straight pin to pop the balloon. Insert the pin on the side of the balloon and tell the students, "If it pops, then it wasn't the mystery word." Continue until a student chooses the word on the balloon with the "X" on it. Take off the word, read the poem aloud, and ask the students if it makes sense. Insert the straight pin into the balloon, through the scotch tape "X." The balloon will not pop because the tape will seal the area around the hole. Continue to hold onto the pin, and remove it while announcing that they discovered the mystery word!

Poetry Treasure Hunt

In this treasure hunt, students will seek the lines from one of Hopkins' poems. Before the celebration, choose four poems (one per small group of students). Divide the poem into four sections (four stanzas, four rhyming couplets, etc.). Type up the poem, using self-adhesive label paper (eight labels per sheet). Type one section per label, and print it out on the label paper. Cut the labels apart. Type up the four hunt clues, and print them on colorful card stock. Cut each clue apart, and staple the clue to the corresponding label. Hide the labels around the classroom or library before the children enter the room. Here is a sample set of clues and poem:

- Clue #1: Please help! I'm a poem whose lines are missing.
  Here is my first line:
  - *Last Laugh,* by Lee Bennett Hopkins
    They all laughed when I told them
    I wanted to be . . .
    Find my next line! Look by the fish tank.
- Clue #2:
  - *A woman in space*
    Floating so free.
    What comes next? Check by the writing center!
- Clue #3:
  - *But they won't laugh at me*
    When they finally see . . .
    Almost done! Go to the author wall for the poem's ending!
- Clue #4:
  - *My feet up on Mars*
    And my face on TV.
    You did it! Now practice reading this poem aloud with your group! You will perform this poem to the whole class once every other group has found their poems.

Provide each group with a handout that serves as the template on which they will adhere their poem lines by peeling the labels from their self-adhesive backing. Make the template by creating four text boxes, each with the same dimensions as the adhesive labels, lined up vertically down the middle of the page. Add color to the handout by placing images of book covers from several of Hopkins' anthologies around the border of the template.

Hand in Hand: An American History Through Poetry

This unique poetry anthology is organized into chapters based on historical events (the first Thanksgiving, Revolutionary War, pioneers,

etc.). If the students are learning about one of these periods in their Social Studies class, share the corresponding poems throughout the month. On the day of the celebration, have the students think about their lives and memorable events that have happened in recent years. Make a list on the board. Next, have the students each trace their own hand, with fingers extended, and cut it out. The students will select one event from the list on the board and write it on their handprints. Finally, have the students write five sentences about the event, one per finger. Display their "hand poems" on a bulletin board, or have them each read their "hand poems" aloud.

Show It, Poet!

Play this fun game during the celebration, or whenever there is time for a quick activity. Choose one student to begin the game. The student will stand at the front of the room and think of a word or a topic from one of Hopkins' anthologies. The student should say, "I am thinking of a word from one of Lee Bennett Hopkins' poems that rhymes with _____." The rest of the students must try to guess the word. For example, if the word is *sport,* the student will say, "I am thinking of a word from one of Lee Bennett Hopkins' poems that rhymes with *court.*" Students will raise their hands to play. When the player calls on a student, that student must ask a question that defines the word, such as, "Is it a place for ships to dock?" The player would then answer, "No, it is not a *port.*" If the player can't think of the rhyming word to answer the student's question, that student can ask a second question. Play continues until the correct word is guessed. The student who guesses the correct word gets to think of a new target word.

School Supplies: A Book of Poems

Most of the poems in this anthology describe an item, such as a book, a compass, or a paperclip. The content of the poem does not name the item, so this anthology makes for a fun interactive read aloud. Read a poem aloud and have the students try to guess the "mystery school supply." Another creative way to share these poems is to read them aloud to the class and then dump out a backpack full of a variety of school supplies. Allow the students to look at the pile of objects for a minute, then put them back into the backpack. Give the students a sheet of paper and a new pencil to use for this activity. Tell them to try to remember all the school supplies that were in the backpack. Set a timer for a minute, and have them write as many items as they can remember. The child who has the longest list of items from the backpack is the winner.

Party Food

Provide a sheet cake that is decorated to resemble an opened book of poetry. Write a birthday wish for Lee Bennett Hopkins and place a candle on it. Sing "Happy Birthday, Dear Lee Bennett Hopkins!"

Party Favors

Use brown paper lunch bags and decorate them to resemble houses (in honor of *City I Love* and *Home to Me: Poems Across America*). Fill the bags with small favors as mementos of Hopkins' various anthologies. Some ideas include school supplies, baseball cards (*Opening Days: Sports Poems*; *Extra Innings: Baseball Poems*), bookmarks with lists of Hopkins' anthologies, small notebooks for encouraging the writing of poetry, Tootsie Pop™ lollipop to remind the students that poetry gets to the heart of an idea with a few words—just like the heart of these lollipops has a special treat inside of them!

Happy Birthday, Lee Bennett Hopkins!

Born April 13, 1938

Easy Readers

- *Dizzy Dinosaurs: Silly Dino Poems*
- *Hamsters, Shells, and Spelling Bees: School Poems*
- *A Pet for Me: Poems*
- *Sports! Sports! Sports! A Poetry Collection*
- *Surprises*
- *Weather: Poems for all Seasons*

Poetry Anthologies

- *A-Haunting We Will Go*
- *Alphathoughts: Alphabet Poems*
- *City I Love*
- *Climb Into My Lap: First Poems To Read Together*
- *Dinosaurs*
- *Easter Buds are Springing: Poems for Easter*
- *Extra Innings*
- *Good Books, Good Times!*
- *Good Rhymes, Good Times*
- *Got Geography!*
- *Hand In Hand*
- *Home To Me: Poems Across America*
- *Hoofbeats, Claws, and Rippled Fins: Creature Poems*
- *Incredible Inventions*
- *LIVES: Poems About Famous Americans*
- *Marvelous Math: A Book of Poems*
- *My America: A Poetry Atlas of the United States*

- *Opening Days: Sports Poems*
- *School Supplies: A Book of Poems*
- *Spectacular Science: A Book of Poems*
- *Wonderful Words: Poems About Reading, Writing, Speaking, and Listening*
- *Witching Time*

Autobiography

- *Been to Yesterdays: Poems of a Life*
- *The Writing Bug*

Lee Bennett Hopkins Reading Log

Read 5 books by **April** _____.

On each line, write the title you've read and have your parent/guardian sign that you read it.

Bring this completed reading log to me by **April** _____ and receive your invitation to attend our birthday celebration on

_____.
Date/Time

_____
Title   Parent/Guardian Signature

_____
Title   Parent/Guardian Signature

_____
Title   Parent/Guardian Signature

_____
Title   Parent/Guardian Signature

_____
Title   Parent/Guardian Signature

Happy Birthday, Dear Authors Born in May!

May 1	Robert Bender	May 13	Bernadette Watts
May 2	Mary Quattlebaum	May 14	Eoin Colfer
	Susan Shreve	May 15	Kadir Nelson
May 3	Karen Heywood	May 16	Caroline Arnold
	Mavis Jukes		Bruce Coville
May 4	Doug Cushman	May 17	Eloise Greenfield
	Don Wood		Gary Paulsen
May 5	**J. Patrick Lewis***	May 18	Debbie Dadey
	Leo Lionni		Lillian Hoban
	Todd Strasser	May 19	Arthur Dorros
May 6	Randall Jarrell		Sarah Ellis
	Ted Lewin		Tom Feelings
	Giulio Maestro	May 20	Caralyn Buehner
	Kristin O'Connell George		Carol Carrick
May 7	Erik Craddock		Mary Pope Osborne
	Nonny Hogrogian	May 21	Bonnie Bryant
May 8	Ellen Howard	May 23	Susan Cooper
	Milton Meltzer	May 24	Diane DeGroat
May 9	Richard Adams	May 25	Martha Alexander
	Eleanor Estes		Barbara Bottner
May 10	Christopher Paul Curtis		Ann McGovern
	Bruce McMillan	May 26	Ruth M. Arthur
May 11	**Juanita Havill***		Sheila Greenwald
	Peter Sís*	May 28	Debby Atwell
	Jane Sutton	May 29	Eleanor Coerr
May 12	Jennifer Armstrong		Brock Cole
	Betsy Lewin		Andrew Clements
	*Author featured in this chapter	May 30	Millicent Selsam

Happy Birthday, Dear Peter Sís!

About Peter Sís

- Peter Sís was born on May 11, 1949, in Brno, Czechoslovakia.
- He attended the Academy of Applied Arts in Prague and the Royal College of Art in London.
- He began his career as a filmmaker, and he won several prestigious awards throughout Europe for his animated films.
- He came to the United States in 1982 in order to film the 1984 Winter Olympics, but when Czechoslovakia and the other Eastern European Communist Countries decided to boycott the Olympics, he was told to return to Czechoslovakia.
- Peter decided to stay in the United States, and he was granted asylum.
- In 1986, Peter wrote to Maurice Sendak and he began to shift careers, from filmmaker to children's book illustrator.
- The first book he illustrated, *The Whipping Boy* by Sid Fleishman, won the Newbery Medal in 1986. Since then he has written and/or illustrated over 30 books for children!
- Peter earned a Caldecott Honor for his book, *Starry Messenger: Galileo Galilei*, and for *The Wall: Growing Up Behind the Iron Curtain*.
- He won the Robert F. Sibert Medal for the best work of nonfiction published in the United States in a given year for his book, *The Wall: Growing Up Behind the Iron Curtain*.
- Peter designed the poster for the 1984 Academy Award winning film, *Amadeus*, directed by Milos Forman.
- He has painted murals for the Washington/Baltimore airport, and for a New York City subway station.
- Peter lives in New York City with his wife and children.
- He is the first children's book illustrator to be named a MacArthur Fellow.

Celebration Ideas

Tell a Story about the Author

Peter Sís often includes mazes in his illustrations. Based on this unique visual element, create a story about his life using a template of a maze. Connect the idea of a maze to the fact that Peter's life took many twists and turns. Use a search engine to find a maze template, and copy it into a PowerPoint™ slide. Conduct an image search for the following pictures: map of Czechoslovakia, photograph of Prague, Communist symbol (scythe and pick ax), paintbrush, film reel, music note, American flag, one of his book covers, home.

Copy these images into the maze, placing them in the order that you will talk about them. Place the final image at the end of the maze. The pictures suggested above could be used as prompts to tell about his life:

- Map of Czechoslovakia: Peter Sís' birthplace. At some point in your discussion, explain that this country is now separated into Slovakia and the Czech Republic.
- Photo of Prague: City where he grew up
- Communist symbol: Discuss his life while living behind the "iron curtain"
- Paintbrush: He's loved to draw and paint since he was a toddler.

- Film Reel: He was a filmmaker, and he came to America in 1982 to film the 1984 Winter Olympics.
- Music Note: While he was living in Prague, he was in a rock band, and he worked as a disc jockey.
- American Flag: Did not return to Prague in 1984, instead he was granted asylum in the United States and became a citizen in 1989.
- Book Cover: He became interested in utilizing his love of art by illustrating children's books after discussing the idea with Maurice Sendak.
- Home: He now lives in New York with his wife and children.

Write to the Author

Have the students celebrate citizenship and the fact that Peter Sís decided to become an American citizen in birthday cards that they create. Inside the cards, the students could write an ending to the sentence starter, "I'm proud to be an American because _____." They could decorate their cards with American symbols, such as the flag, liberty bell, patriotic colors, etc.

Madlenka's Mission

Peter Sís has written three books about a young girl who lives in New York City: *Madlenka, Madlenka's Dog,* and *Madlenka: Soccer Star.* In honor of these wonderful stories about a girl with a creative imagination, plan a treasure hunt activity in which students must think of themselves as friends of Madlenka's who are helping her to find her missing apartment key in her neighborhood. Here is a sample set of clues for one of the small groups of 3–4 students to follow:

- "Madlenka is walking around her neighborhood, and she realized that she misplaced the key to her apartment. Now she must retrace her steps to find the key! Go to the cookbook section of the library (*or a book display in the classroom*) to see if Mr. Gaston, the French baker, can help her."
- (*Photocopy Sís' illustration of Gaston from* Madlenka *and write the following on its reverse side. Place the clue on the shelf near the cookbook section or display.*) "Bonjour! I have not seen your key! Go to the magazine rack and ask Mr. Singh if he has seen the key."
- (*Photocopy the drawing of Mr. Singh and write the following on its reverse side. Place the clue on the shelf near the magazine rack in the library/classroom.*) "No, I do not know where your key is. But if you can walk on tiptoe to Ms. Grimm's home in the folktale neighborhood (398.2), she may have an answer for you!"
- (*Photocopy the picture of Ms. Grimm and write the following on its reverse side. Place the clue on the shelf near the folktale collection in the library/classroom.*) "Guten tag, Kinder! I was just reading my favorite folktale, Snow White! I haven't seen any keys near my books, though. Perhaps Mrs. Kham will know—march over to the section of books about Asia (950) and ask her."
- (*Photocopy the picture of Mrs. Kham and write the following on its reverse side. Place the clue on the shelf near the books about Asia.*) "Where in the world could it be? The key to your quest lies in a basket near the front desk!"

The students will find the keys hidden in a basket on either the circulation desk, or the teacher's desk. The keys could be made from chocolate molds (key-shaped molds are available from candy making supply companies). If this is not an option, simply copy key pictures from clip art, and tape the image to a small cardboard tube that has been wrapped in paper and filled with small candies.

Other hunt clues might revolve around Madlenka walking her dog and losing her key, or Madlenka kicking her soccer ball around her neighborhood and losing her key.

Musical Chairs

Play this familiar party game in honor of *Play, Mozart, Play!* To make a connection between the game and the book, play Mozart's "A Little Night Music." Since Sís created the poster for the movie, Amadeus, project an image of this poster on the screen while playing the game!

USA Bingo

Use Peter Sís' book *The Train of States* as the source of clues for this twist on the popular game of Bingo.

Before the Celebration

Print a copy of an outline of a United States map, or use the reproducible on page 17. Hand out one map to each student.

During the Celebration

Instruct the students to choose ten random states and only color those ten states on their maps. Once they are ready, hold up the book by Peter Sís, and tell them that you will randomly open up to one page. On each page, Sís has illustrated a boxcar for one particular state. Each state's flag, symbols, and key facts are listed on the page. You will share the state's facts with the students without showing the picture or revealing the name of the state. The students must raise their hands to guess the correct identity of the state. Once the state is identified, only those students that had previously colored it on their maps may mark the state (use beans as markers). The first student to get five, or all 10 depending on their knowledge about the states, is the winner. Award a small prize to all participants, such as globe erasers, map books for their own states (available from most state tourism agencies), or other souvenirs related to the United States.

Freedom Banners

Two of Peter Sís' books are autobiographical accounts of his childhood in Communist Czechoslovakia: *TIBET Through the Red Box*, and *THE WALL: Growing Up Behind the Iron Curtain*. Talk with the students about the freedoms they have as citizens of the United States. Use their ideas as inspiration for making personal banners. Provide each student with construction paper, markers, crayons, and pencils. The students will begin their banner by drawing a picture of themselves and cutting it out. Next, they will draw pictures of the freedoms that they enjoy, such as freedom to worship as they please, freedom to talk about their ideas, freedom to draw their own pictures, freedom to read books of their own choice, freedom to set their own goals for their careers, etc. After they've drawn, colored, and cut out their various pictures, give them red or blue 12" x 18" construction paper. Instruct them to glue their self-portraits in the middle of the large paper and to place their freedom pictures around their portraits. Hang these banners on a bulletin board or hallway, with a title: "Peter Sís Reminds Us to Remember Our Freedoms!"

I Spy!

Use a document camera to ensure that all students can examine the illustrations in *Beach Ball*. Each page is a search-and-find experience, with categories such as: items beginning with each letter in the alphabet, colors, numbers, opposites, etc. Create an "I Spy" activity by lining a large shoe box with aluminum foil and then wrapping the outside of the box, and the lid separately with colorful wrapping paper. Place small toys and objects inside the box and have students look inside for a limited amount of time before closing the lid and telling them to write down everything they can remember that fits a specific category (list items in alphabetical order; items of a specific color or shape, etc.). Create one shoebox for each group of 3–4 students to avoid difficulty in passing around 1 box for all to view. Challenge students to make their own "I Spy" boxes from old toys at home. As they bring them in, put them on display in the classroom or library, along with a list of categories that students must use in listing the items they've found in their classmates' boxes.

Family Memories

Many of Peter Sís' books were inspired by his personal experiences growing up. Talk to the students about their own family experiences and memories, and make a list of ideas. Have the students use the list to help them think about a favorite memory from a family event or experience.

1. Distribute 6" x 18" sheets of construction paper, one per child. Show them how to fold the paper into thirds (making three 6" x 6" boxes).

2. Set this aside and distribute 4" x 5" sheets of white construction paper. Instruct the children to draw a picture of their family event. Glue this onto the middle square of the 6" x 18" sheet of construction paper, centering it near the top so that the students can write a title/caption below the picture.

3. Distribute a sheet of 5" x 5" lined paper. The students will use this to write the story about their event. They will glue this onto the first 6" x 6" square.

4. Distribute a 3" x 5" sheet of construction paper. Instruct the students to use a glue stick to glue around three edges of the rectangle. They will glue it into place along the bottom half of the last 6" x 6" square, leaving the unglued edge open at the top. This will provide a pocket for students to fill with a memento, such as a ticket stub or card, related to their family event.

5. Students will fold the 6" x 18" sheet up into thirds and write a title on the cover. Instruct them to bring these home to give to their parents, or to their mothers for Mother's Day.

Stories to Solve

All of the activities for Peter Sís' birthday celebration are based on the books that he has written and illustrated. He has also, however, illustrated many books by other authors, including George Shannon's *Stories to Solve* and *More Stories to Solve*. Throughout the month, share one of the stories with the students, along with Sís' illustrations, and challenge them to solve the mysteries or problems imbedded in the stories. This could be used as a month-long learning center in a classroom or a display activity in the library. Change the stories to solve each week to maintain interest in the center/display.

Party Food

Kolaches—a favorite Central European pastry! Kolaches can be ordered online from bakeries, or choose an enticing recipe online and make your own!

Party Favors

Create a small booklet of mazes. There are a variety of free mazes to download from the Internet. Copy and paste them into a Word document. Set up the page in landscape format and create two columns, so that two mazes will fit on each page. Print and copy into booklets.

Other favors could include biography-related gifts, such as

- Glow-in-the-dark stars, for his biographical account of Galileo Galilei in *Starry Messenger*
- Magnifying lens or plant seeds, for his biographical account of Charles Darwin in *The Tree of Life*
- Small boat or compass key chain, for his biographical account of Christopher Columbus in *Follow the Dream*

Happy Birthday, Peter Sís!

Born May 11, 1949

Booklist

- *Ballerina!*
- *Beach Ball*
- *Dinosaur!*
- *Fire Truck*
- *Follow the Dream: The Story of Christopher Columbus*
- *Going Up: A Color Counting Book*
- *Komodo!*
- *Madlenka*
- *Madlenka's Dog*
- *Madlenka: Soccer Star*
- *An Ocean World*
- *Play, Mozart, Play!*
- *Rainbow Rhino*
- *Rumpelstiltskin*
- *Ship Ahoy!*
- *A Small Tall Tale From the Far, Far North*
- *Starry Messenger: Galileo Galilei*
- *The Three Golden Keys*
- *Tibet Through the Red Box*
- *Train of States*
- *The Tree of Life: Charles Darwin*
- *Trucks, Trucks, Trucks*
- *The Wall: Growing Up Behind the Iron Curtain*
- *Waving: A Counting Book*

Peter Sís Reading Log

Read 5 books by **May** ____.

On each line, write the title you've read and have your parent/guardian sign that you read it.

Bring this completed reading log to me by **May** ____ and receive your invitation to attend our birthday celebration on

_____.
Date/Time

_____

Title   Parent/Guardian Signature

_____

Title   Parent/Guardian Signature

_____

Title   Parent/Guardian Signature

_____

Title   Parent/Guardian Signature

_____

Title   Parent/Guardian Signature

Happy Birthday, Dear J. Patrick Lewis!

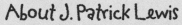

About J. Patrick Lewis

- J. Patrick Lewis was born on May 5, 1942, in Gary, Indiana.
- The "J" stands for John, but he goes by Pat. His grandchildren call him "Grandpat."
- He was born 20 minutes after his twin brother, Leo, was born.
- He is also known as "Dr. Lewis." He earned his Ph.D. at Ohio State University in 1974.
- He was a professor of economics for many years before he discovered his love of poetry.
- J. Patrick Lewis is the father of three children and the stepfather of two children.
- Visit his website, jpatricklewis.com, for information about his life through photographs.

Celebration Ideas

Tell the Author's Story

J. Patrick Lewis has published a variety of riddle poems. Therefore, it seems natural to tell his story in a series of rhyming riddles! Place a copy of a photograph of Lewis on an easel or bulletin board. After reading each riddle-poem, the students must guess the answers. Once they've solved the riddles, tape or staple the poem (printed on various colors of paper) and its answer around the perimeter of his photo. This will create an eye-catching and informative display! Challenge the students to write their own riddle-poems about the author or his books.

Try these riddle-culous poems with your students:

- Hey!
  What's that J?
  In the front of your name;
  Can you explain?
  It isn't Jat, or Jave, or Jike!
  Is it a name you like?
  Why do you hide it away?
  Come clean and say it today!
  Does it rhyme with toe?
  No, not Joe.
  Does it rhyme with slim?
  No, not Jim.
  It must rhyme with Ron!
  Yes! It's _____!
  [John!]

- Not from the wild west,
  No gold, no bandannas.
  He's from the Midwest,
  Wanderer of _____!
  [Indiana]

- Whose resumé is this?
  Look at this job list!
  Economist
  Father,
  Like no other!
  Writer
  Versifier
  Professor
  Orator
  Rhymester
  Any time-ster!
  Financial wizard
  Lyrical word blizzards!
  Picture book pleaser
  And wordy brainteaser!
  His poems spoke to us like they knew us,
  He's no stranger, he's _____!
  [J. Patrick Lewis!]

Write to the Author

Teach the students to make flap books.

To Make a Flap Book

1. Fold a 12" x 18" sheet of construction paper in half lengthwise.
2. Unfold the paper, then cut it into fourths from the bottom edge to the crease at the middle.
3. Have the students refold the paper along the crease so that the four flaps open along the bottom and the crease is the top edge.
4. Tell the students to think of four words to describe J. Patrick Lewis's books, and have them write one word per flap. When they open the flap, the students can write why they used that word, draw a picture, or simply write a birthday greeting on the inside

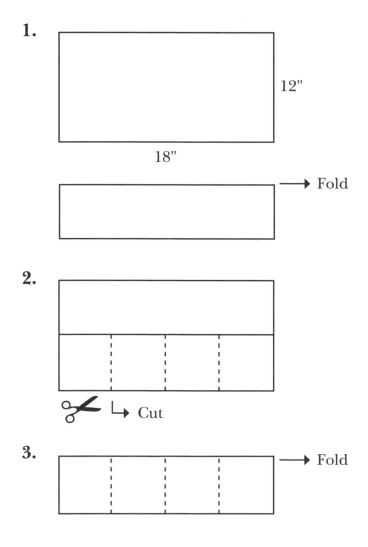

of the flap. Mail these off to the author, along with a cover letter and self-addressed stamped envelope.

Doggone Fun!

In Lewis's and Zappitello's picture book, *First Dog*, a homeless dog travels around the world in search of the perfect canine companion and home. Lewis describes dogs that are native to a variety of countries. Play "Find the Dog" in honor of this book.

Before the Celebration

Use a search engine to find pictures of dogs mentioned in the book and print them, along with their breed's name. Hide the pictures of the dogs around the classroom or library.

During the Celebration

Distribute the names of the dogs to the children, one per child. On signal, have the children roam the classroom/library in search of the picture that matches their dog's breed name. If they see pictures of dogs that are not of their breed, they must not tell anyone where the picture is located. Encourage them to keep their dog's breed name a secret until everyone has found their matching picture. Award small prizes, such as cookies cut in the shape of dog bones.

Riddle Bingo!

Lewis's book, *Riddle-icious* contains 28 riddle poems with answers. Give each student a blank 4 x 4 grid, and write the 28 answers, in random order, on the board. Tell the students to copy down 16 of the answers, and write them in the boxes in any order they'd like. After each child has his filled in completely, open the book to any random page, and read the riddle poem aloud. Students can raise their hand if they have a guess for the answer. Once the answer is revealed, those who had written that answer down can cross it off in their box. The first to get four answers crossed off in a row is the winner! This game provides appropriate scaffolding for helping students to make logical guesses, since the answer is provided somewhere in the list of words!

Arithme-tickle

Read aloud several of Lewis's clever poems in this book, and challenge your students to solve the math problems imbedded in each. Tell them that they are ready for some Mental Math Magic! Before the celebration, print out a set of 10 numeral cards, 0–9, for each child. Next, plan out a set of math problems whose answers use the numerals 0–9 only once. During the celebration, instruct the children to cut them apart so that they'll have 10 separate numeral cards. Tell the students that you are going to ask a set of questions and they must use their "Math Magic" cards to display each question's answer. They must keep the cards displayed until all the questions have been asked and answered. By the time they answer the last question, they should have used each card only once. Here is a sample set of "Math Magic" questions:

- This is the day in May that J. Patrick Lewis was born. It is also the answer to 15–10. (5)
- He has written a few poems and books about baseball. This is the number of players on a baseball team. It is also the answer to 3 x 3. (9)
- In *The Fantastic 5 & 10¢ Store*, Benny Penny visits this magical shop. If he had with him 2 nickels, 2 dimes, and 2 pennies, how much money would he have to spend? (32¢).
- This is how old he was when he published his first children's book. It is also the answer to: 32 + 14 (46: He published his first children's book in 1988).
- This is how old J. Patrick Lewis turns in 2012. It is also the answer to 3 quarters – 1 nickel (70).
- If J. Patrick Lewis wrote a dozen and a half poems in one book, how many poems would he have written for that book? (18)

After this last question, all of the magic cards will be used. Each student's desk should have his/her cards displayed as follows:

5

9

32

46

70

18

This is an effective way to review math skills and logical thinking throughout the school year. It is also metacognitive, as it allows students to think about their thinking and check their own work (i.e., if they've already used a numeral in an earlier problem, but they need that card for another answer, one of those answers must be incorrect).

Crafty 5 & 10¢ Creations

After reading Lewis's *The Fantastic 5 & 10¢ Store: A Rebus Adventure*, tell the children that they will imagine that they are shopping in the craft section of the store, and they'll need to purchase the items they'd like to use to embellish their own spring kites!

Before the Celebration

Cut large construction paper kites (12" x 18" paper cut into diamond shapes). Next, assemble a variety of crafty items for the students to use as kite decorations, such as: 18-inch lengths of crepe paper streamers, buttons, foam shapes, stickers, pom poms, 10-inch lengths of yarn, pipe cleaners, tissue paper squares, etc. Finally, decide on a price for each item, ranging between 1¢ and 10¢. Create a price list to post near the display, and provide a copy of the price list for each student.

During the Celebration

Provide each student with a set amount of play coins and a price list. Instruct them to plan how they want to spend their money to purchase items in order to decorate their kites. Allow small groups to shop, and have the class decorate their kites, then hang them up for a colorful spring display!

Spot the Plot

This wonderful poetry collection of riddles about classic children's books makes for a fun guessing game . . . with a twist!

Before the Celebration

Write 6–8 titles from the 13 titles that Lewis writes about in this book. Put each title on a 4" x 6" index card and tape it to an inflated balloon. Tape the balloons to the board at the front of the room. Choose one title to be the "mystery title" (it could be a book that you plan to read aloud during the celebration). Make an "X" with tape on the side of the balloon containing the mystery title.

During the Celebration

Tell the students that they'll need to listen as you read poems from this book, and they'll have to raise their hand if they can "spot the plot" and name the book's title. Tell them that once they've figured out which title is correct, you will pop the balloon. If the balloon contains the mystery title, however, it will not pop when it is stuck with a safety pin! Save the mystery title for the end. Pop each balloon by inserting a safety pin into the side of the balloon as its title is revealed. When the last title (mystery title) is revealed, insert the safety pin into the tape "X." the tape will form a seal around the pin, thereby keeping the balloon inflated. Remove the pin, and tell the students that this is the mystery title, and read the book aloud to the class. As you read, the balloon will slowly deflate, as air seeps through the pinhole. The students will be amazed!

Wordles™

J. Patrick Lewis has written several books devoted to his love of language and words, such as: *Please Bury Me in the Library*, and *Doodle Dandies*. Capitalize on his play with words by instructing the students to make their own "Wordles." Go to www.wordle.net/create and have the students each choose one word about literacy, reading, writing, books, etc. Then have them type in words related to that topic. The site will automatically create a colorful, visually appealing word wall of the students' ideas related to their topic. These can be printed and posted around the classroom or library. It is a very effective way to capture their thoughts and feelings about the importance of books in children's lives.

Party Favors

Pocket-size dictionaries or thesauruses (in honor of J. Patrick Lewis's word wizardry); snack bags of animal crackers (in honor of his poems about animals in *A Hippopotamusn't*); book coupons, such as "Guaranteed for one extra check out week without a late fee," "Good for one library book above the school limit," "Good for an extra turn to read a favorite book aloud to the class," etc.

Party Food

- Alphabet cookies or cereal—have the students use the letters to spell as many words as possible before eating them!
- Fruit salad science experiment on oxidation processes—a treat and activity inspired by Lewis' book, *Scien-trickery: Riddles in Science*. Use the experiment found in Vicki Cobb's *Science Experiments You Can Eat*.
- Sheet cake decorated to resemble a book, in honor of Lewis' poems and riddles about books and literacy.

Happy Birthday, J. Patrick Lewis!

Born May 5, 1942

Picture Books

- *At the Wish of the Fish: An Adaptation of a Russian Folktale*
- *The Boat of Many Rooms*
- *The Christmas of the Reddle Moon*
- *The Fantastic 5 & 10¢ Store: A Rebus Adventure*
- *The Fat-Cats at Sea*
- *First Dog* (with Beth Zappitello)
- *The Frog Princess*
- *The House*
- *The Kindergarten Cat*
- *July is a Mad Mosquito*
- *The La-Di-Da Hare*
- *Long Was the Winter Road they Traveled: Tale of the Nativity*
- *The Moonbow of Mr. B. Bones*
- *One Dog Day*
- *The Snowflake Sisters*
- *The Tsar and the Amazing Cow*
- *Tulip at the Bat*

Poetry

- *Arithme-Tickle: An Even Number of Odd Riddle-Rhymes*
- *Birds on a Wire: A Renga 'Round Town,* (with Paul Janeczko)
- *Black Swarn/White Crow* (haiku)
- *The Bookworm's Feast: A Potluck of Poems*
- *BoshBlobberBosh: Runcible Poems for Edward Lear*
- *Castles: Cold Stone Poems* (with Rebecca Kai Dotlich)
- *Countdown to Summer: 180 Poems for Every Day of the School Year*
- *Doodle Dandies: Poems that Take Shape*
- *Earth Verses and Water Rhymes*
- *Freedom Like Sunlight: Praisesongs for Black Americans*
- *God Made the Skunk, and Other Animal Poems*
- *Good Mornin', Ms. America: The U.S.A. in Verse*
- *Good Mousekeeping, and Other Animal Home Poems*
- *Heroes and She-roes: Poems of Amazing and Everyday Heroes*
- *A Hippopotamusn't and Other Animal Verses*
- *The Little Buggers: Insect and Spider Poems*
- *Monumental Verses*
- *Please Bury Me in the Library*
- *Once Upon a Tomb: Gravely Humorous Verses*
- *Richicholas Nicholas: More Animal Poems*
- *Riddle-icious*
- *Riddle-lightful*
- *Scien-trickery: Riddles in Science*
- *Skywriting: Poems to Fly*
- *Spot the Plot*
- *Swan Songs: Poems of Extinction*
- *Two-legged, Four-legged, No-legged Rhymes*
- *Vherses: A Celebration of Outstanding Women*
- *Wing Nuts: Screwy Haiku* (Paul Janeczko)
- *A World of Wonders: Geographic Travels in Verse and Rhyme*

Nonfiction

- *Big Is Big (and Little Little): A Book of Contrasts*
- *Black Cat Bone: A Life of Blues Legend Robert Johnson in Verse*
- *Blackbeard the Pirate King*
- *A Burst of Firsts: Doers, Shakers, and Record Breakers*

J. Patrick Lewis Reading Log

Read 5 books by **May ____**.

On each line, write the title you've read and have your parent/guardian sign that you read it.

Bring this completed reading log to me by **May ____** and receive your invitation to attend our birthday celebration on

_____.

Date/Time

_____

Title   Parent/Guardian Signature

_____

Title   Parent/Guardian Signature

_____

Title   Parent/Guardian Signature

_____

Title   Parent/Guardian Signature

_____

Title   Parent/Guardian Signature

Happy Birthday, Dear Juanita Havill!

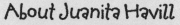

About Juanita Havill

- Juanita Havill was born on May 11, 1949, in Evansville, Indiana.
- She is married to Pierre Masure and has two children: Laurence and Pierre.
- Juanita Havill likes to walk and swim and work in her garden.
- She likes to go to the movies and to see live theater.
- She graduated from the University of Illinois with a B.A. in 1971 and a M.A. in 1973.
- She has worked as a translator for companies in France and the United States.
- Juanita Havill wrote for her high school's newspaper.
- She realized that she wanted to write children's books after taking a writing class while living in Minneapolis.

Celebration Ideas:

Tell the Author's Story

Juanita Havill has written a variety of stories, covering many topics. Capitalize on this by presenting her biography as a "Suitcase Story."

<u>Before the Celebration</u>

Gather the following items: a package of seeds, a map of France, a baseball, a medallion (or a picture of the Ezra Jack Keats Award for New Writers), a picture of 3 children: 2 boys and 1 girl, stuffed animal: cat or horse, 2–3 books by Havill, a newspaper, a pair of gym shoes, and a small bag of sand. Place all of the items into a suitcase.

<u>During the Celebration</u>

Don a wide-brimmed gardening hat and introduce yourself as Juanita Havill. Tell them that you are in town and have packed up many souvenirs of your life. You use your life experiences to inspire many of the books you write for children. Tell the class that as you pull each item from the suitcase, you will explain why it is significant to you. If one of the items is prevalent in one of her books, ask the students to guess to which book the item relates.

- Package of seeds: Juanita Havill loves to garden and remembers working in a garden when she was only six years old! This artifact relates to two of her books: *Grow: A Novel in Verse*, and *I Heard it From Alice Zucchini*.
- Map of France: Juanita Havill has lived in France as an English translator.
- Baseball: As a child, Juanita Havill enjoyed playing sports such as baseball, basketball, and football.
- Medallion: Juanita Havill won the Ezra Jack Keats Award for New Writers for her first book, *Jamaica's Find*.
- Picture of two boys and one girl: Juanita Havill is the middle child of two brothers, so she drew from the experience of wanting to be included in their games when she wrote her series of picture books about a girl named Jamaica, as well as her novel, *It Always Happens to Leona*.
- Stuffed animal (cat or horse): Juanita Havill loved animals, especially cats and horses, when she was a girl. Perhaps her love of animals inspired her writing of *Sato and the Elephants*.
- Books: Juanita Havill has loved to read books since she was a young girl.

- Pair of gym shoes: Her current hobbies are walking, swimming, and gardening.
- Newspaper: Juanita Havill wrote for her high school newspaper.
- Bag of sand: Juanita Havill currently lives in the desert climate of Arizona, where she raised two children with her husband.

Write to the Author

Send a birthday garden mural to the author, to honor her love of gardening! Provide each student with a sheet of 6" x 9" colored construction paper. Instruct them to use the paper to draw a large flower shape, such as the head of a daisy or tulip. After they cut it out, they will use a dark marker to write a birthday greeting to Juanita Havill. Hang up a large sheet of light blue bulletin board paper, and have the students each paint a green stem along the bottom of the paper, then glue their flower head to the top of the stem. Use bright tempera paints to write, "Happy Birthday, Juanita Havill!" across the top of the mural. Send it off to the author, along with a cover letter explaining your author program.

Jamaica's Book Fun

Juanita Havill has authored seven picture books about a young girl named Jamaica. Celebrate this young heroine with the following activities.

- What is your favorite book about Jamaica? Create a large, colorful graph that poses this question to your students. Use photocopies of their individual school pictures as the graph markers. Write the book titles along the bottom, and have students use their school photographs to create a bar graph. Use the graph's results as the stimulus for a variety of math problems, such as; "Which book was most popular?" "What were the total votes for the books, *Jamaica's Blue Marker* and *Jamaica Tag-Along*?" "How many more votes did [book title] get than [book title]?" etc.
- Spelling Bee: Have a quick spelling bee as a tribute to the lesson Jamaica learned about cheating in the book, *Jamaica and the Substitute Teacher.*

- Statue Charades: Play a combination of Statues and Charades in honor of the book, *Brianna, Jamaica, and the Dance of Spring.*

<u>Before the Celebration</u>

Write down a variety of occupations, one per strip of paper.

<u>During the Celebration</u>

Choose one student to be the "Sculptor" who selects students, one at a time, to come forward and pick the name of an occupation from a bowl. That person must not read it aloud, but must think of a pose that would indicate the occupation to the rest of the group. When the student is ready, the Sculptor joins hands with the student and twirls him around three times. The student must stop twirling and stand in the pose that he has thought of for that particular occupation (for example, a police office pose might involve standing straight, with one hand by the mouth as if blowing a whistle and the other arm extended forward as if telling people to stop). Once the student is in position, he must hold that position until the rest of the group can guess the correct occupation.

- What Would Jamaica Do?: In each story, Jamaica learns a valuable life lesson (such as sharing, telling the truth, being thankful, including young children in games, etc.). As each book in this series is read throughout the month, fill in a large chart to keep track of these lessons. Chart headings could include: Title, Problem, Solution, Life Lesson.

<u>Before the Celebration</u>

Make a list of school situations that would involve the students in learning a variety of life lessons.

<u>During the Celebration</u>

Divide the students into small groups, and give a situation to each group. They must discuss how they believe Jamaica would handle the situation and then create a skit to perform for the rest of the group about it. Integrate a craft by having the students create puppets for a puppet show about their situation.

- Cards for Kids: Are there children in your area that could use a card to cheer them up? Perhaps there is a local children's hospital, or other such agency in your community. Discuss the powerful use of cards to cheer up Jamaica's classmate in *Jamaica's Blue Marker*. Instruct the students to use their colorful markers to make "Get Well" cards for patients at a children's hospital. This is a wonderful way to connect the students to their peers in the community.

Craft: Soap Carvings

In honor of *Sato and the Elephants*, provide the students with a soft bar of soap and a craft stick. Tell them to think about an animal or simple object, and have them carve it out of the soap, just like Sato learned to do from his father using blocks of ivory.

As a variation, provide students with baking clay (such as Sculpey™), and instruct them to make a "netsuke" (a Japanese miniature sculpture) about one-inch in diameter. Use a wooden skewer to make a hole through it, and bake them in a low-temperature oven for 15 minutes. Once cooled, provide students with a leather cord to run through the netsuke's hole and wear around their necks, just like Sato.

The Magic Fort

Ask the students what adventures they'd pretend to have if they had a playhouse or a fort in their backyard. Brainstorm ideas together. Following the discussion, teach students how to make a paper box mini-fort from a sheet of 8 ½" x 11" card stock. Once they've made their mini-forts, provide colored construction paper for a setting and have the students integrate their forts into an imaginary adventure (such as a pirate ship at sea, a covered wagon rolling across the prairie, a basket for a hot air balloon, etc.). Create a display and allow time for students to write about their adventures in their magic forts.

To Make the Paper Box Mini-fort

Take the students through the process below, one step at a time. They will be able to follow your directions and successfully make these paper forts!

1. Fold the paper in half lengthwise and width-wise twice, so that when you unfold the paper, you should see 16 boxes.
2. Fold each 8 ½" side's edge to the center crease. Both edges must meet in the center and not overlap.
3. Fold each of the four corners to the closest crease, forming triangles.
4. Fold the edges of each 8 ½" side, which are meeting in the center, over the corner folds. The resulting shape will be octagonal, and the center edges will resemble lips, folded over the corners.
5. Gently pull apart the center "lips" so that a box form begins to take shape. Crease the corners to define them and to form the box.
6. The box is now a magical fort! Embellish it any way you wish and use construction paper to provide a setting.

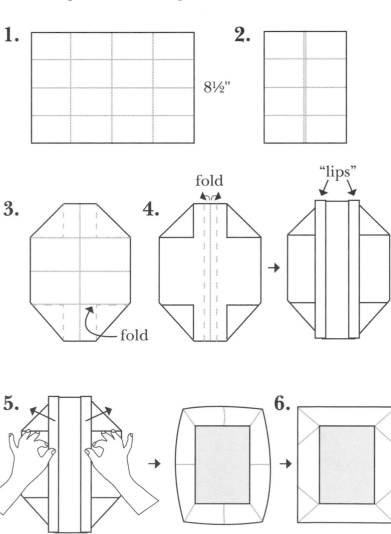

Grow a Flower!

After reading Havill's *Grow: A Novel in Verse*, have the students take advantage of the spring season and plant flower seeds. The seeds could be planted early in the month, thereby allowing time for the teacher or librarian to integrate the book into a science unit. The students could graph the development of their plants' growth. Connect this activity to Mother's Day by having the students paint/decorate terra cotta pots and then transplanting their flowers into the pots to give as presents.

Endangered Species Awareness

Havill promotes environmental awareness regarding endangered elephants through her book, *Sato and the Elephants.* Use a search engine to find information about other endangered animals. Divide the students into groups, one per endangered animal, and charge each group with the task of researching the issues that are causing their animal's endangerment. Provide poster board for each group, and have them make posters to hang up in the school, teaching their peers about how they can help prevent the extinction of these animals.

Read Alouds

Juanita Havill has written several novels that will serve well as read alouds throughout her birthday month. Additionally, her novel for beginning readers, *Jennifer, Too*, is well suited for first and second graders to read for literature circles.

Party Food

Dirt cups, in honor of her gardening hobby, as well as her books, *Grow: A Novel in Verse* and *I Heard it From Alice Zucchini.* Use the following recipe, from www.kraftrecipes.com.

Dirt Cups

Ingredients:	1 package chocolate instant pudding (3.9 oz.)
	2 cups cold milk
	8 oz. frozen whipped topping (thawed)
	15 chocolate sandwich cookies
	10 chewy fruit-flavored worms.
Directions	1. Mix together chocolate pudding mix and cold milk. Let stand 5 minutes.
	2. Fold in whipped topping.
	3. Crush the cookies into crumbs and stir in ¼ cup of crumbs.
	4. Pour the mixture into 10 7-ounce plastic cups.
	5. Refrigerate 1 hour.
	6. Sprinkle remaining cookie crumbs over top of mixture and place one chewy fruit-flavored worm into mixture.
	7. Eat and enjoy! Makes 10 dirt cups.

Party Favors

Marker sets (in honor of *Jamaica's Blue Marker*), small stuffed toys (*Jamaica's Find*), jump ropes or jacks (useful toys for best friends, like Jamaica and Brianna), seed packets (gardening), small candies.

Happy Birthday, Juanita Havill!

Born May 11, 1949

Picture Books

- Jamaica Series:
    - *Jamaica's Find*
    - *Jamaica Tag-Along*
    - *Jamaica and Brianna*
    - *Jamaica's Blue Marker*
    - *Jamaica and the Substitute Teacher*
    - *Brianna, Jamaica, and the Dance of Spring*
    - *Jamaica is Thankful*
- *Call the Horse Lucky*
- *Just Like a Baby*
- *Kentucky Troll*
- *The Magic Fort*
- *Sato and the Elephants*
- *Saving Owen's Toad*
- *Treasure Nap*

Poetry

- *I Heard it From Alice Zucchini*

Novels

- *Eyes Like Willy's*
- *Grow: A Novel in Verse*
- *It Always Happens to Leona*
- *Jennifer, Too*
- *Leona and Ike*

Juanita Havill Reading Log

Read 5 books by **May** ____.

On each line, write the title you've read and have your parent/guardian sign that you read it.

Bring this completed reading log to me by **May** ____ and receive your invitation to attend our birthday celebration on

_____.

Date/Time

_____

Title   Parent/Guardian Signature

_____

Title   Parent/Guardian Signature

_____

Title   Parent/Guardian Signature

_____

Title   Parent/Guardian Signature

_____

Title   Parent/Guardian Signature

Resources

Games and Activity Books

- *Dynamic Physical Education for Elementary School Children* (16th ed.) by Robert P. Pangrazi and Aaron Beighle. Benjamin Cummings Publishing, 2009.

- *Follow the Trail: A Young Person's Guide to the Great Outdoors* by Jessica Loy. Henry Holt & Company, 2003.

- *Great Theme Parties for Children* by Irene N. Watts. Sterling Publishing Company, 1991.

- *Hopscotch, Hangman, Hot Potato, & Ha Ha Ha: A Rulebook of Children's Games* by Jack Maguire. Simon and Schuster, 1992.

- *Hug a Tree and Other Things to do Outdoors with Young Children* by Robert E. Rockwell et al. Gryphon House, Inc., 1986.

- *I Love Dirt! 52 Activities to Help You and Your Kids Discover the Wonders of Nature* by Jennifer Ward. Trumpeter Books, 2008.

- *Kids' Outdoor Parties: Hundreds of Fun Things to Do at Outdoor Parties for Kids 4–12* by Penny Warner. Meadowbrook Press, 1999.

- *Leading Kids to Books Through Magic* by Caroline Feller Bauer. American Library Association, 1996.

- *Miss Mary Mack and Other Children's Street Rhymes* by Joanna Cole, and Stephanie Calmenson. HarperCollins, 1990.

- *The New Games Book* edited by Andrew Fluegelman. New Games FoundationHeadlands Press, 1976.

- *The New Handbook for Storytellers: With Stories, Poems, Magic, and More* by Caroline Feller Bauer. American Library Association, 1993.

- *Parachute Games* by Todd Strong and Dale LeFevre. Human Kinetics, 1996

- *The Phonics They Use: Words for Reading and Writing* (5th ed.) by Patricia Cunningham. Allyn and Bacon, 2008.

- *Science Experiments You Can Eat* by Vicki Cobb. HarperCollins, 1984.

- *Sharing Nature With Children* by Joseph Cornell. Dawn Publications, 1979.

- *Steven Caney's Toy Book* by Steven Caney. Workman Publishing, 1972.

- *The Worst-Case Scenario Survival Handbook* by Joshua Piven. Chronicle Books, 1999.

Craft Books

- *Artstarts: Drama, Music, Movement, Puppetry, and Storytelling Activities* by Martha Brady and Patsy T. Gleason. Teacher Ideas Press, 1994.

- *The Big Green Book of Recycled Crafts: Over 100 Earth-Friendly Projects* by Susan White Sullivan, ed. Leisure Arts Publications, 2009.

- *Crafts from Salt Dough* by Audrey Gessat. Bridgestone Books, 2003.

- Crafts 'n Things Magazine: www.craftsnthings.com

- *Doodle Diary: Art Journaling for Girls* by Dawn DeVries Sokol. Gibbs Smith Publishers, 2010.

- *Mobiles & Other Paper Windcatchers* by Noel and Phyllis Fiarotta. Sterling Publishing Company, 1996.

- *Paper-Folding Fun! 50 Awesome Crafts to Weave, Twist & Curl: A Williamson Kids Can!® Book* by Ginger Jonson. Williamson Publishing, 2002.

- *Simple Puppets From Everyday Materials* by Barbara MacDonald Buetter. Sterling Publishing, 1996.
- *Steven Caney's Toy Book* by Steven Caney. Workman Publishing, 1972.
- *The Ultimate Book of Kid Concoctions* by John E. Thomas and Danita Pagel. The Kids Concoctions Company, 1998.
- *Usborne Big Book of Things to Do: Lots of Make and Play Ideas* by Ray Gibson. Usborne Books, 2003.
- *The Usborne Book of Art Skills* by Fiona Watt. Usborne Books, 2002.
- *You Can Weave! Projects for Young Weavers* by Kathleen Monaghan and Hermon Joyner. Davis Publications, Inc., 2000.

Sources for Prizes and Party Favors

- **Kimbo Educational**

  www.kimboed.com

  Musical activities, CDs, and DVDs

- **Oriental Trading Company**

  www.orientaltrading.com

  Party favors, school supplies, party supplies, craft supplies, holiday items, candy, carnival novelties

- **Rhode Island Novelty**

  www.rinovelty.com

  Party favors, school supplies, party supplies, craft supplies, candy, carnival novelties

- **Toy Connection**

  www.toyconnection.com

  Party favors, school supplies, stationary, holiday items, candy, carnival novelties

- **U.S. Toy Company**

  www.ustoy.com

  Party favors, school supplies, party supplies, craft supplies, candy, carnival novelties

- **Upstart**

  www.upstartpromotions.com

  Reading awards, bookmarks, bookbags, stickers, incentives

Bibliography by Author

September

Paul Goble

- *Adopted by the Eagles* (Bradbury Press, 1994)
- *All Our Relatives: Traditional Native American Thoughts About Nature* (World Wisdom, 2005)
- *Beyond the Ridge* (Simon & Schuster, 1989)
- *The Boy and His Mud Horses and Other Stories from the Tipi* (World Wisdom, 2010)
- *Buffalo Woman* (Aladdin, 1987)
- *Crow Chief* (Orchard Books, 1992)
- *Death of the Iron Horse* (Atheneum, 1987)
- *The Earth Made Me New: Plains Indians' Stories of Creation* (World Wisdom, 2009)
- *The Gift of the Sacred Dog* (Perfection Learning, 1984)
- *The Girl Who Loved Wild Horses* (Bradbury Press, 1978)
- *The Great Race of the Birds and Animals* (Perfection Learning, 1991)
- *Hau Kola: Hello Friend* (Meet the Author) (with Gerry Perrin, Richard C. Owen Publishers, 1994)
- *Her Seven Brothers* (Perfection Learning, 1993)
- *Iktomi and the Berries* (Orchard Books, 1989)
- *Iktomi and the Boulder* (Orchard Books, 1991)
- *Iktomi and the Buffalo Skull* (Orchard Books, 1991)
- *Iktomi and the Buzzards* (Orchard Books, 1994)
- *Iktomi and the Ducks* (Orchard Books, 1990)
- *Iktomi Loses His Eyes* (Scholastic, 1999)
- *The Legend of the White Buffalo Woman* (National Geographic Children's Books, 2002)
- *Love Flute* (Perfection Learning, 1997)
- *Mystic Horse* (HarperCollins, 2003)
- *Remaking the Earth* (Orchard Books, 1996)
- *The Return of the Buffalo* (National Geographic Children's Books, 2002)
- *Star Boy* (Perfection Learning, 1991)
- *Storm Maker's Tipi* (Atheneum, 2001)
- *Tipi: Home of the Nomadic Buffalo Hunters* (with Rodney Frey, World Wisdom, 2007)
- *The Woman Who Lived With Wolves and Other Stories from the Tipi* (World Wisdom, 2010)
- *Hau Kola: Hello Friend (Meet the Author)* (with Gerry Perrin, Richard C. Owen Publishers, 1994)

Jack Prelutsky

- *A. Nonny Mouse Writes Again* (Knopf Books for Young Readers, 1993)
- *Awful Ogre's Awful Day* (Greenwillow Books, 2001)
- *Awful Ogre Running Wild* (Greenwillow Books, 2008)
- *The Baby Uggs Are Hatching* (Greenwillow Books, 1982)
- *The Beauty of the Beast: Poems from the Animal Kingdom* (Knopf, 1997)
- *Behold the Bold Umbrellaphant* (Greenwillow Books, 2006)
- *Beneath a Blue Umbrella* (Greenwillow Books, 1990)
- *Dog Days: Rhymes Around the Year* (Knopf, 1999)
- *The Dragons Are Singing Tonight* (Greenwillow Books, 1993)
- *For Laughing Out Loud* (Knopf, 1991)
- *The Frogs Wore Red Suspenders* (Greenwillow Books, 2002)
- *The Gargoyle On The Roof* (Greenwillow Books, 1999)
- *Good Sports* (Knopf Books for Young Readers, 2007)
- *The Headless Horseman Rides Tonight* (Greenwillow Books, 1980)
- *If Not For the Cat* (Greenwillow Books, 2004)
- *Imagine That! Poems of Never Was* (Knopf Books for Young Readers, 1998)
- *In Aunt Giraffe's Green Garden* (Greenwillow Books, 2007)
- *It's Christmas!* (Greenwillow Books, 1981)
- *It's Halloween!* (Greenwillow Books, 1977)
- *It's Raining Pigs & Noodles* (Greenwillow Books, 2000)
- *It's Snowing! It's Snowing!* (Greenwillow Books, 1984)
- *It's Thanksgiving!* (Greenwillow Books, 1982)
- *It's Valentine's Day!* (Greenwillow Books, 1983)
- *Jack Prelutsky Holiday CD Audio Collection* (Greenwillow Books, 2005)
- *Monday's Troll* (Greenwillow Books, 1996)
- *My Dog May Be a Genius* (Greenwillow Books, 1998)
- *My Parents Think I'm Sleeping* (Greenwillow Books, 1985)
- *The New Kid On The Block* (Greenwillow Books, 1984)
- *Nightmares: Poems to Trouble Your Sleep* (Greenwillow Books, 1976)

- *Pizza, Pigs, and Poetry: How to Write a Poem* (Greenwillow Books, 2008)
- *A Pizza The Size of the Sun* (Greenwillow Books, 1996)
- *Poems of A. Nonny Mouse* (Knopf, 1989)
- *Rainy, Rainy Saturday* (William Morrow & Co., 1980)
- *Read a Rhyme, Write a Rhyme* (Knopf Books for Young Readers, 2005)
- *Read Aloud Rhymes For The Very Young* (Knopf Books for Young Readers, 1986)
- *Ride A Purple Pelican* (Greenwillow Books, 1986)
- *Rolling Harvey Down The Hill* (Greenwillow Books, 1980)
- *Scranimals* (Greenwillow Books, 2002)
- *Something BIG Has Been Here* (Greenwillow Books, 1990)
- *The Way of Living Things* (with Alma Flor Ada, SRA, 1997)
- *What a Day It Was At School* (Greenwillow Books, 2006)
- *Wild Witches' Ball* (Harper Festival Books, 2004)
- *The Wizard* (Greenwillow Books, 2007)

John Scieszka

- *Baloney, Henry P.* (Viking Junior, 2001)
- *The Book That Jack Wrote* (Penguin Putnam, 1994)
- *Cowboy & Octopus* (Viking Juvenile, 2007)
- *The Frog Prince, Continued* (Scholastic, 1991)
- *Guys Write for Guys Read* (ed. by Jon Scieszka) (Viking, 2008)
- *Knucklehead: Tall Tales & Mostly True Stories About Growing Up Scieszka* (Viking, 2008)
- *Math Curse* (Viking, 1995)
- *Robot Zot!* (Simon & Schuster, 2009)
- *Science Verse* (Viking, 2004)
- *Seen Art?* (Viking Juvenile, 2005)
- *Spaceheads: SPHDZ Book 1* (Simon & Schuster Books for Young Readers, 2010)
- *Squids Will Be Squids* (Viking, 1998)
- *The Stinky Cheese Man and Other Fairly Stupid Tales* (Viking, 1992)
- *The True Story of the 3 Little Pigs* (Viking, 1989)

Time Warp Trio Series
- *Knights of the Kitchen Table (#1)* (Viking, 1991)
- *The Not-So-Jolly Roger (#2)* (Viking, 1991)
- *The Good, The Bad & the Goofy (#3)* (Viking, 1992)
- *Your Mother was a Neanderthal (#4)* (Viking, 1993)
- *2095 (#5)* (Viking, 1995)

- *Tut, Tut (#6)* (Viking, 1996)
- *Summer Reading is Killing Me (#7)* (Viking, 1998)
- *It's All Greek To Me (#8)* (Viking, 1999)
- *See You Later, Gladiator (#9)* (Viking, 2000)
- *Sam Samurai (#10)* (Viking, 2001)
- *Hey Kid, Want to Buy a Bridge? (#11)* (Viking, 2002)
- *Viking It and Liking It (#12)* (Viking, 2002)
- *Me Oh Maya (#13)* (Viking, 2003)
- *Da Wild, Da Crazy da Vinci (#14)* (Viking, 2004)
- *Oh Say, I Can't See (#15)* (Viking, 2005)
- *Marco? Polo! (#16)* (Viking, 2006)

October

Joseph Bruchac

- *Between Earth and Sky: Legends of Native America* (Harcourt Brace, 1996)
- *A Boy Called Slow: Sitting Bull* (Philomel Books, 1994)
- *The Boy Who Lived With The Bears and Other Iroquois Stories* (HarperCollins, 1995)
- *A Circle of Thanks: Thanksgiving* (Bridgewater Books, 1996)
- *Crazy Horse's Vision* (Lee & Low Books, 2000)
- *Eagle Song* (Puffin, 1999)
- *The Earth Under Sky Bear's Feet: Native American Poems of the Land* (Putnam & Grosset, 1998)
- *The First Strawberries: A Cherokee Story* (Dial Books for Young Readers, 1993)
- *Gluskabe and the Four Wishes* (Cobblehill Books/ Dutton, 1995)
- *The Great Ball Game: A Muskogee Story* (Dial Books for Young Readers, 1994)
- *How Chipmunk Got His Stripes* (Puffin Books, 2001)
- *Many Nations: An Alphabet of Native Americans* (Cartwheel Books, 1997)
- *Native American Animal Stories* (Fulcrum Publishers, 1992)
- *Native Plant Stories* (Fulcrum Publishers, 1995)
- *Pushing Up The Sky and Other Native American Plays For Children* (Dial Books for Young Readers, 2000)
- *Raccoon's Last Race* (Dial Books for Young Readers, 2004)
- *Seeing The Circle: Autobiography of Joseph Bruchac* (Richard C. Owen, 1999)
- *Squanto's Journey* (Silver Whistle, 2000)
- *Thirteen Moons on Turtle's Back: A Native American Year of Moons* (Philomel Books, 1992)
- *The Trail of Tears* (Random House, 1999)
- *Turtle's Race With Beaver* (Dial Books for Young Readers, 2003)

Steven Kellogg

- *A-Hunting We Will Go!* (William Morrow & Co., 1998)
- *Best Friends* (Dial Books for Young Readers, 1986)
- *Can I Keep Him?* (Dial Books for Young Readers, 1971)
- *Chicken Little* (HarperCollins, 1987)
- *The Christmas Witch* (Dial Books for Young Readers, 1992)
- *Give the Dog a Bone* (Chronicle Books, 2004)
- *I Was Born 10,000 Years Ago* (William Morrow & Co., 1996)
- *The Island of the Skog* (Dial Press, 1973)
- *Jack and the Beanstalk* (HarperCollins, 1991)
- *Johnny Appleseed: A Tall Tale* (Morrow Junior Books, 1988)
- *Mike Fink: A Tall Tale* (Morrow Junior Books, 1992)
- *The Missing Mitten Mystery* (A Reworking of *The Mystery of the Missing Red Mitten*, Dial Press, 2000)
- *Much Bigger Than Martin* (Dial Books for Young Readers, 1976)
- *The Mysterious Tadpole* (Dial Press, 1977)
- *The Mystery of the Flying Orange Pumpkin* (Dial Books for Young Readers, 1980)
- *The Mystery of the Missing Red Mitten* (Dial Books for Young Readers, 1974)
- *The Mystery of the Stolen Blue Paint* (Dial Books for Young Readers, 1982)
- *Paul Bunyan: A Tall Tale* (William Morrow & Co., 1984)
- *Pecos Bill: A Tall Tale* (William Morrow & Co., 1986)
- *A Penguin Pup for Pinkerton* (Dial Books for Young Readers, 2001)
- *The Pied Piper's Magic* (Dial Books for Young Readers, 2009)
- *Pinkerton, Behave!* (Dial Books for Young Readers, 1979)
- *Prehistoric Pinkerton* (Dial Books for Young Readers, 1987)
- *Ralph's Secret Weapon* (Dial Books for Young Readers, 1983)
- *A Rose for Pinkerton* (Dial Books for Young Readers, 1981)
- *Sally Ann Thunder Ann Whirlwind Crockett* (Morrow Junior Books, 1995)
- *Tallyho, Pinkerton!* (Dial Books for Young Readers, 1983)
- *There Was an Old Woman* (Frederick Warne Publishers Ltd., 1978)
- *The Three Little Pigs* (HarperTrophy, 1997)
- *The Three Sillies* (Candlewick Press, 1999)
- *The Wicked Kings of Bloon* (Prentice-Hall, 1970)
- *Won't Somebody Play With Me?* (Dial Press, 1972)
- *Yankee Doodle* (Simon & Schuster, 1994)

Robert D. San Souci

- *Brave Margaret* (Simon & Schuster, 1999)
- *Cendrillon: A Caribbean Cinderella* (Simon & Schuster, 1998)
- *The Christmas Ark* (Random House, 1991)
- *Cinderella Skeleton* (Silver Whistle/Harcourt, 2000)
- *Cut From the Same Cloth: American Women of Myth, Legend, and Tall Tale* (Philomel Books, 1993)
- *The Enchanted Tapestry: A Chinese Folktale* (Penguin Putnam, 1987)
- *Even More Short and Shivery: Thirty Spine-Tingling Stories* (Random House, 1997)
- *Fa Mulan: The Story of a Woman Warrior* (Hyperion, 1998)
- *The Faithful Friend* (Four Winds Press, 1995)
- *Feathertop: Based on the Tale by Nathaniel Hawthorne* (Doubleday, 1992)
- *The Firebird* (Dial Books for Young Readers, 1992)
- *The Hired Hand: An African American* (Dial Books for Young Readers, 1997)
- *The Hobyahs* (Doubleday, 1994)
- *Kate Shelley: Bound For Legend*
- *Larger Than Life: The Adventures of American Legendary Heroes* (Dial Books for Young Readers, 1991)
- *The Legend of Scarface* (Doubleday, 1978)
- *The Legend of Sleepy Hollow* (Doubleday, 1986)
- *Little Gold Star: A Spanish-American Cinderella* (William Morrow & Co., 2000)
- *More Short and Shivery: Thirty Terrifying Tales* (Dell/Yearling, 1994)
- *Nicholas Pipe* (Dial Books for Young Readers, 1997)
- *Pedro and the Monkey* (HarperCollins, 1996)
- *The Samarai's Daughter: A Japanese Legend* (Dial Books for Young Readers, 1992)
- *The Secret of the Stones* (Phyllis Fogelman Book, 2000)
- *Short and Shivery: Thirty Chilling Tales* (Dell/Yearling, 1987)
- *The Silver Charm: A Folktale from Japan* (Doubleday, 2002)
- *Six Foolish Fishermen* (Hyperion Books for Children, 2000)
- *Sootface: An Ojibwa Cinderella Story* (Doubleday, 1994)
- *Sukey and the Mermaid* (Four Winds Press, 1992)
- *The Talking Eggs: A Folktale from the American South* (Dial Books for Young Readers, 1989)

- *Tarzan* (Hyperion, 1999)
- *A Terrifying Taste of Short and Shivery* (Delacorte, 1998)
- *The Twins and the Bird of Darkness* (Simon & Schuster, 2002)
- *Two Bear Cubs* (Yosemite Association, 1997)
- *A Weave of Words: An Armenian Tale* (Orchard Books, 1997)
- *The White Cat: An Old French Fairy Tale* (Orchard Books, 1990)
- *Young Arthur* (Doubleday, 1997)
- *Young Guinevere* (Doubleday, 1993)
- *Young Lancelot* (Doubleday, 1996)
- *Young Merlin* (Doubleday, 1990)

November

Lois Ehlert

- *Boo To You!* (Beach Lane Books, 2009)
- *Circus* (HarperCollins, 1992)
- *Color Farm* (Lippincott, 1990)
- *Color Zoo* (Lippincott, 1989)
- *Eating the Alphabet: Fruits & Vegetables From A to Z* (Voyager Books, 1989)
- *Feathers for Lunch* (Harcourt Brace, 1990)
- *Fish Eyes: A Book You Can Count On* (Harcourt Brace Jovanovich, 1990)
- *Growing Vegetable Soup* (Harcourt Brace Jovanovich, 1987)
- *Hands* (Harcourt, 1997)
- *In My World* (Harcourt, 2002)
- *Leaf Man* (Harcourt, 1995)
- *Market Day* (Harcourt Brace, 2000)
- *Mole's Hill* (Voyager Books, 1994)
- *Moon Rope/ Un Lazo a la Luna* (Harcourt Brace Jovanovich, 1992)
- *Nuts to You!* (Harcourt, Brace, Jovanich, 1993)
- *Oodles of Animals* (Harcourt, 2008)
- *Pie in The Sky* (Harcourt, 2004)
- *Planting a Rainbow* (Harcourt Brace, 1988)
- *Red Leaf, Yellow Leaf* (Harcourt Brace Jovanovich, 1991)
- *Snowballs* (Harcourt Brace, 1995)
- *Top Cat* (Harcourt Brace, 1998)
- *Waiting for Wings* (Harcourt, 2001)

Daniel Pinkwater

- *Aunt Lulu* (Macmillan, 1988)
- *Author's Day* (Macmillan, 1993)
- *Bear's Picture* (Holt, Rinehart, Winston, 1972; reillustrated version: Houghton Mifflin, 2008)
- *The Big Orange Splot* (Scholastic, 1977)

- *Cone Kong: The Scary Ice Cream Giant* (Cartwheel Books, 2002)
- *Guys From Space* (Macmillan, 1989)
- *I Was a Second Grade Werewolf* (Dutton, 1983)
- *Ned Feldman, Space Pirate* (Atheneum, 1994)
- *The Picture of Morty and Ray* (HarperCollins, 2003)
- *Rainy Morning* (Atheneum, 1999)
- *Second-Grade Ape* (Cartwheel Books, 1998)
- *Yo-Yo Man* (HarperCollins, 2007)

Bad Bears Series
- *Bad Bears and a Bunny: An Irving & Muktuk Story* (Houghton Mifflin, 2005)
- *Bad Bear Detectives: An Irving and Muktuk Story* (Houghton Mifflin, 2006)
- *Bad Bears Go Visiting: An Irving & Muktuk Story* (Houghton Mifflin, 2007)
- *Bad Bears in the Big City: An Irving & Muktuk Story* (Houghton Mifflin, 2003)
- *Irving and Muktuk: 2 Bad Bears* (Houghton Mifflin, 2001)

Big Bob and Gloria Series
- *Big Bob and the Magic Valentine's Day Potatoes* (Scholastic, 1999)
- *Big Bob and the Thanksgiving Potatoes* (Scholastic, 1998)
- *Big Bob and the Winter Holiday Potatoes* (Scholastic, 1999)

The Blue Moose Series
- *The Blue Moose* (Blackie and Son, 1977)
- *Return of the Moose* (Mead, Dodd, 1979)
- *Moosepire* (Little, Brown and Company, 1986)

Fat Camp Commandos Series
- *Fat Camp Commandos* (Scholastic Press, 2001)
- *Fat Camp Commandos Go West* (Scholastic, 2002)

Hoboken Chicken Series
- *The Hoboken Chicken Emergency* (Prentice-Hall, 1977)
- *Looking For Bobowicz: A Hoboken Chicken Story* (HarperCollins, 2004)
- *The Artsy-Smartsy Club* (HarperCollins, 2005)

Larry Series
- *At The Hotel Larry* (Marshall Cavendish, 1997)
- *Bongo Larry* (Marshall Cavendish, 2004)
- *Dancing Larry* (Marshall Cavendish, 2006)
- *Ice Cream Larry* (Marshall Cavendish, 1999)
- *Sleepover Larry* (Marshall Cavendish, 2007)
- *Young Larry* (Marshall Cavendish, 2004)

Mush Series
- *Mush, A Dog From Space* (Macmillan Books for Young Readers, 1995)
- *Mush's Jazz Adventure* (Aladdin, 2002)

The Werewolf Club Series
- *The Lunchroom of Doom* (Aladdin, 2000)
- *The Magic Pretzel* (Aladdin, 2000)
- *The Werewolf Club Meets Dorkula* (Aladdin, 2001)
- *The Werewolf Club Meets the Hound of the Basketballs* (Aladdin, 2001)
- *The Werewolf Club Meets Oliver Twit* (Aladdin, 2002)

Ed Young

- *Beyond the Great Mountains: A Visual Poem About China* (Chronicle Books, 2005)
- *Cat and Rat: The Legend of the Chinese Zodiac* (Henry Holt & Company, 1998)
- *Donkey Trouble* (Atheneum, 1995)
- *Hook* (Roaring Brook Press, 2009)
- *I, Doko: The Tale of a Basket* (Philomel Books, 2004)
- *Lon Po Po: A Red-Riding Hood Story From China* (Philomel Books, 1989)
- *The Lost Horse* (Silver Whistle/Harcourt Brace, 1998)
- *Monkey King* (HarperCollins, 2001)
- *Moon Mother: A Native American Creation Tale* (HarperCollins, 1993)
- *Mouse Match* (Silver Whistle, 1997)
- *My Mei Mei* (Philomel Books, 2006)
- *The Rooster's Horns: A Chinese Puppet Play to Make and Perform* (Putnam, 1983)
- *Seven Blind Mice* (Philomel Books, 1992)
- *The Sons of the Dragon King* (Atheneum, 2004)
- *What About Me?* (Philomel Books, 2002)

Illustrated by Ed Young

- *Birches* (by Robert Frost; Henry Holt & Company, 1988)
- *Chinese Mother Goose Rhymes* (by Robert Wyndham; Putnam, 1998)
- *Dreamcatcher* (by Audrey Osofsky; Orchard Books, 1992)
- *The Emperor and the Kite* (by Jane Yolen; Philomel Books, 1967; revised edition 1988)
- *Foolish Rabbit's Big Mistake* (by Rafe Martin; Putnam, 1985)
- *The Hunter: A Chinese Folktale* (by Mary Casanova; Atheneum, 2000)
- *I Wish I Were A Butterfly* (by James Howe; Harcourt, Brace, Jovanovich, 1987)
- *Moon Bear* (by Brenda C. Guiberson, Henry Holt, 2010)

- *A Pup Just For Me/ A Boy Just For Me* (by Dorothea P. Seeber; Philomel Books, 2000)
- *Sadako and the Thousand Paper Cranes* (by Eleanor Coerr; Putnam, 1993)
- *Tsunami!* (by Kimiko Kajikawa; Philomel, 2009)
- *The Turkey Girl: A Zuni Cinderella Story* (by Penny Pollock; Little, Brown, and Company, 1996)
- *Twenty Heartbeats* (by Dennis Haseley; Roaring Brook Press, 2008)
- *Wabi Sabi* (by Mark Reibstein; Little, Brown, 2008)
- *White Wave: A Chinese Tale* (by Diane Wolkstein; Harcourt Brace, 1996)
- *Yeh-Shen: A Cinderella Story From China* (by Ai-Ling Louie; Philomel Books, 1982)

December

Jan Brett

- *Annie and the Wild Animals* (Houghton Mifflin, 1985)
- *Armadillo Rodeo* (G.P. Putnam's Sons, 1995)
- *Beauty and the Beast* (Clarion Books, 1989)
- *Berlioz the Bear* (Putnam, 1991)
- *Christmas Trolls* (Putnam, 1993)
- *Comet's Nine Lives* (Putnam, 2001)
- *Daisy Comes Home* (Putnam, 2002)
- *The Easter Egg* (G.P. Putnam's Sons, 2010)
- *The First Dog* (Harcourt Children's Books, 1988)
- *Fritz and the Beautiful Horses* (Houghton Mifflin, 1981)
- *Gingerbread Baby* (Putnam, 1999)
- *Gingerbread Friends* (Putnam, 2008)
- *Goldilocks and the 3 Bears* (Putnam, 1987)
- *The Hat* (G.P. Putnam's Sons, 1997)
- *Hedgie Blasts Off!* (Putnam, 2006)
- *Hedgie Loves to Read* (Scholastic, 2006)
- *Hedgie's Surprise* (Putnam, 2000)
- *Home for Christmas* (G.P. Putnam's Sons, 2011)
- *Honey, Honey, Lion!* (G.P. Putnam's Sons, 2005)
- *The Mitten: A Ukrainian Folktale* (Putnam, 1989)
- *On Noah's Ark* (G.P. Putnam's Sons, 2003)
- *The 3 Little Dassies* (G.P. Putnam's Sons, 2010)
- *The Three Snow Bears* (G.P. Putnam's Sons, 2007)
- *Town Mouse, Country Mouse* (Putnam, 1994)
- *Trouble With Trolls* (G.P. Putnam's Sons, 1992)
- *The Twelve Days of Christmas* (Putnam & Grosset Group, 1997)
- *The Umbrella* (G.P. Putnam's Sons, 2004)
- *Who's That Knocking On Christmas Eve?* (Putnam, 2002)
- *The Wild Christmas Reindeer* (Putnam, 1990)

Jerry Pinkney

- *Aesop's Fables* (SeaStar Books, 2000)
- *The Lion and the Mouse* (Little, Brown and Company, 2009)
- *The Little Match Girl* (P. Fogelman Books, 1999)
- *The Little Red Hen* (Dial Books for Young Readers, 2006)
- *Little Red Riding Hood* (Little, Brown, and Company, 2007)
- *The Nightingale* (P. Fogelman Books, 2002)
- *Noah's Ark* (Sea Star Books, 2002)
- *The Three Little Kittens* (Dial Books for Young Readers, 2010)
- *The Ugly Duckling* (Morrow Junior Books, 1999)

Books by Rudyard Kipling
- *The Jungle Book* (HarperCollins, 1995)
- *Rikki-Tikki-Tavi* (Morrow Junior Books, 1997)

Collaborations with Valerie Flournoy
- *The Patchwork Quilt* (Dial Books for Young Readers, 1985)
- *Tanya's Reunion* (Dial Books for Young Readers, 1995)

Collaborations with Julius Lester
- *Black Cowboy, Wild Horses* (Dial Books for Young Readers, 1998)
- *The Complete Tales of Uncle Remus* (Dial Books for Young Readers, 1999)
- *John Henry* (Dial Books for Young Readers, 1994)
- *The Old African* (Dial Books for Young Readers, 2005)
- *Sam and the Tigers: A Retelling of Little Black Sambo* (Dial Books for Young Readers, 1996)

Collaborations with Patricia McKissack
- *The All-I'll-Ever-Want Christmas Doll* (Schwartz & Wade Books, 2007)
- *Goin' Someplace Special* (Atheneum, 2001)
- *Mirandy and Brother Wind* (Knopf Books for Young Readers, 1988)

Collaborations with Gloria Jean Pinkney
- *Back Home* (Dial Books for Young Readers, 1992)
- *The Sunday Outing* (Dial Books for Young Readers, 1994)

Collaborations with Robert D. San Souci
- *The Hired Hand* (Dial Books for Young Readers, 1997)

- *The Talking Eggs: A Folktale from the American South* (Dial Books for Young Readers, 1989)

Collaborations with Other Authors
- *Minty: A Story of Young Harriet Tubman* (by Alan Schroeder, Dial Books for Young Readers, 1996)
- *The Moon Over Star* (by Dianna Hutts Aston, Dial Books for Readers, 2008)
- *Rabbit Makes a Monkey of Lion* (by Verna Aardema, Dial Books for Young Readers, 1989)
- *Undersea Animals: A Dramatic Dimensional Visit to Strange Underwater Realms* (by Jane Buxton, National Geographic Children's Books, 2008)

Diane Stanley

- *Elena* (Hyperion, 1996)
- *The Gentleman and the Kitchen Maid* (Dial, 1994)
- *The Giant and the Beanstalk* (HarperCollins, 2004)
- *Goldie and the Three Bears* (HarperCollins, 2003)
- *Joan of Arc* (Morrow Junior Books, 1998)
- *Leonardo daVinci* (Morrow Junior Books, 1996)
- *Michelangelo* (HarperCollins, 2000)
- *Moe the Dog in Tropical Paradise* (Putnam, 1992)
- *Mozart, the Wonder Child: A Puppet Play in 3 Acts* (HarperCollins, 2009)
- *Peter the Great* (HarperCollins, 1999)
- *Raising Sweetness* (G.P. Putnam's Sons, 1995)
- *Rumpelstiltskin's Daughter* (Morrow Junior Books, 1997)
- *Saladin: Noble Prince of Islam* (HarperCollins, 2002)
- *Saving Sweetness* (G.P. Putnam's Sons, 1996)
- *The Trouble with Wishes* (HarperCollins, 2007)
- *Woe is Moe* (Putnam, 1995)

Collaborations with Peter Vennema
- *Bard of Avon: The Story of William Shakespeare* (Morrow Junior Books, 1992)
- *Charles Dickens: The Man Who Had Great Expectations* (HarperCollins, 1993)
- *Cleopatra* (Morrow Junior Books, 1994)
- *Good Queen Bess: The Story of Elizabeth 1 of England* (HarperCollins, 2001)
- *Shaka, King of the Zulus* (HarperCollins, 1994)

Time-Traveling Twins Series (with Holly Berry)
- *Joining the Boston Tea Party* (HarperCollins, 2001)
- *Roughing it on the Oregon Trail* (HarperCollins, 1999)
- *Thanksgiving on Plymouth Plantation* (Joanna Cotler Books, 2004)

January

Gerald McDermott

- *Anansi the Spider: A Tale From the Ashanti* (Holt, Rinehart, Winston, 1972)
- *Arrow to the Sun: A Pueblo Indian Tale* (Viking, 1974)
- *Coyote: A Trickster Tale From the American Southwest* (Harcourt Brace, 1994)
- *Creation* (Dutton Children's Books, 2003)
- *Daniel O'Rourke: An Irish Tale* (Puffin, 1986)
- *The Fox and the Stork* (Harcourt, 2003)
- *Jabutí the Tortoise: A Trickster Tale from the Amazon Rain Forest* (Harcourt, 2001)
- *The Magic Tree: A Tale from the Congo* (Henry Holt & Company, revised issue 1994)
- *Monkey: A Trickster Tale from India* (Houghton Mifflin, 2011)
- *Musicians of the Sun* (Simon & Schuster, 1997)
- *Papagayo: The Mischief Maker* (Harcourt Brace Jovanovich, 1992)
- *Pig Boy: A Trickster Tale from Hawai'i* (Harcourt, 2009)
- *Raven: A Trickster Tale From the Pacific Northwest* (Harcourt, 2001)
- *The Stonecutter: A Japanese Folktale* (Puffin, 1975)
- *Sun Flight* (Four Winds Press, 1980)
- *Tim O'Toole and the Wee Folk: An Irish Tale* (Puffin, 1992)
- *Zomo the Rabbit: A Trickster Tale From West Africa* (Harcourt Brace, 1996)

Pat Mora

- *Abuelos* (Groundwood Books, 2008)
- *Agua, Agua, Agua* (Good Year Books, 1994)
- *The Bakery Lady/La señora de la panadería* (Piñata Books, 2001)
- *A Birthday Basket for Tía* (Simon & Schuster, 1992)
- *Book Fiesta* (Rayo, 2009)
- *Confetti: Poems for Children* (Lee & Low Books, 1996)
- *Delicious Hullabaloo/Pachana deliciosa* (Piñata Books, 1998)
- *The Desert is My Mother/El Desierto es mí madre* (Piñata Books, 1994)
- *Doña Flor: A Tall Tale About a Gian Woman with a Great Big Heart* (Knopf, 2005)
- *The Gift of the Poinsettia, with Charles Ramirez Berg* (Arte Publico, 1995)
- *Gracias ~ Thanks* (Lee & Low Books, 2009)
- *Here, Kitty, Kitty!/¡Ven, gatita, ven!* (Rayo, 2008)
- *Join Hands! The Ways We Celebrate Life* (Charlesbridge, 2008)
- *Let's Eat! / A Comer!* (Rayo, 2007)
- *A Library for Juana: The World of Sor Juana Inés* (Knopf, 2002)
- *Listen to the Desert/Oye al desierto* (Clarion Books, 1994)
- *Love to Mamá: A Tribute to Mothers* (Lee & Low Books, 2001)
- *¡Marimba! Animales from A to Z* (Groundwood Books, 2006)
- *Maria Paints the Hills* (Museum of New Mexico Press, 2002)
- *My Own True Name: New and Selected Poems for Young Adults* (Perfection Learning, 2000)
- *The Night the Moon Fell: A Maya Myth* (Groundwood Books, 2000)
- *Pablo's Tree* (Macmillan, 1994)
- *A Piñata in a Pine Tree!* (Clarion Books, 2009)
- *The Race of Toad and Deer* (Groundwood Books, 2001)
- *The Rainbow Tulip* (Viking, 1999)
- *The Song of Francis and the Animals* (Eerdmans Books for Young Readers, 1980)
- *Sweet Dreams/Dulces Sueños* (Rayo, 2008)
- *This Big Sky* (Scholastic, 1998)
- *Tomás and the Library Lady* (Knopf, 1997)
- *Uno, Dos, Tres/ One, Two, Three* (Clarion Books, 1996)
- *Wiggling Pockets/Tus Bolsillos Se Mueven* (Rayo, 2009)
- *Yum! Mmmm! Que Rico! Americas' Sproutings* (Lee & Low Books, 2007)

Janet Stevens

Written and Illustrated by Janet Stevens

- *Coyote Steals the Blanket: A Ute Tale* (Holiday House, 1993)
- *From Pictures to Words: A Book About Making a Book* (Holiday House, 1994)
- *How the Manx Cat Lost its Tail* (Harcourt, 1990)
- *Old Bag of Bones: A Coyote Tale* (Holiday House, 1996)
- *The Princess and the Pea* (Holiday House, 1989)
- *The Three Billy Goats Gruff* (Harcourt Brace Jovanovich, 1987)
- *Tops and Bottoms* (Harcourt Brace, 1995)
- *The Tortoise and the Hare* (Holiday House, 1984)

Collaborations with Eric Kimmel

- *Anansi and the Magic Stick* (Holiday House, 2001)
- *Anansi and the Moss-Covered Rock* (Holiday House, 1988)

- *Anansi and the Talking Melon* (Holiday House, 1994)
- *Anansi Goes Fishing* (Holiday House, 1992)
- *Anansi's Party Time* (Holiday House, 2008)

Collaborations with Coleen Salley
- *Epossumondas* (Harcourt, 2002)
- *Epossumondas Plays Possum* (Harcourt, 2009)
- *Epossumondas Saves the Day* (Harcourt, 2006)
- *Why Epossumondas Has No Hair on his Tail* (Holiday House, 1994)

Collaborations with Susan Stevens Crummel
- *And the Dish Ran Away with the Spoon* (Harcourt, 2001)
- *Cook-A-Doodle-Doo!* (Harcourt, 1999)
- *The Great Fuzz Frenzy* (Harcourt, 2005)
- *Help Me, Mr. Mutt!* (Harcourt, 2008)
- *Jackalope* (Harcourt, 2003)
- *The Little Red Pen* (Harcourt, 2011)
- *My Big Dog* (Golden Books, 2008)
- *Plaidypus Lost* (Holiday House, 2004)

Collaborations with Other Authors
- *The Dog Who Had Kittens* (by Polly M. Robertus, Holiday House, 1991)
- *Gates of the Wind* (by Kathryn Lasky, Harcourt Brace, 1995)
- *To Market, To Market* (by Anne Miranda, Harcourt Brace, 1997)

February

Mo Willems

- *City Dog, Country Frog* (Hyperion Books for Children, 2010)
- *Don't Let the Pigeon Drive the Bus* (Hyperion Books for Children, 2003)
- *Don't Let the Pigeon Stay Up Late* (Hyperion Books for Children, 2006)
- *Edwina, The Dinosaur Who Didn't Know She Was Extinct* (Hyperion Books for Children, 2006)
- *Hooray for Amanda and Her Alligator!* (Balzer & Bray, 2011)
- *Knuffle Bunny: A Cautionary Tale* (Hyperion Books for Children, 2004)
- *Knuffle Bunny Free* (Balzer & Bray, 2010)
- *Knuffle Bunny Too: A Case of Mistaken Identity* (Hyperion Books for Children, 2007)
- *Leonardo the Terrible Monster* (Hyperion, 2005)

- *Naked Mole Rat Gets Dressed* (Hyperion Books for Children, 2009)
- *The Pigeon Finds a Hot Dog!* (Hyperion Books for Children, 2004)
- *The Pigeon Has Feelings, Too* (Hyperion, 2005)
- *The Pigeon Loves Things That Go!* (Hyperion, 2004)
- *The Pigeon Wants a Puppy* (Hyperion Books for Children, 2008)
- *Time to Pee!* (Hyperion Books for Children, 2003)
- *Time to Say, "Please!"* (Hyperion Books for Children, 2005)

Elephant and Piggie Series
- *Are You Ready to Play Outside?* (Hyperion Books for Children, 2008)
- *Can I Play, Too?* (Hyperion Books for Children, 2010)
- *Elephants Cannot Dance!* (Hyperion Books for Children, 2009)
- *Happy Pig Day!* (Hyperion Books for Children, 2011)
- *I Am Going!* (Hyperion Books for Children, 2010)
- *I Am Invited to a Party!* (Hyperion Books for Children, 2007)
- *I Broke My Trunk!* (Hyperion Books for Children, 2011)
- *I Love My New Toy!* (Hyperion Books for Children, 2008)
- *I Will Surprise My Friend!* (Hyperion Books for Children, 2008)
- *My Friend is Sad* (Hyperion Books for Children, 2007)
- *Pigs Make Me Sneeze!* (Hyperion Books for Children, 2009)
- *There is a Bird on Your Head!* (Hyperion Books for Children, 2007)
- *Today I Will Fly!* (Hyperion Books for Children, 2007)
- *Watch Me Throw the Ball!* (Hyperion Books for Children, 2009)
- *We Are In a Book!* (Hyperion Books for Children, 2010)

Cat the Cat Series
- *Cat the Cat, Who is That?* (Balzer & Bray, 2010)
- *Let's Say Hi to Friends Who Fly!* (Balzer & Bray, 2010)
- *Time to Sleep, Sheep the Sheep* (Balzer & Bray, 2010)
- *What's Your Sound, Hound the Hound?* (Balzer & Bray, 2010)

Jane Yolen

- *A Letter From Phoenix Farm* (Richard C. Owens, 1992)
- *A Sip of Aesop* (The Blue Sky Press, 1995)
- *All Those Secrets of the World* (Little, Brown, 1991)
- *An Invitation to the Butterfly Ball* (St. Martin's Press, 1991)
- *And Twelve Chinese Acrobats* (Putnam & Grosset Group, 1995)
- *The Ballad of the Pirate Queens* (Harcourt Brace, 1995)
- *Birds of a Feather* (Wordsong/Boyds Mills Press, 2011)
- *Color Me A Rhyme* (Wordsong/Boyds Mills Press, 2000)
- *Come to the Fairies Ball* (Wordsong, 2009)
- *Commander Toad and the Dis-asteroid* (Puffin, 1996)
- *Commander Toad and the Voyage Home* (G.P. Putnam's Sons, 1998)
- *Commander Toad in Space* (Puffin, 1996)
- *Creepy Monsters, Sleeping Monsters* (Candlewick Press Press, 2011)
- *The Day Tiger Rose Said Good-bye* (Random House Books for Children, 2011)
- *Dinosaur Dances* (G.P. Putnam's Sons, 1990)
- *Elfabet: An ABC of Elves* (Little, Brown, and Company, 1990)
- *Elsie's Bird* (Philomel Books, 2010)
- *Fairy Tale Feasts* (Interlink, 2009)
- *Encounter* (Harcourt, 1992)
- *Fairy Tale Feasts* (Interlink Books, 2009)
- *The Flying Witch* (HarperCollins, 2003)
- *The Girl in the Golden Bower* (Little, Brown, and Company, 1995)
- *Grandad Bill's Song* (Philomel, 1994)
- *Greyling* (Philomel Books, 1991)
- *Honkers* (Little, Brown, and Company, 1993)
- *Hoptoad* (Silver Whistle/Harcourt, 2003)
- *Horizons: Poems As Far As the Eye Can See* (Wordsong/Boyds Mills Press, 2003)
- *How Do Dinosaurs Get Well Soon?* (Blue Sky Press, 2003)
- *How Do Dinosaurs Laugh Out Loud?* (Cartwheel Books, 2010)
- *How Do Dinosaurs Say Good Night?* (Blue Sky Press, 2000)
- *How Do Dinosaurs Say I Love You?* (Blue Sky Press, 2009)
- *Hush Little Horsie* (Random House, 2010)
- *King Long Shanks* (Harcourt Brace, 1998)
- *Least Things: Poems About Small Natures* (Wordsong/Boyds Mills Press, 2003)
- *Letting Swift River Go* (Little, Brown, and Company, 1991)
- *Lost Boy* (Dutton, 2010)
- *The Mary Celeste* (Simon & Schuster, 1999)
- *Merlin and the Dragons* (Dutton, 1995)
- *Mightier Than the Sword* (Silver Whistle, 2003)
- *Miz Berlin Walks* (Philomel Books, 1997)
- *Mouse's Birthday* (Putnam's Sons, 1993)
- *My Brothers' Flying Machine* (Little, Brown, 2003)
- *My Father Knows the Names of Things* (Simon & Schuster, 2010)
- *Nocturne* (Harcourt, Brace, 1997)
- *Not All Princesses Dress in Pink* (Simon & Schuster, 2010)
- *Not One Damsel in Distress* (Silver Whistle, 2000)
- *Off We Go!* (Little, Brown, and Comany, 2000)
- *Old Dame Counterpane* (Philomel Books, 1994)
- *The Originals: Animals That Time Forgot* (Philomel Books, 1998)
- *Owl Moon* (Philomel Books, 1987)
- *Picnic With Piggins* (Harcourt Brace Jovanovich, 1988)
- *Piggins* (Harcourt Brace Jovanovich, 1987)
- *Piggins and the Royal Wedding* (Harcourt Brace Jovanovich, 1989)
- *Pretty Princess Pig* (Little Simon, 2011)
- *Raining Cats & Dogs* (Harcourt Brace, 1993)
- *Raising Yoder's Barn* (Little, Brown, and Company, 1998)
- *Sea Watch: A Book of Poetry* (Philomel Books, 1996)
- *The Seeing Stick* (Crowell, 1977)
- *Snow, Snow: Winter Poems* (Wordsong/Boyds Mills Press, 1998)
- *Switching on the Moon* (Candlewick Press, 2010)
- *Twelve Impossible Things Before Breakfast: Stories* (Sandpiper, 2001)
- *Welcome to the Green House* (G.P. Putnam, 1993)
- *Welcome to the Ice House* (G.P. Putnam, 1998)
- *Welcome to the Sea of Sand* (Putnam's Sons, 1996)
- *Wild Wings: Poems for Young People* (Wordsong/Boyds Mills Press, 2002)
- *Wings* (Harcourt Brace Jovanovich, 1991)

Paul O. Zelinsky

- *Awful Ogre's Awful Day* (by Jack Prelutsky, Greenwillow Books, 2001)
- *Awful Ogre Running Wild* (by Jack Prelutsky, Greenwillow Books, 2008)
- *Doodler Doodling* (by Rita Golden Gelman, Greenwillow Books, 2004)

- *Dust Devil* (by Anne Isaacs, Schwartz & Wade Books, 2010)
- *Hansel and Gretel* (retold by Rika Lesser, Dutton, 1999)
- *Knick-Knack Paddywhack* (adapted by Paul O. Zelinsky, Dutton, 2002)
- *Rapunzel* (retold by Paul O. Zelinsky, Dutton, 1997)
- *Rumpelstiltskin* (retold by Paul O. Zelinsky, Dutton, 1986)
- *The Shivers in the Fridge* (by Fran Manushkin, Dutton, 2006)
- *Swamp Angel* (by Anne Isaacs, Dutton, 1994)
- *The Story of Mrs. Loveright and Her Purrless* Cat (by Lore Segal, Atheneum, 1985)
- *Toy Dance Party* (by Emily Jenkins, Schwartz & Wade Books, 2008)
- *Toys Go Out* (by Emily Jenkins, Schwartz & Wade Books, 2006)
- *The Wheels on the Bus* (adapted by Paul O. Zelinsky, Dutton, 1990)
- *Zoo Doings: Animal Poems* (by Jack Prelutsky, Greenwillow Books, 1983)

March

Leo and Diane Dillon

- *Aida* (by Leontyne Price, Harcourt, 1990)
- *Ashanti to Zulu: African Traditions* (by Margaret Musgrove, Dial Books for Young Readers, 1976)
- *Behind the Back of the Mountain* (by Verna Aardema, Dutton, 1973)
- *Earth Mother* (by Ellen Jackson, Walker Books for Young Readers, 2005)
- *The Girl Who Dreamed Only Geese* (by Howard Norman, Harcourt Brace, 1997)
- *The Girl Who Spun Gold* (by Virginia Hamilton, The Blue Sky Press, 2000)
- *Her Stories* (by Virginia Hamilton, Blue Sky Press, 1995)
- *Honey, I Love and Other Love Poems* (by Eloise Greenfield, HarperCollins, 1978)
- *The Hundred Penny Box* (by Sharon Bell Mathis, Viking, 1975)
- *Jazz on a Saturday Night* (by Leo & Diane Dillon, Blue Sky Press, 2007)
- *Mama Says: A Book of Love for Mothers and Sons* (by Rob D. Walker, Blue Sky Press, 2009)
- *Mansa Musa* (by Khephra Burns, Harcourt Brace, 2001)
- *Many Thousand Gone* (by Virginia Hamilton, Knopf, 1992)

- *Mother Goose: Numbers on the Loose* (by Leo & Diane Dillon, Harcourt, 2007)
- *Never Forgotten* (by Patricia McKissack, Schwartz & Wade Books, 2011)
- *Northern Lullaby* (by Nancy White Carlstrom, Philomel Books, 1992)
- *One Winter's Night* (by John Herman, Philomel Books, 2003)
- *The People Could Fly: The Picture Book* (by Virginia Hamilton, Knopf, 2004)
- *Pish, Posh, Said Hieronymous Bosch* (by Nancy Willard, Harcourt, Brace, Jovanovich, 1991)
- *Rap a Tap Tap: Here's Bojangles—Think of That!* (by Leo & Diane Dillon, The Blue Sky Press, 2002)
- *The Secret River* (by Marjorie Kinnan Rawlings, Atheneum, 2009)
- *Switch on the Night* (by Ray Bradbury, Alfred A. Knopf, 1993)
- *Tale of the Mandarin Ducks* (by Katherine Paterson, Puffin, 1995)
- *To Every Thing There is a Season* (by Leo & Diane Dillon, Blue Sky Press, 1998)
- *Two Little Trains* (by Margaret Wise Brown, HarperCollins, 2001)
- *Two Pairs of Shoes* (by P.L. Travers, Viking, 1980)
- *Where Have You Been?* (by Margaret Wise Brown, HarperCollins, 2004)
- *Who's In Rabbit's House?* (by Verna Aardema, Dial Books for Young Readers, 1977)
- *Why Mosquitoes Buzz in People's Ears* (by Verna Aardema, Dial Press, 1975)
- *Wind Child* (by Shirley Rousseau Murphy, HarperCollins, 1999)

Douglas Florian

- *A Beach Day* (Greenwillow Books, 1990)
- *A Chef: How We Work* (Greenwillow Books, 1992)
- *A Fisher: How We Work* (Greenwillow Books, 1994)
- *A Painter: How We Work* (Greenwillow Books, 1993)
- *A Pig is Big* (Greenwillow Books, 2000)
- *A Potter: How We Work* (Greenwillow Books, 1991)
- *A Summer Day* (William Morrow & Co., 1988)
- *A Winter Day* (Greenwillow Books, 1987)
- *A Year in the Country* (Greenwillow Books, 1989)
- *Airplane Ride* (T. Y. Crowell, 1984)
- *An Auto Mechanic: How We Work* (Greenwillow Books, 1991)
- *At the Zoo* (Greenwillow Books, 1992)
- *Autumnblings* (Greenwillow Books, 2003)
- *Beast Feast* (Voyager Books, 1998)

- *Bing Bang Boing* (Harcourt, 1994)
- *bow wow meow meow: it's rhyming cats and dogs* (Harcourt, 2003)
- *The City* (HarperCollins, 1982)
- *City Street* (Greenwillow Books, 1990)
- *Comets, Stars, the Moon and Mars: Space Poems & Paintings* (Harcourt, 2007)
- *Dinothesaurus* (Atheneum, 2009)
- *Handsprings* (Greenwillow Books, 2005)
- *In the Swim* (Harcourt, 1997)
- *Insectlopedia* (Harcourt, 1998)
- *Laugheteria* (Harcourt, 1999)
- *Lizards, Frogs, and Polliwogs* (Harcourt, 2001)
- *Mammalabilia* (Harcourt, 2000)
- *Monster Motel: Poems and Paintings* (Harcourt Brace, 1993)
- *Omnibeasts* (Harcourt, 2004)
- *On the Wing* (Harcourt, 1996)
- *Poetrees* (Beach Lane Books, 2010)
- *See For Yourself: Meet the Author* (Richard C. Owens Pubs., 2005)
- *Summersaults* (Greenwillow Books, 2002)
- *Vegetable Garden* (Harcourt Brace Jovanovich, 1991)
- *Winter Eyes* (Greenwillow Books, 1999)
- *Zoo's Who* (Harcourt, 2005)

Dav Pilkey

- *The Adventures of Captain Underpants: An Epic Novel* (Scholastic, 1997)
- *The Adventures of Ook and Gluk: Kung-Fu Cavemen from the Future* (Blue Sky Press, 2010)
- *The Adventures of Super Diaper Baby: The First Graphic Novel* (Blue Sky Press, 2002)
- *Captain Underpants and the Attack of the Talking Toilets* (Scholastic, 1999)
- *Captain Underpants and the Big, Bad Battle of the Bionic Booger Boy, Part 1* (Scholastic, 2003)
- *Captain Underpants and the Big, Bad Battle of the Bionic Booger Boy, Part 2* (Scholastic, 2003)
- *Captain Underpants and the Invasion of the Incredibly Naughty Cafeteria Ladies From Outer Space* (Scholastic, 1999)
- *Captain Underpants & the Perilous Plot of Professor Poopypants* (Scholastic, 2000)
- *Captain Underpants & the Wrath of the Wicked Wedgie Woman* (Scholastic, 2001)
- *Dog Breath* (Blue Sky Press, 1994)
- *Dogzilla* (Harcourt, 1993)
- *Dragon Gets By* (Orchard Books, 1991)
- *Dragon's Fat Cat* (Orchard Books, 1992)
- *Dragon's Halloween* (Orchard Books, 1992)
- *Dragon's Merry Christmas* (Orchard Books, 1991)
- *The Dumb Bunnies* (by Sue Denim, Blue Sky Press, 1994)
- *The Dumb Bunnies' Easter* (by Sue Denim, Scholastic, 1995)
- *The Dumb Bunnies go to the Zoo* (by Sue Denim, Scholastic, 1997)
- *A Friend For Dragon* (Orchard Books, 1991)
- *God Bless the Gargoyles* (Harcourt, 1996)
- *The Hallo-wiener* (Blue Sky Press, 1995)
- *Juliius* (by Angela Johnson, Orchard Books, 1993)
- *Kat Kong* (Harcourt Brace, 1993)
- *Make Way for Dumb Bunnies* (by Sue Denim, Blue Sky Press, 1996)
- *The Moonglow Roll-O-Rama* (Scholastic, 1995)
- *The Paperboy* (Orchard Books, 1996)
- *Ricky Ricotta's Mighty Robot* (Scholastic, 2000)
- *Ricky Ricotta's Mighty Robot vs. the Jurassic Jack Rabbits from Jupiter* (Scholastic, 2002)
- *Ricky Ricotta's Mighty Robot vs. The Mecha Monkeys from Mars* (Scholastic, 2000)
- *Ricky Ricotta's Mighty Robot vs. The Mutant Mosquitoes . . .* (Scholastic, 2000)
- *Ricky Ricotta's Mighty Robot vs. the Stupid Stinkbugs from Saturn* (Scholastic, 2003)
- *Ricky Ricotta's Mighty Robot vs. The Voodoo Vultures . . .* (Blue Sky Press, 2001)
- *The Silly Gooses* (Scholastic, 1998)
- *'Twas the Night Before Thanksgiving* (Orchard Books, 1990)
- *When Cats Dream* (Orchard Books, 1992)
- *World War Won* (Landmark Editions, 1987)

April

Lee Bennett Hopkins

- *A-Haunting We Will Go* (Albert Whitman, 1977)
- *A Pet for Me: Poems* (HarperCollins, 2003)
- *Alphathoughts: Alphabet Poems* (Wordsong, 2003)
- *Been to Yesterdays: Poems of a Life* (Wordsong/Boyds Mills Press, 1995)
- *City I Love* (Abrams Books for Young Readers, 2009)
- *Climb Into My Lap: First Poems To Read Together* (Simon & Schuster, 1998)
- *Dinosaurs* (Harcourt Brace, 1987)
- *Dizzy Dinosaurs: Silly Dino Poems* (Harper, 2011)
- *Easter Buds are Springing: Poems for Easter* (Harcourt Brace, 1979)

- *Extra Innings: Baseball Poems* (Harcourt Brace Jovanovich, 1993)
- *Good Books, Good Times!* (Harper & Row, 1990)
- *Good Rhymes, Good Times* (HarperCollins, 1995)
- *Got Geography!* (Greenwillow Books, 2006)
- *Hamsters, Shells, and Spelling Bees: School Poems* (HarperCollins, 2008)
- *Hand In Hand* (Simon & Schuster, 1994)
- *Happy Birthday* (Simon & Schuster, 2000)
- *Home To Me: Poems Across America* (Orchard Books, 2002)
- *Hoofbeats, Claws, and Rippled Fins: Creature Poems* (HarperCollins, 2002)
- *Incredible Inventions* (Greenwillow Books, 2009)
- *LIVES: Poems About Famous Americans* (HarperCollins, 1999)
- *Marvelous Math: A Book of Poems* (Simon & Schuster, 1997)
- *My America: A Poetry Atlas of the United States* (Simon & Schuster, 2000)
- *Opening Days: Sports Poems* (Harcourt Brace, 1996)
- *Pass the Poetry, Please* (Trophy, 1987)
- *School Supplies: A Book of Poems* (Simon & Schuster, 1996)
- *Spectacular Science: A Book of Poems* (Simon & Schuster, 1999)
- *Sports! Sports! Sports! A Poetry Collection* (HarperCollins, 1999)
- *Surprises* (Harper & Row, 1984)
- *Weather: Poems for all Seasons* (HarperCollins, 1995)
- *Witching Time* (Albert Whitman, 1977)
- *Wonderful Words: Poems About Reading, Writing, Speaking, and Listening* (Simon & Schuster, 2004)
- *The Writing Bug: Meet the Author* (Richard C. Owens Pubs., 1993)

April Pulley Sayre

- *Ant, Ant, Ant: An Insect Chant* (NorthWord Books, 2005)
- *Army Ant Parade* (Henry Holt, 2002)
- *Bird, Bird, Bird: A Chirping Chant* (Cooper Square Publishing, 2007)
- *The Bumblebee Queen* (Charlesbridge, 2005)
- *Crocodile Listens* (Greenwillow Books, 2001)
- *Dig, Wait, Listen: A Desert Toad's Tale* (Greenwillow Books, 2001)
- *Home at Last: A Song of Migration* (Henry Holt & Company, 1998)
- *Honk, Honk, Goose! Canada Geese Start a Family* (Henry Holt & Company, 2009)
- *The Hungry Hummingbird* (Scholastic, 2003)

- *Hush Little Puppy* (Henry Holt & Company, 2007)
- *If You Should Hear a Honey Guide* (Henry Holt & Company, 1995)
- *If You're Hoppy* (Greenwillow Books, 2011)
- *It's My City! A Singing Map* (Greenwillow Books, 2001)
- *Meet the Howlers* (Charlesbridge, 2010)
- *Noodle Man: The Pasta Superhero* (Orchard Books, 2002)
- *One is a Snail, Ten is a Crab* (Candlewick Press, 2003)
- *Rah, Rah, Radishes! A Vegetable Chant* (Beach Lane Books, 2011)
- *Shadows* (Henry Holt & Company, 2002)
- *Splish, Splash! Animal Baths!* (Millbrook Press, 2000)
- *Stars Beneath Your Bed: The Surprising Story of Dust* (Greenwillow Books, 2005)
- *Trout Are Made of Trees* (Charlesbridge, 2008)
- *Trout, Trout, Trout: A Fish Chant* (Charlesbridge, 2008)
- *Turtle, Turtle, Watch Out!* (Charlesbridge, 2010)
- *Vulture View* (Henry Holt & Company, 2007)

Gary Soto

- *A Fire in My Hands* (Harcourt, 2006)
- *Baseball In April and Other Stories* (Harcourt Brace Jovanovich, 1990)
- *Big Bushy Mustache* (Knopf, 1998)
- *Canto Familiar* (Harcourt Brace, 1995)
- *The Cat's Meow* (Scholastic, 1995)
- *Chato Goes Cruisin'* (G.P. Putnam's Sons, 2004)
- *Chato's Kitchen* (G.P. Putnam's Sons, 1995)
- *Chato and the Party Animals* (Puffin, 2004)
- *Fearless Fernie* (G.P. Putnam's Sons, 2002)
- *If The Shoe Fits* (G.P. Putnam's Sons, 2002)
- *Marisol: An American Girl Story* (Pleasant Company Publications, 2005)
- *My Little Car* (G.P. Putnam's Sons, 2006)
- *Neighborhood Odes* (Harcourt Brace Jovanovich, 1992)
- *The Old Man and His Door* (Putnam's Sons, 1996)
- *Partly Cloudy: Poems of Love and Longing* (Harcourt, 2009)
- *The Skirt* (Delacorte Press, 1992)
- *Snapshots From The Wedding* (G.P. Putnam's Sons, 1997)
- *Too Many Tamales* (Putnam, 1993)
- *Worlds Apart: Traveling with Fernie and Me* (G.P. Putnam's Sons, 2005)

May

Juanita Havill

- *Brianna, Jamaica, and the Dance of Spring* (Houghton Mifflin, 2002)
- *Call the Horse Lucky* (The Gryphon Press, 2010)
- *Eyes Like Willy's* (HarperCollins, 2004)
- *Grow: A Novel in Verse* (Peachtree Publishers, 2008)
- *I Heard it From Alice Zucchini* (Chronicle Books, 2006)
- *It Always Happens to Leona* (Crown, 1989)
- *Jamaica and Brianna* (Houghton Mifflin, 1993)
- *Jamaica and the Substitute Teacher* (Houghton Mifflin, 1999)
- *Jamaica is Thankful* (Houghton Mifflin, 2009)
- *Jamaica Tag-Along* (Houghton Mifflin, 1989)
- *Jamaica's Blue Marker* (Houghton Mifflin, 1995)
- *Jamaica's Find* (Houghton Mifflin, 1986)
- *Jennifer, Too* (Hyperion, 1994)
- *Just Like a Baby* (Chronicle Books, 2009)
- *Kentucky Troll* (Lothrop, Lee & Shepard Books, 1993)
- *Leona and Ike* (Knopf, 1990)
- *The Magic Fort* (Houghton Mifflin, 1991)
- *Sato and the Elephants* (Lothrop, Lee & Shepard Books, 1993)
- *Saving Owen's Toad* (Hyperion, 1994)
- *Treasure Nap* (Houghton Mifflin, 1992)

J. Patrick Lewis

- *Arithme-Tickle: An Even Number of Odd Riddle-Rhymes* (Harcourt, 2002)
- *At the Wish of the Fish: An Adaptation of a Russian Folktale* (1999)
- *Big Is Big (and Little Little): A Book of Contrasts* (Holiday House, 2007)
- *Birds on a Wire: A Renga 'Round Town*, with Paul Janeczko (Wordsong, 2008)
- *Black Cat Bone: A Life of Blues Legend Robert Johnson in Verse* (Creative Editions, 2006)
- *Black Swarn/White Crow* (Atheneum, 1995)
- *Blackbeard the Pirate King* (National Geographic Children's Books, 2006)
- *The Boat of Many Rooms: The Story of Noah in Verse* (Atheneum, 1996)
- *The Bookworm's Feast: A Potluck of Poems* (Dial, 1999)
- *BoshBlobberBosh: Runcible Poems for Edward Lear* (Creative Editions, 1998)
- *A Burst of Firsts: Doers, Shakers, and Record Breakers* (Dial, 2001)
- *Castles: Cold Stone Poems*, with Rebecca Kai Dotlich (Boyds Mills Press, 2007)
- *The Christmas of the Reddle Moon* (Dial, 1994)
- *Countdown to Summer: 180 Poems for Every Day of the School Year* (Little, Brown, and Company, 2009)
- *Doodle Dandies: Poems that Take Shape* (Atheneum, 1998)
- *Earth Verses and Water Rhymes* (Atheneum, 1991)
- *The Fantastic 5 & 10¢ Store: A Rebus Adventure* (Schwartz & Wade Books, 2010)
- *The Fat-Cats at Sea* (Random House, 1994)
- *First Dog*, with Beth Zappitello (Sleeping Bear Press, 2009)
- *Freedom Like Sunlight: Praisesongs for Black Americans* (Creative Editions, 2003)
- *The Frog Princess* (Dial Books for Young Readers, 1994)
- *God Made the Skunk, and Other Animal Poems* (Doggerel Daze, 2005)
- *Good Mornin', Ms. America: The U.S.A. in Verse* (Brighter Child, 2006)
- *Good Mousekeeping, and Other Animal Home Poems* (Atheneum, 2001)
- *Heroes and She-roes: Poems of Amazing and Everyday Heroes* (Dial Books for Young Readers, 2005)
- *A Hippopotamusn't and Other Animal Verses* (Dial Books for Young Readers, 1990)
- *The House* (Creative Editions, 2009)
- *July is a Mad Mosquito* (Atheneum, 1994)
- *The Kindergarten Cat* (Schwartz & Wade Books, 2010)
- *The La-Di-Da Hare* (Atheneum, 1997)
- *The Little Buggers: Insect and Spider Poems* (Dial, 1997)
- *Long Was the Winter Road they Traveled: Tale of the Nativity* (Dial, 1997)
- *Monumental Verses* (National Geographic, 2005)
- *The Moonbow of Mr. B. Bones* (Knopf, 1992)
- *Once Upon a Tomb: Gravely Humorous Verses* (Candlewick Press, 2006)
- *One Dog Day* (Atheneum, 1993)
- *Please Bury Me in the Library* (Harcourt, 2004)
- *Ridicholas Nicholas: More Animal Poems* (Dial, 1995)
- *Riddle-icious* (Knopf, 1996)
- *Riddle-lightful* (Knopf, 1998)
- *Scien-trickery: Riddles in Science* (Harcourt, 2004)
- *Skywriting: Poems to Fly* (Creative Editions, 2009)
- *The Snowflake Sisters* (Atheneum, 2003)
- *Spot the Plot* (Chronicle Books, 2009)
- *Swan Songs: Poems of Extinction* (Creative Editions, 2003)
- *The Tsar and the Amazing Cow* (Dial, 1988)

- *Tulip at the Bat* (Little, Brown, and Company, 2007)
- *Two-legged, Four-legged, No-legged Rhymes* (Knopf, 1991)
- *Vherses: A Celebration of Outstanding Women* (Creative Editions, 2005)
- *Wing Nuts: Screwy Haiku,* with Paul Janeczko (Little, Brown, and Company, 2006)
- *A World of Wonders: Geographic Travels in Verse and Rhyme* (Dial, 2002)

Peter Sís

- *Ballerina!* (Greenwillow Books, 2001)
- *Beach Ball* (Greenwillow Books, 1990)
- *Dinosaur!* (Greenwillow Books, 2000)
- *Fire Truck* (Greenwillow Books, 1998)
- *Follow the Dream: The Story of Christopher Columbus* (Knopf, 1991)
- *Going Up: A Color Counting Book* (Greenwillow Books, 1989)
- *Komodo!* (Greenwillow Books, 1993)
- *Madlenka* (Farrar, Strauss and Giroux, 2000)
- *Madlenka: Soccer Star* (Farrar, Strauss and Giroux, 2010)
- *Madlenka's Dog* (Farrar, Strauss and Giroux, 2002)
- *An Ocean World* (Greenwillow Books, 1992)
- *Play, Mozart, Play!* (Greenwillow Books, 2006)
- *Rainbow Rhino* (Random House, 1987)
- *Rumpelstiltskin* (by Christopher Noel, Simon & Schuster, 1995)
- *Ship Ahoy!* (Greenwillow Books, 1999)
- *A Small Tall Tale From the Far, Far North* (Knopf, 1993)
- *Starry Messenger: Galileo Galilei* (Farrar, Strauss and Giroux, 1996)
- *The Three Golden Keys* (Doubleday, 1994)
- *Tibet Through the Red Box* (Farrar, Strauss and Giroux, 1998)
- *Train of States* (Greenwillow Books, 2004)
- *The Tree of Life: Charles Darwin* (Farrar, Strauss, & Giroux, 2003)
- *Trucks, Trucks, Trucks* (Greenwillow Books, 1999)
- *The Wall: Growing Up Behind the Iron Curtain* (Farrar, Strauss and Giroux, 2007)
- *Waving: A Counting Book* (Greenwillow Books, 1988)

Notes

Notes

Notes

APR 2013

Notes

CLIFTON PARK-HALFMOON PUBLIC LIBRARY, NY

0 00 06 04132746